MONEY, EMPLOYMENT AND INFLATION

Money, employment and inflation

ROBERT J. BARRO
UNIVERSITY OF CHICAGO

HERSCHEL I. GROSSMAN
BROWN UNIVERSITY

CAMBRIDGE UNIVERSITY PRESS
CAMBRIDGE
LONDON · NEW YORK · MELBOURNE

Published by the Syndics of the Cambridge University Press
The Pitt Building, Trumpington Street, Cambridge CB2 1RP
Bentley House, 200 Euston Road, London NW1 2DB
32 East 57th Street, New York, NY 10022, USA
296 Beaconsfield Parade, Middle Park, Melbourne 3206, Australia

Library of Congress catalogue card number: 75–13449

ISBN: 0 521 20906 4

First published 1976

Text set in 10/12 pt. Monotype Times New Roman
at The Pitman Press, Bath

Printed in the United States of America

Contents

TO JUDY AND BETSY

Preface

This monograph is the outgrowth of ideas developed while we were colleagues at Brown University from 1968 to 1971. During that period, we became aware that we shared similar reservations about the weak foundations of conventional macro-economic analysis. We both felt the need for a substantial restructuring of these foundations, especially to deal adequately with the problem of exchange under non-market-clearing conditions. Unfortunately, earlier efforts by other authors, especially Patinkin (1956, chapter 13) and Clower (1965), along lines which seemed promising had apparently made little impact on the profession. However, the publication of the argumentative book by Leijonhufvud (1968) did succeed in stimulating interest in these issues.

Our first joint paper dealing with the reformulation of macro-economic analysis built on the foundations suggested by the work of Patinkin and Clower and was published in the *American Economic Review* in 1971. The ideas in this paper provide the basis for the analytical core of the present monograph. The present work also makes use of ideas developed in our subsequent individual and joint papers which are listed in the references at the end of the book.

Although the principal motivation for this monograph is to recast macro-economic analysis in terms of a theory of exchange under non-market-clearing conditions, we have also tried to incorporate into the analysis other recent and important contributions to the reformulation of macro-economic theory. We discuss in detail the role of inflationary expectations, especially their relation to interest rates and unemployment. This analysis derives from the work of Mundell (1965), Phelps (1967), and Friedman (1968). We also analyze in detail the dynamics of aggregate demand, building on ideas attributable to Tucker (1966) and Laidler (1968). In addition, we consider in detail an alternative approach to recasting macro-economic theory based on the notion of incomplete information regarding the spatial distribution of wages and prices.

This analysis derives largely from the work of Mortensen (1970, 1974).

We are grateful to several years' worth of first-year graduate students at Brown and Chicago who participated in the development of this material and who also provided valuable responses to a number of alternative approaches. Grants from the National Science Foundation supported most of the research on which this monograph is based. We appreciate the encouragement of James Blackman, NSF Program Director for Economics. Marion Anthony of Brown University typed the several drafts of each chapter with great skill and a cheerful disposition.

Robert J. Barro
Herschel I. Grossman

July 1975

Introduction

This monograph presents a comprehensive choice-theoretic analysis of the determination of the level of employment and the rate of inflation. This analysis has two principal and closely related objectives: first, to identify the interrelations between the behavior of individual economic units and the realization of macro-economic phenomena; and second, to explain the critical aspects of individual behavior in terms of the motivation of the individuals involved and the constraints which they face. In brief, this monograph attempts to rework the theory of macro-economic relations through a reexamination of their micro-economic foundations.

The point of departure for the study, in chapter 1, is the basic model of Walrasian general equilibrium in an intertemporal context. This model involves three forms of economic decision-making units – firms, households, and government – and four economic goods – labor services, consumable commodities, public services, and fiat money. Within this framework, this chapter analyzes profit maximizing behavior of firms, life-cycle utility maximizing behavior of households, and the results of the implied harmonization of firm, household, and government behavior for the determination of the wage rate, price level, employment, and output. This idealized representation provides a useful basis for identifying the implications of relaxing various crucial abstractions. The Walrasian model, however, does not provide an adequate basis for theorizing about employment and inflation.

An unfortunate aspect of the evolution of conventional post-Keynesian macro-economics has been a chronic attempt to coax a theory of employment and inflation out of a framework of general market clearing.[1] The result of these efforts has been to leave conventional macro-economics with an embarrassingly weak choice-theoretic

---

[1] Leijonhufvud (1968) elaborates extensively on this theme. For a critical evaluation of Leijonhufvud's exegesis, see Grossman (1972a) and Yeager (1973).

basis, and to associate with it important implications which are difficult to reconcile with observed phenomena.

A classic example of such a difficulty concerns the relationship between the level of employment and the real wage rate. In the conventional analysis, the demand for labor is inversely and uniquely related to the level of real wages. This assumption accords with Keynes, who, in this respect, had adhered to received pre-Keynesian doctrine.[2] Given this assumption, cyclical variations in the quantity of labor demanded and the amount of employment must imply countercyclical variation in real wage rates. As is well known, however, such a pattern of real wages has not been observed.[3]

Chapter 2 departs from the Walrasian framework to consider output and employment under non-market-clearing conditions. This chapter provides the analytical core of the monograph. The crucial assumption is that wages and prices respond sluggishly to shifts in demand. Consequently, exchange may take place at wages and prices which are inconsistent with general market clearing. In this chapter, we first generalize the analysis of profit maximizing behavior and the analysis of life-cycle utility maximizing behavior to allow for the constraints imposed by the failure of markets to clear. We then use these results to develop a general model of the determination of output and employment at given levels of wages and prices.

This analysis enables us to derive some familiar results, such as the notion that insufficient commodity demand depresses employment through a multiplier process, with more generality and rigor than is possible in conventional analysis. In addition, the explicit modelling of exchange under non-market-clearing conditions leads to some unfamiliar results. One such example is that the impact of excess supply of commodities on effective labor demand removes the necessary inverse classical relationship between the real wage rate and employment.

---

[2] Keynes wrote:
> 'with a given organization, equipment and technique, real wages and the volume of output (and hence of employment) are uniquely correlated, so that, in general, an increase in employment can only occur to the accompaniment of a decline in the rate of real wages. Thus, I am not disputing this vital fact which the classical economists have (rightly) asserted. . . . The real wage earned by a unit of labor has a unique inverse correlation with the volume of employment.' (1936, p. 17.)

[3] Kuh (1966) and Bodkin (1969) have recently reviewed the relevant evidence. Keynes himself (1939) recognized this discrepancy, and offered a rather contrived explanation for it in terms of monopoly and procyclical variation in demand elasticities.

Another important example is the analysis of the relative importance of the life-cycle budget constraint and of liquidity considerations in determining the size of the demand multiplier in a context of general excess supply. A third example is the derivation of the supply multiplier which determines income and employment in a context of general excess demand and which is analogous to the more conventional demand multiplier.

Chapter 3 introduces capital, financial assets, and a rate of return into the analytical framework. In this chapter, we first generalize the analysis of firm behavior to allow for investment and the issue of equity shares, and, second, we revise the analysis of the household's life-cycle plan and asset choice to take account of the availability of a positive rate of return. We also introduce the possibility of government borrowing, which allows us to draw an explicit distinction between monetary and fiscal policy. We then investigate the implications of the harmonization of this generalized firm, household, and government behavior within a context of general market clearing and a context of general excess supply. The analysis of the general excess supply case in this chapter is analogous to conventional IS–LM analysis.

Chapter 4 focuses on inflation and considers the relation between inflation and rates of return. In this chapter, we first generalize the analysis of household behavior to allow for inflationary expectations. We then analyze how this revised household behavior interacts with firm and government behavior to determine real and nominal rates of return. The final section of this chapter develops a dynamic analysis of the interplay between inflation, expected inflation, and rates of return.

Chapter 5 develops a model of the relation between inflation and unemployment. This model derives from the analytical framework of chapter 2, but focuses in detail on the market for labor services. The innovation here is the introduction of heterogeneous labor services. The analysis generates the so-called Phillips Curve, but also brings out the interplay between aggregate demand, unemployment, inflationary expectations, and actual wage inflation.

The analysis of the interplay between inflation and inflationary expectations in both chapter 4 and chapter 5 involves two essential elements. The first of these is the familiar adaptive expectations mechanism by which actual inflation generates inflationary expectations. The second essential element is the less familiar idea that wage and price adjustment results from the summation of two component forces: The first force attempts to correct for any existing discrepancy between actual wages and prices and market-clearing wages and prices, a discrepancy which can itself depend on inflationary expectations. The second force attempts to anticipate and prevent any potential future discrepancies between actual wages and prices and market-clearing wages and prices. This second force produces a direct one-for-one effect of inflationary expectations on actual inflation.

Chapter 6 analyzes the dynamics of aggregate demand. Here, we use the analytical framework of chapter 3 to explore the implications of various structural lags for the time paths of output, employment, and the rate of return within a context of general excess supply. We focus specifically on the responses of effective demands to their proximate determinants, the adjustment of expectations regarding future levels of income and the rate of return, and the response of the rate of return to divergences between the demand and supply of financial assets.

Finally, chapter 7 returns to the basic model of chapter 1 and considers an alternative departure from the Walrasian framework – namely, that economic units have incomplete information regarding the spatial dispersion of wages and prices. Under these conditions, speculative behavior by households can lead to a positive causal relation between aggregate demand and employment. However, this model has some additional implications which are difficult to reconcile with experience – specifically, its predictions about the cyclical behavior of quits, real wages, and consumption, and its failure to account for layoffs. For these reasons, we are led to conclude that the speculative behavior which results from this incomplete information probably plays a relatively small role in the determination of the actual cyclical pattern of output and employment.

Before we develop the basic model, it will be useful for us to note here some interesting and potentially important considerations which our analysis neglects. With regard to our analytical framework, one obvious abstraction is that we ignore considerations of risk and uncertainty. Although expectations play a key role in the analysis, and we often consider the possibility that expectations may not be fulfilled, the analysis of firm and household behavior always treats expectations as if they were held with certainty. Specifically, households maximize the utility of expected consumption and leisure rather than the expected utility of consumption and leisure. Abstracting from risk and uncertainty does permit a clearer development of many essential points, but it also means that we are only approximating the results of a more extended analysis.

Because we neglect an explicit treatment of uncertainty, our mechanisms for generating expectations – for example, on price and wage changes – are of the simple adaptive type. In particular, these expectations are not derived as optimal predictions from a model with a specified information structure. Accordingly, our assumed processes for generating expectations may not be 'rational', in the sense of fully incorporating the information available to market participants. Our analysis could be usefully extended to include a rational – that is, optimal – basis for forming expectations. However, this extension will require a detailed consideration of uncertainty, together with an explicit treatment of the information costs associated with alternative expectations mechanisms.

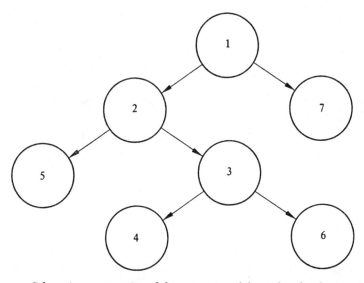

Schematic representation of the progression of the analysis by chapters

Another notable abstraction is that our models do not consider financial intermediation. This simplification follows directly from our neglect of risk and uncertainty. That is to say, a useful analysis of the role of financial intermediation would require explicit analysis of the implications of risk and uncertainty.

We should also note that, with some exceptions, the analysis largely ignores distributional considerations. Again, this abstraction permits a clearer development of many essential points, but introduces a degree of approximation into the results.

Considerations of time and space have also caused us to limit the scope of our inquiry. One such limitation is that our analysis deals entirely with a closed economy. Extensions to consider an open economy seem straightforward and worthwhile. Similarly, we have not dealt with the long-term implications of growth in population or technology, although the analytical framework could readily encompass these phenomena.

One other omission from our discussion is especially embarrassing and should be explicity noted. Although the discussion stresses the implications of exchange at wages and prices which are inconsistent with general market clearing, we provide no choice-theoretic analysis of the market-clearing process itself. In other words, we do not analyze the adjustment of wages and prices as part of the maximizing behavior of firms and households. Consequently, we do not really explain the failure of markets to clear, and our analyses of wage and price dynamics are based on ad hoc adjustment equations.

Unfortunately, the development of a convincing theory of the market-clearing process represents a still unsolved puzzle. The existing literature provides few clues as to useful approaches.[4] The development of such a theory ranks high on our agenda for current and future research.

[4] Examples of models which do suggest explanations for market-clearing friction include Barro (1972), who emphasizes lumpy costs of changing prices and the stochastic nature of demand, and Sweezy (1939), who emphasizes competitive strategy. More recent contributions, which emphasize risk aversion and implicit contracts, include Azariadis (1974) and Baily (1974).

1 *The basic model*

This chapter develops a simple model which serves as our basic
analytical framework. Section 1.1 outlines the essentials of
this model. Section 1.2 analyzes the behavior of individual
economic units within the basic model. Section 1.3 develops
comparative-statics analysis. Section 1.4 analyzes wage and
price dynamics.

1.1   The essentials of the basic model

The basic model involves four economic goods – labor services, consumable commodities, public services, and fiat money – and three forms
of economic decision-making unit – a fixed number of firms, a fixed
number of households, and government. Labor services and public
services are the only variable inputs into the production process. Other
inputs have a fixed quantity, no alternative use, and zero user cost.
Current output consists of consumable commodities and public services.
All current output is produced by the same technology, and only assumes
its specific identity according to the identity of its purchaser. In particular,
household purchases are consumables and government purchases are
public services. Fiat money is the only store of value; it also serves as
a medium of exchange and unit of account. Transactions involving
money are costless, and receipts and disbursements of money are
perfectly synchronized.

Firms demand labor and supply both consumable commodities
and public services. They attempt to maximize profits. These profits
represent a return to the nonvariable inputs, of which each firm possesses
a predetermined and fixed amount. Profits are essentially economic
rents earned by the nonvariable inputs.

Households may be either working or retired. Working households supply labor and demand consumables and money balances.
Retired households demand consumables and money balances. All
households also receive the profits of the firms and pay taxes according
to predetermined patterns. Households attempt to maximize utility.
The government collects taxes, demands and distributes public services,
and supplies money balances.

The use of money as a medium of exchange implies that exchange takes place at two market places – a labor market, in which
labor services are exchanged for money, and a commodity market, in

which consumable commodities and public services are exchanged for money. In general, each good, other than money, has its own market in which it is traded for money. In contrast, money has no market of its own, but is traded in each of the markets associated with the other goods.

In most general terms, the analysis in this book is concerned with the determination of the quantities of the economic goods and their exchange ratios. Regarding quantities, we shall be concerned, at various times, with two sorts of distinction. First, quantities are either stock or flow variables. Second, we distinguish among quantities actually held or exchanged, quantities supplied, and quantities demanded. To emphasize these distinctions, we conform throughout to three notational conventions. First, lower case letters denote flow variables and upper case letters denoted stock variables. Thus, in the basic model, we have

l: flow of labor services, measured in man-hours per year,

c: flow of consumables, measured in physical units per year,

g: flow of public services, measured in units of consumables per year,

y: flow of current output, measured in units of consumables per year, $y \equiv c + g$,

π: flow of profits, measured in units of consumables per year,

τ: flow of tax revenues (net of transfers), measured in units of consumables per year,

M.   nominal stock of money balances, measured in dollars, and

m: flow of nominal money balances, measured in dollars per year, $m \equiv dM/dt$.

Second, the superscripts s and d denote quantities supplied and demanded, respectively, of the attached variable. Variables written without a superscript denote the actual flow exchanged or the actual stock held.

In general, the number of independent exchange ratios is one less than the number of economic goods. Because both consumables and public services are produced by the same technology, they are perfectly substitutable on the supply side. This substitutability effectively fixes the exchange ratio between consumables and public services. Thus, the basic model involves two independent exchange ratios. Since labor services and commodities are both actually exchanged for money, we focus on the exchange ratios between money and labor services and between money and commodities. In particular, we have

P: the price of commodities, both consumables and public services, which is the number of dollars per unit of commodities, and

W: the nominal wage rate, which is the number of dollars per man-hour of labor services.

The real wage rate, which is the number of units of commodities per man-hour of labor services, is given by the ratio W/P.

When analyzing the behavior of firms, working households, and retired households, we consider the 'representative' unit; that is, a unit whose behavior, except for its atomistic scale, is identical to the behavior of the aggregate of such units. The representative unit is essentially an average unit. Consequently, we are able to move freely between the individual and aggregate, and we use the same notation to represent both. Note, however, that in employing the concept of the representative unit we abstract from distributional effects. Therefore, the validity of the analysis depends either on the smallness of changes in distribution, or on the negligible impact on variables of interest of those variations in distribution which do occur.

We also assume that firms and households are atomistic units–that is, that each one contributes only negligibly to the total quantity supplied or demanded of each good. Consequently, each unit acts as a price-taker with respect to P and W – that is, each unit neglects the impact of its own supply or demand on market price and wage. In addition, the basic model assumes that each unit acts as though it can sell or buy any amount which it supplies or demands of each good at the going market price or wage. In particular, firms believe that they can buy the quantity of labor services which they demand and sell the quantity of commodities which they supply; households believe that they can sell the quantity of labor services which they supply and buy the quantity of consumables which they demand; and government believes that it can buy the quantity of public services which it demands. This assumption is justified, *ex post*, only when aggregate supply and demand balance in each market; in symbols, when $l^d = l^s = l$ and $c^d + g^d = y^s = y$. Thus, in the basic model, exchanges are assumed to take place only under these market-clearing conditions. (Section 1.4 below discusses the possible rationalization of this assumption.) Under these circumstances, each atomistic unit's assumed ability to buy or sell any amount desired at the existing P and W is always borne out by the actual transactions which occur in the markets.

The possibility of exchange taking place under non-market-clearing conditions would introduce the possibility that actual transactions and quantities supplied or demanded might be unequal for some economic units. In this case individual units may consider possible constraints on purchases or sales in the formulation of supply and demand. The form of the demand and supply functions derived for the basic model depends crucially on the absence of this possibility. We denote these functions as 'notional' – in the sense of assumed ability to conduct all desired trades at the going P and W. The more general demand and supply functions, which allow for the possibility of exchange under non-market-clearing conditions, are called 'effective' functions. We begin consideration of effective functions in chapter 2. In chapter 1, we confine attention to the notional functions.

The purpose of the basic model is to provide a choice-theoretic basis for the analysis of the relationships between aggregate variables. Because the underlying behavior of individual units is explicitly represented, the implications of relaxing various abstractions are readily identifiable. Along these lines, in subsequent chapters, we introduce into this basic framework many complicating aspects of reality, such as (1) constraints imposed on individual behavior by exchange under non-market-clearing conditions, (2) investment goods and financial assets, (3) expectations, and (4) transactions costs.

1.2 The behavior of firms, households, and government in the basic model

1.2.1 *The firms*

The objective of the firms is to maximize profits. This objective may be thought of as imposed on the firms by the households, who own the firms in the sense that the households receive the profits. Given this imposed objective, we view the firms as separate decision-making units from the households.

Profits are the difference between revenue from sales and payments to productive inputs. The basic model assumes labor services to be the only input which must be purchased. The government makes public services available without charge to the firms.[1] Consequently, profit is given by

$$\pi \equiv y - \frac{W}{P} l.$$

Because we assume that firms are able to sell the quantity of output which they supply and to buy the quantity of labor services which they demand, profit as viewed by the representative firm may also be expressed as

$$\pi \equiv y^s - \frac{W}{P} l^d, \tag{1.1}$$

---

[1] Although firms use money as a medium of exchange, their activities do not involve the holding of money balances. This phenomenon reflects the assumption that transactions are costless and that receipts and disbursements are prefectly synchronized.

where y^s is the firm's supply of commodities, l^d its demand for labor services, and where W/P is exogenous to the firm – that is independent of the firm's choice of y^s and l^d.

The firm chooses y^s and l^d so as to maximize π. The production function, which relates the quantities of inputs of labor and public services to the quantity of output, constrains this choice. For the representative firm, we assume the production function to be

$$y = \Phi(l, g), \tag{1.2}$$

where Φ exhibits positive and diminishing marginal product with respect to each input, as well as diminishing returns to scale. We also assume, for simplicity, that the marginal product of labor is independent of the level of g.[2] Since commodities are assumed to be nonstorable, firms do not hold inventories. Further, since adjustment costs are zero, firms set output to be equal to sales at all times. Therefore, y may be viewed alternatively as representing either sales or output of commodities per year. Profit maximization requires the equation of the marginal product of labor to the real wage – that is, the selection of

$$l^d = l^d \underset{(-)}{\left(\frac{W}{P}\right)} \text{ and}^3 \tag{1.3}$$

$$y^s = \Phi\left[l^d\left(\frac{W}{P}\right), g\right] \equiv y^s \underset{(-)\,(+)}{\left(\frac{W}{P}, g\right),^4} \tag{1.4}$$

such that

$$\frac{\delta\Phi}{\delta l} = \frac{W}{P}.$$

Profit maximization subject to the assumed production function implies that both notional labor demand and notional commodity supply are inversely related to the real wage. Commodity supply also depends directly on the level of public services.

1.2.2 The households
The objective of the households is to maximize utility. We assume that utility depends directly on the level of consumption and inversely on

[2] The signs of the partial derivatives of Φ are $[\Phi_l, \Phi_g] > 0$, $[\Phi_{ll}, \Phi_{gg}] < 0$, and $\Phi_{lg} = 0$.

[3] Because we have assumed that $\Phi_{lg} = 0$, l^d is independent of g.

[4] The sign in parentheses below an argument of a function indicates the sign of the derivative, partial or total as the case may be, of the dependent variable with respect to that argument.

the amount of time devoted to employment. Note that consumption, c, refers here to consumables purchased for money in the market place and employment, l, refers to employment for money wages obtained in the market place. By definition, all time not spent at employment in the market is spent at leisure. The analysis does not distinguish between various possible leisure time activities, e.g., rest, home production.

With the existence of a store of value, utility maximization is an intertemporal problem. By appropriate management of its money balance over time, money being the only store of value in the basic model, the household may select from a wide range of lifetime consumption and employment patterns. In order to illustrate this problem of choice, we first specify the momentary utility function

$$u(t) = u[c(t), l(t)], \tag{1.5}$$

which exhibits positive and diminishing marginal utility with respect to consumption and positive and increasing marginal disutility with respect to employment.[5]

We then assume that the household attempts to maximize total utility over its planning horizon, which is

$$U = \int_0^N u(t) \, dt,^6 \tag{1.6}$$

where N represents the number of years until the household's planning horizon. The planning horizon consists of N' working years and $N - N'$ retirement years. We take N' and N to be exogenously determined parameters. For households which are currently retired, $N' = 0$.

Because we assume that households are able to sell the quantity of labor which they supply and to buy the quantity of commodities which they demand, the actual quantities c and l are equivalent to the notional consumables demand c^d and the notional labor supply l^s. At the present moment, the household chooses $c^d(0)$ and $l^s(0)$ to be consistent with the maximization of U. This choice calculus also implies the entire planned time paths of c^d and l^s.

[5] The signs of the partial derivatives of u are $u_c > 0$, $u_l < 0$, $u_{cc} < 0$, $u_{ll} < 0$, and $u_{cl} \gtrless 0$. This utility function abstracts from any effect of governmental activity either on the level of utility or on the marginal utility of private consumption or employment. Cf. Bailey (1971, chapter 9).

[6] The total utility expression may be generalized to include a discount factor for the instantaneous utility flow, $u(t)$. In addition, some intertemporal dependence among utility flows at different points in time can be introduced. These complications would not affect the general forms of the resulting supply and demand functions and are not treated explicitly here.

Holdings of money balances provide a medium which ties together the time paths of c^d and l^s. Assuming P to be constant, the household's disposable income consists of its wage income plus its profit income less its tax liabilities. Recall that we assume that all households receive a share of the profits of the firms and pay taxes according to predetermined patterns.[7] Saving, which is the rate of change of real money holdings, is the difference between real disposable income and consumption. Thus, for working households,

$$\frac{1}{P}\left(\frac{\mathrm{d}M}{\mathrm{d}t}\right)^d \equiv \frac{m^d}{P} \equiv \frac{W}{P}l^s + \pi - \tau - c^d. \tag{1.7}$$

By determining its consumption and employment, the household simultaneously determines the rate of change of its real money balance. Only two of these three decisions are independent. Equation (1.7) applies also to retired households, but with l^s set at zero. If P is regarded as constant over time, the household's planned real asset holdings at any point in time, $M(t)/P$, can be calculated by adding to initial real asset holdings, $M(0)/P$, the integral of m^d/P from time 0 to time t.

Since no utility accrues from consumption beyond the planning horizon, the household's optimal intertemporal plan entails the exhaustion of asset holdings at date N.[8] We have assumed the variables W, P, π, and τ to be exogenous to the household – that is, independent of its own actions. We assume, in addition, that the household takes these variables to be constant over time in formulating its consumption and employment plans. Consequently, the household's planned time pattern of consumption and leisure will satisfy

$$\frac{M(N)}{P} = \frac{M(0)}{P} + N(\pi - \tau) + \frac{W}{P}\int_0^{N'} l^s(t)\mathrm{d}t$$

$$- \int_0^N c^d(t)\mathrm{d}t = 0. \tag{1.8}$$

This condition says that total consumption until its planning horizon must equal the sum of total real wages earned until retirement plus total profits received less taxes paid until its planning horizon plus its present holding of real money balances. The latter two items would delimit lifetime consumption if no employment were taken, and they

---

[7] Chapter 3 modifies this assumption regarding profit distribution with the introduction of an equity market. The assumption regarding tax payments could be easily modified to allow tax liabilities to depend on household income or wealth.

[8] We rule out the possibility of negative legacies.

represent a basic constraint on household behavior. We refer to this constraint as nonwage wealth, and denote its value by Ω, where

$$\Omega \equiv \frac{M(0)}{P} + N(\pi - \tau).$$

Again, equation (1.8) also applies to retired households, but with wage income set at zero.

The optimal time time pattern of consumption and employment depends on the specification of the momentary utility function as given in equation (1.5), on the additive nature of lifetime utility as given in equation (1.6), on the lengths of the working and planning horizons, N' and N, on the relative price of leisure and consumption during working years, which is the real wage rate W/P, and on Ω. In particular, given equations (1.5) and (1.6) and the values of N' and N, the maximization of U, subject to the asset exhaustion condition of equation (1.8),[9] requires, for working households, the following time pattern for l^s and c^d: The level of l^s is constant from now, date 0, until retirement, date N'. The level of c^d is constant from date 0 until date N' and is also constant, but generally at a different level, from date N' until the planning horizon, date N. However, if consumption and employment are independent influences on utility, before- and after-retirement levels of consumption would be the same – that is, c^d would be constant from date 0 until date N. In this case, the asset-exhaustion condition of equation (1.8) simplifies to

$$\Omega + N' \frac{W}{P} l^s - Nc^d = 0.$$

The maximization calculus implies, specifically, that the current levels of c^d and l^s are determined by functions of the following form:

$$c^d = c^d \underset{(+)\ \ (+)}{(\Omega,\ W/P)} \tag{1.9}$$

and

$$l^s = l^s \underset{(-)\ \ (+)}{(\Omega,\ W/P)}. \tag{1.10}$$

The mathematical note at the end of this section details the derivation of these functions. However, we can readily explain their form intuitively.

Changes in $M(0)/P$, π, and τ involve pure wealth effects; they affect c^d and l^s only through their effect on Ω. In particular, increases

---

[9] The maximization of U is also subject to the inequality constraints $[c^d(t),\ l^s(t),\ M(t)] \geq 0$. We assume these constraints to be ineffective, except for $M(N) = 0$, and we therefore deal only with interior solutions for c^d and l^s, subject to equation (1.8).

in $M(0)/P$ and π and reductions in τ raise Ω and, since both consumption and leisure are assumed to be normal goods, such increases in Ω raise c^d and lower l^s.

The effects of changes in W/P are more complicated, since both income and substitution effects are involved. On the one hand, an increase in W/P increases the real income associated with any amount of employment, and induces an increase in c^d and a decrease in l^s (increase in leisure). On the other hand, an increase in W/P raises the cost of leisure relative to consumption during working years, and induces increases in both c^d and l^s. Consequently, the total effect of an increase in W/P on c^d would be positive, but the net effect on l^s involves a weighing of income and substitution effects and, in general, is ambiguous. We shall assume that the substitution effect outweighs the income effect in the relevant range, so that, on balance, an increase in W/P raises l^s.

Given the definition of saving as specified by equation (1.7), the optimal time patterns for c^d and l^s imply an optimal time pattern for m^d/P. In particular, m^d/P is constant from date 0 until N', and constant at a different level from date N' until N. Whether m^d/P is positive or negative during the working years depends on the values of Ω and W/P. Typically we would expect Ω to be small enough and W/P to be large enough that the incentive to provide for consumption during retirement would induce the representative working household to engage in positive saving.

Substitution of the optimal values for c^d and l^s from equations (1.9) and (1.10) into equation (1.7) yields for working households the following expression for the current notional real flow demand for money balances:

$$\frac{m^d}{P} = \frac{m^d}{P} \underset{(-)\ (+)\ \ \ (+)}{(\Omega,\ W/P,\ \pi - \tau)}. \tag{1.11}$$

An increase in Ω raises current c^d and lowers current l^s, and so, given W/P and $\pi - \tau$, lowers current m^d/P. An increase in W/P raises planned c^d during retirement years, and so, given Ω and $\pi - \tau$, must also raise m^d/P during working years. Finally, given Ω and W/P, which determine c^d and $(W/P)l^s$, an increase in $\pi - \tau$ increases current disposable income and raises current m^d/P.

Retired households differ from working households in that, for retired households, l^s is zero and no possibility exists for substitution between consumption and leisure. Consequently, the real wage rate has no effect on the optimal behavior of retired households. However, the directions of effect of Ω and $\pi - \tau$ on c^d and m^d/P for retired households are the same as those for working households. Thus, the aggregate notional demand and supply functions, combining both working and retired households, have the same forms as the functions given in equations (1.9–1.11), where Ω and $\pi - \tau$ are interpreted as aggregate quantities.[10] Aggregate Ω has the same definition as individual Ω, but with $M(0)/P$, π, and τ representing aggregates and N representing the average number of years until the planning horizon for all households.

Mathematical note

The interior solution for optimal values of $c^d(t)$ and $l^s(t)$ satisfies the following conditions:

$$\frac{\delta u}{\delta c^d(t)} = \lambda \qquad \text{for } 0 \leq t \leq N,$$

$$\frac{\delta u}{\delta l^s(t)} = -\lambda \cdot \frac{W}{P} \qquad \text{for } 0 \leq t \leq N', \text{ and}$$

$$l^s(t) = 0 \qquad \text{for } N' < t \leq N$$

where λ is a constant determined so as to satisfy the asset-exhaustion condition of equation (1.8). These conditions imply that

$$c^d(t) = c^d(0) \qquad \text{for } 0 \leq t \leq N',$$
$$c^d(t) = c^d(N) \qquad \text{for } N' < t \leq N,$$
$$l^s(t) = l^s(0) \qquad \text{for } 0 \leq t \leq N', \text{ and}$$
$$l^s(t) = 0 \qquad \text{for } N' < t \leq N.$$

Further, if consumption and employment are independent influences on utility – that is, if $\delta^2 u/\delta c(t)\delta l(t) = 0$ – then $c^d(0) = c^d(N)$. For a

[10] This formulation abstracts from the effects of the distribution of wealth both among working and retired households and between these two groups. In fact, such effects may be important. For example, working and retired housholds should have predictably different reactions to changes in nonwage wealth. In particular, *ceteris paribus*, an increase in the share of a given aggregate Ω owned by retired households would have the following effects: Working households would decrease their notional consumption demand and increase their notional labor supply and saving. However, retired households would increase their notional consumption demand and decrease their saving, and because of their shorter planning horizons, their changes in consumption and saving would tend to outweigh those of the working households. Consequently, on net c^d and l^s would tend to rise, and m^d/P would tend to fall.

further discussion of the nature and form of this intertemporal maximization problem, see, for example, Intriligator (1971, chapter 14).

1.2.3 Government

The basic model treats government behavior as exogenous, and does not attempt to explain its three activites – g^d, m^s/P, and τ – as responses to changes in wages, prices, etc. However, government activity is subject to the budget constraint,

$$g^d \equiv \tau + \frac{m^s}{P}. \tag{1.12}$$

This constraint says that government demand for commodities, i.e., provision of public services, must be financed by some combination of taxation (net of transfers) and flow supply of money, money being the only form of government debt in the basic model. The total outstanding real stock of government debt is M/P, which, treating P as constant, is the integral of past creations of new money balances, m/P. In the basic model the stock of government debt coincides with the stock of private wealth. Finally, we assume that the quantity of public services which the government chooses to provide is such that the marginal productivity of public services is less than unity. In other words, we assume $\Phi_g(g^d) < 1$. From a resource allocation standpoint, this assumption implies that, at least under general-market-clearing conditions, the public sector is too large.[11]

> [11] This assumption about the marginal productivity of public services refers to the effect on aggregate output of a change in the aggregate amount of public services. The choice of an optimal aggregate level of g would require the government to maximize $u[c^*(g), l^*(g)]$, where $c^*(g)$ and $l^*(g)$ represent the solutions to the systems of market-clearing conditions specified in the next section. The first-order condition for this maximum would be $u_c c_g^* + u_l l_g^* = 0$. The production function, $c + g = \Phi(l, g)$, implies $c_g^* - \Phi_l l_g^* + 1 - \Phi_g = 0$, and profit maximization implies $\Phi_l = W/P$. Thus, the first-order condition can be expressed as $\left(\dfrac{W}{P} + \dfrac{u_l}{u_c}\right) l_g^* = 1 - \Phi_g$. Moreover, for working households, utility maximization implies $\dfrac{W}{P} + \dfrac{u_l}{u_c} = 0$. For retired households, $l^* = 0$, so that $l_g^* = 0$. Consequently, the first-order condition reduces to $\Phi_g[l_g^*(g), g] = 1$. If, as we are assuming, $\Phi_{lg} = 0$, the calculation of the optimal g^d simplifies to satisfying the condition $\Phi_g(g) = 1$. See Grossman and Lucas (1974) for a fuller discussion of the implications of the level of g relative to the optimal level. See Buchanan and Tullock (1962, Chapters 10, 11), Niskanen (1971), and Barro (1973) for rationalizations of over-expansion of the public sector from the viewpoint of political economy.

1.3   Comparative-statics analysis in the basic model

1.3.1   *Market-clearing conditions*

The basic model assumes that exchange takes place only under market-clearing conditions. These conditions require a harmonization of the behavior of the firms, households, and government, which was analyzed in the preceding section. In the basic model, exchange takes place at two market places – the labor market and the commodity market. In the labor market, market clearing requires that both the quantity of labor services demanded by the firms and the quantity of labor services supplied by the households be equal to the actual level of employment. Thus, the labor-market-clearing condition is

$$l^d \underset{(-)}{\left(\frac{W}{P}\right)} = l^s \underset{(-)(+)}{\left(\Omega, \frac{W}{P}\right)} = l. \tag{1.13}$$

In the commodity market, market clearing requires that both the quantity of commodities supplied by the firms and the quantity of commodities demanded by the households and the government be equal to actual production. Thus, the commodity-market-clearing condition is

$$y^s \underset{(-)(+)}{\left(\frac{W}{P}, g^d\right)} = c^d \underset{(+)(+)}{\left(\Omega, \frac{W}{P}\right)} + g^d = y. \tag{1.14}$$

We can analyze the implications of these market-clearing conditions most readily through graphical representations. Figure 1.1 represents the labor market. The vertical axis measures the real wage rate, and the horizontal axis measures the quantity of labor services. Notional labor demand is uniquely related to W/P and is represented as a single downward sloping curve. Notional labor supply depends on nonwage-wealth Ω and W/P, and is represented as a family of upward sloping curves. Figure 1.1 explicitly depicts three of these l^s curves, corresponding to three values of Ω, where $\Omega_2 > \Omega^* > \Omega_1$.

Observe that labor-market clearing would be consistent with various combinations of Ω and W/P. The combination $[\Omega^*, (W/P)^*]$ is one of these. Suppose that Ω is equal to Ω^*. In that situation, at real wage rates above $(W/P)^*$ there would be excess supply of labor services, i.e., l^d would be less than l^s. At real wage rates below $(W/P)^*$, there would be excess demand for labor services, i.e., l^d would be greater than l^s. Similarly, with W/P equal to $(W/P)^*$, Ω greater than Ω^* would make l^d greater than l^s, whereas Ω less than Ω^* would make l^d less than l^s.

Figure 1.2 represents the commodity market. The vertical axis again measures the real wage rate, and the horizontal axis now

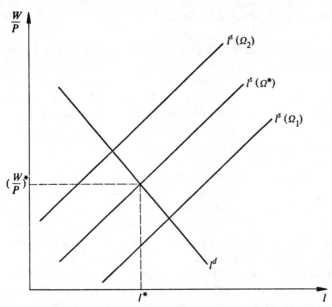

Figure 1.1
The labor market in the basic model

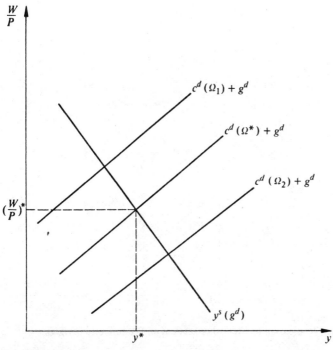

Figure 1.2
The commodity market in the basic model

measures the quantity of commodities. Notional commodity supply depends on W/P, as well as on g^d which we hold fixed for the moment, and is represented as a single downward sloping curve. Notional commodity demand depends on Ω and W/P, in addition to g^d. Thus, notional commodity demand is represented as a family of upward sloping curves, three of which, corresponding to the three values of nonwage wealth Ω_2, Ω^*, and Ω_1, are explicitly depicted in figure 1.2.

Observe that commodity-market clearing would also be consistent with various combinations of Ω and W/P. The combination $[\Omega^*, (W/P)^*]$ is again one of these. With Ω equal to Ω^*, W/P greater than $(W/P)^*$ would make $c^d + g^d$ greater than y^s, whereas W/P less than $(W/P)^*$ would make $c^d + g^d$ less than y^s. Similarly, with W/P equal to $(W/P)^*$, Ω greater than Ω^* would make $c^d + g^d$ greater than y^s, whereas Ω less than Ω^* would make $c^d + g^d$ less than y^s.

The combination $[\Omega^*, (W/P)^*]$ is consistent with market clearing in both markets. A little experimentation would reveal that this combination is also the only one consistent with general market clearing. To demonstrate this uniqueness property, it is convenient to combine the analysis depicted in figures 1.1 and 1.2 into a single diagram, repre-

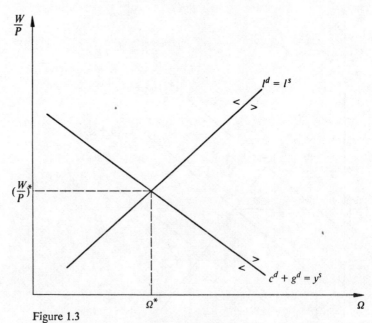

Figure 1.3
Market-clearing loci for labor services and commodity markets

sented by figure 1.3. In this figure, the locus labeled $l^d = l^s$ depicts the combinations of values of Ω and W/P which are consistent with the labor-market-clearing condition. The above discussion of the effects of Ω and W/P on the state of excess labor supply or demand implies that this locus is upward sloping. To verify this result, consider the following experiment: Suppose that the labor-market-clearing condition were initially satisfied, but that Ω was then increased. The effect would be a decrease in l^s, which would cause excess demand in the labor market. What change in W/P would be required to reestablish the labor-market-clearing condition? Clearly, W/P would have to rise, causing l^s to increase and l^d to decrease. The $(>, <)$ signs bordering the $l^d = l^s$ locus indicate that combinations of Ω and W/P below and to the right imply excess demand for labor services, whereas combinations above and to the left imply excess supply.

Similarly, the locus labeled $c^d + g^d = y^s$ depicts the combinations of values of Ω and W/P which are consistent with the commodity-market-clearing condition. To determine the slope of this locus, consider the following experiment: Suppose that the commodity-market-clearing condition were initially satisfied, but that Ω was then increased. The effect would be an increase in c^d, which would cause excess demand in the commodity market. What change in W/P would be required to reestablish the commodity-market-clearing condition? Clearly, W/P would have to decrease, causing c^d to decrease and y^s to increase. The commodity-market-clearing locus is thus downward sloping. The $(<, >)$ signs here indicate that this locus separates the region of excess supply, below and to the left of the locus, from the region of excess demand, above and to the right of the locus.

The two market-clearing loci intersect at the point $[\Omega^*, (W/P)^*]$. This intersection indicates that, as we discussed above, only this combination of nonwage wealth and real wage rate is consistent with both market-clearing conditions. We denote Ω^* as the general-market-clearing level of nonwage wealth and $(W/P)^*$ as the general-market-clearing real wage rate. The combination $[\Omega^*, (W/P)^*]$ also implies values for l, y, c, P, W, and π – denoted l^*, y^*, c^*, P^*, W^*, and π^* – which are consistent with general market clearing. We can determine l^* and y^* by substituting Ω^* and $(W/P)^*$ into conditions (1.13) and (1.14). We can then determine π^* from $\pi^* = y^* - (W/P)^* l^*$. Since $\Omega^* = (M/P^*) + N(\pi^* - \tau)$, where M, N, and τ are specified exogenously, P^* follows immediately once Ω^* and π^* are known. The value of W^* is simply the product of P^* and $(W/P)^*$. Finally, c^* equals y^* less g^d.

1.3.2 The supply and demand for money balances

As we indicated in equation (1.7) above, the behavior of the households in the basic model is subject to the momentary budget constraint

$$c^d + \frac{m^d}{P} + \tau \equiv \frac{W}{P} l^s + \pi.$$

This constraint implies that, although the household apparently engages in three activities – demanding consumables and money balances and supplying labor services – it really has only two degrees of freedom. The total value of its demands for consumables and money plus its tax payments to the government must equal the value of its supply of labor services plus its receipts of profits from the firms. In addition, from the government's budget constraint, equation (1.12), household taxes must equal the difference between the value of government demand for commodities and the supply of money,

$$\tau \equiv g^d - \frac{m^s}{P}.$$

From the definition of profit, equation (1.1), household profit receipts must equal the difference between the values of firm supply of commodities and firm demand for labor services,

$$\pi \equiv y^s - \frac{W}{P} l^d.$$

We should note that the above specifications of equations (1.1), (1.7), and (1.12) all involved the assumption that firms, households, and the government could actually transact the quantities which they supply and demand, an assumption which is tenable only if the general-market-clearing conditions are satisfied.

By combining these three conditions, we obtain an economy-wide budget constraint, which is applicable under general-market-clearing conditions:

$$(c^d + g^d - y^s) + \frac{W}{P} (l^d - l^s) + \frac{1}{P} (m^d - m^s) \equiv 0. \tag{1.15}$$

Equation (1.15) implies that if the market-clearing conditions for commodities and labor services are both satisfied, the flow notional demand and supply for money must also be equal. Consequently, even though the basic model involves three economic goods, the conditions of equality between quantities demanded and supplied imply only two independent constraints on the two independent exchange ratios. This property is sometimes referred to as Walras' Law of Markets.

1.3.3 *The effects of exogenous disturbances*

Comparative-statics analysis in the basic model is concerned with the relations between the exogenous variables of the model and the values of the endogenous variables which satisfy the market-clearing conditions. Suppose that some exogenous disturbance occurs. General possibilities include changes in production technology, in household tastes or age structure, which would affect the average values of N' and N, or in government behavior. In order to satisfy the market-clearing conditions, what changes, if any, in Ω^* and $(W/P)^*$, and hence in l^*, y^*, P^* and W^* will be required? We classify this as a question for comparative-statics analysis because it does not inquire into the processes by which these endogenous variables would actually change. The investigation of such processes is called dynamic analysis. The next section considers dynamic analysis within the context of the basic model.

In order to illustrate the nature of the effects of exogenous disturbances in the basic model, we consider three examples of practical interest and apply comparative-statics analysis to each of them. The mathematical note at the end of this section sets out the general form of this analysis.

As the first example, consider a change in government behavior in the form of an increase in m^s/P which is used to finance a reduction in τ. The reduction in τ may be viewed equivalently as either an increase in transfers from government to households or a cut in household taxes. The proximate effect of this disturbance would be to raise Ω and, as a consequence of this increase in nonwage wealth, to induce an increase in c^d and a decrease in l^s.[12] However, this disturbance does not alter the nature of the functional dependence of c^d and l^s on Ω and W/P, nor does it affect the relations between y^s and l^d and W/P. Consequently, the market-clearing loci of figure 1.3 do not shift, and the initial values of Ω and W/P are still consistent with general market clearing. In order to reestablish general market clearing, Ω must return to its original

---

[12] The effect of a reduction in τ in increasing Ω involves the assumption that the representative household anticipates that τ will be constant over time at its current level. Consequently, the representative household regards this reduction in τ as permanent, and calculates the change in Ω as $d\Omega = -Nd\tau$. Alternatively, if the representative household regarded the reduction in τ to be transitory, only a momentary aberration, the reduction in τ, *per se*, would not affect Ω. The flow demand for money would absorb the entire reduction in τ in accordance with equation (1.11), and would thereby balance the increase in m^s/P without any change in Ω or W/P. In that case, the present disturbance would affect the market-clearing conditions only through its effect over time on M, which is discussed in the next paragraph.

value while W/P remains unchanged. This adjustment can be accomplished by an increase in P just sufficient to offset the decrease in τ – more precisely, P increases by NP^2/M times the reduction in τ – accompanied by an equiproportionate increase in W.

This analysis of the immediate effects of the increase in m^s/P is not, however, the end of the story. We must also take account of the relation between m and M, i.e., $m \equiv dM/dt$. For simplicity, assume that m was initially zero, so that the government's budget was initially in balance: $g^d = \tau$. Then the increase in m^s/P, which according to the market-clearing conditions and Walras' Law equals m^d/P and m/P, will mean that m becomes positive and that M continually increases. This continual increase in M tends continually to raise Ω and induces further increases in c^d and decreases in l^s. As we have seen, the sole impact of an exogenous disturbance to Ω is to produce changes in P and W which offset the disturbance and keep W/P unchanged. In this case, P and W must increase over time at the same proportionate rate as M, which will also keep M/P unchanged over time.

Finally, suppose that, after some finite interval, m^s/P were decreased to zero, with τ increased back to its original value. This reversal of the initial disturbance would imply decreases in P and W in order to maintain the values of Ω^* and $(W/P)^*$. However, because of the accumulated increase in M, P and W would not return to their original values. The net increase in P^* and W^* over their original values would be equiproportional to the increase in M over its original value, thereby reestablishing the initial value of M/P, and maintaining the initial values of Ω and W/P. Figure 1.4 depicts the time paths of m/P, M, and P^* in this example.

This example of comparative-statics analysis, which concerned disturbances to the intitial market-clearing conditions involving changes in both m and M, has established an important property of the model with regard to monetary effects. Changes in the rate of monetary expansion, when the additional money is used to reduce taxes, have a direct effect on the nominal values P^* and W^* and an indirect effect on M/P^*, but have no effect on the other real variables of the system – Ω^*, $(W/P)^*$, π^*, y^*, and l^*. Changes in the nominal stock of money have a direct and equiproportionate effect on P^* and W^*, but have no effect on any of the real variables of the system, including M/P^*. This property of the basic model regarding changes in M is referred to as neutrality of money. Neutrality is a consequence of the form of the supply and demand functions in which real supplies and demands depend only on real variables – for example, W/P and M/P – and not separately on nominal variables – for example, W or P. This property of the demand functions, termed lack of money illusion, derives from the underlying maximization of utility by the households, where utility is assumed to depend only on the real amounts of consumption and employment and not on their nominal values. The setting of government demand for commodities in real terms is also necessary for neutrality.

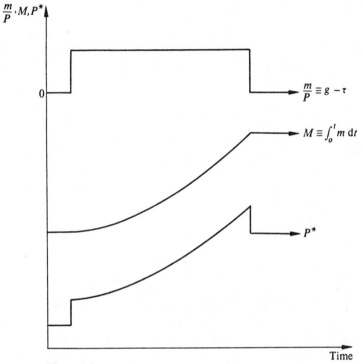

Figure 1.4
Time paths of m/p, M, and P^*

In the preceding example, we considered an increase in m^s/P which had no effect on Ω^*, $(W/P)^*$, π^*, y^*, and l^*. However, this increase in m^s/P was used solely to reduce τ. If, alternatively, any part of the increase in m^s/P had been used to finance an increase in g^d, its effect would have been essentially different. In particular, Ω^*, $(W/P)^*$, π^*, y^*, and l^* would all have been changed.

As a second example of comparative-statics analysis, let us assume that, with τ held fixed, m^s/P is increased and used solely to increase government demand for commodities. This disturbance has no direct effect on household behavior. However, it will shift the y^s

curve and each of the $c^d + g^d$ curves, depicted in figure 1.2, to the right. At any combination of Ω and W/P, both the supply of commodities and the total of government and household demands for commodities will be increased. However, we have assumed that the level of provision of public services is sufficiently high that the marginal product with respect to g^d is less than unity. Consequently, the rightward shift in the $c^d + g^d$ curves is greater than the rightward shift in the y^s curve, and the combination of values of Ω and W/P which originally satisfied the market-clearing conditions will now imply excess demand for commodities.

What changes in Ω and W/P are necessary to reestablish equality between notional demand and notional supply in both markets? Figure 1.5 reproduces the market-clearing loci of figure 1.3 and illustrates the

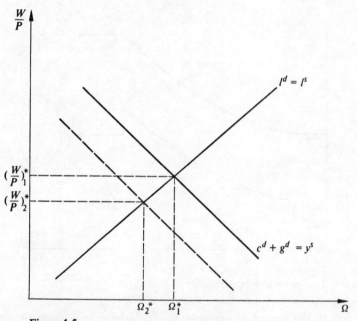

Figure 1.5
Effect of increased government expenditure

effect of this disturbance by a leftward shift in the $c^d + g^d = y^s$ locus. The dashed line represents the new locus. The new intersection of the market-clearing loci is such that Ω_2^* is below Ω_1^* and $(W/P)_2^*$ is below $(W/P)_1^*$.

The reduction in Ω depresses c^d, and the reduction in W/P both further depresses c^d and stimulates y^s. In this way, $c^d + g^d$ and y^s are re-equated. The necessity to maintain the equality between l^d and l^s

determines the relative magnitudes of the declines in Ω and W/P. The reduction in Ω stimulates l^s, whereas the reduction in W/P produces a just offsetting combination of depressant to l^s and stimulant to l^d.

What implications do the reductions in Ω and W/P have for P, W, y, c, and l? We have assumed τ to be unchanged. Moreover, the reduction in W/P implies an increase in π. Consequently, the reduction in Ω requires an increase in P. The effect on W is ambiguous, depending on the quantitative relation between P and Ω and on the relative magnitudes of the reductions in Ω and W/P. The increase in g^d implies a rise in y^s, and the reduction in W/P implies a further increase in y^s and a rise in l^d. With the market-clearing conditions satisfied, these changes imply increases in y and l. However, because the reductions in Ω and W/P depress c^d and c, the induced increase in y is smaller than the increase in g^d. Because we assumed that the provision of public services was initially too large, a further increase in g^d makes households worse off, in the sense that c declines and l increases.[13]

Once again, these effects are not the end of the story. The increase in m^s/P again produces a continual increase in M, which, as in the preceding example, requires that both P and W rise at the same proportionate rate.

Government behavior is, of course, not the only possible source of disturbances. As a final example of comparative-statics analysis, consider a technological innovation which increases the output produced by any given amount of labor services. A simple possibility would assume the production function to have the form

$$\Phi(l,g) = \alpha\phi(l,g),$$

where technical progress would be represented by an increase in the parameter α. As α increases, both $\Phi(l,g)$ and $\delta\Phi/\delta l$ become larger for all values of l and g^d. The effect of this disturbance will be to shift both the l^d and y^s functions, depicted in figures 1.1 and 1.2, to the right. At any real wage rate firms will want to employ more labor and to sell more output. As a result of these shifts, the values of Ω and W/P which originally satisfied the market-clearing conditions will no longer do so. These original values will now imply excess demand for labor services and excess supply of commodities.

Again, we may ask what changes in Ω and W/P are required to reestablish the market-clearing conditions? Figure 1.6 reproduces

[13] A similar result would obtain if public services provided a direct source of utility for households, rather than a productive input for firms, but at the margin substituted for private consumption on a less than one-for-one basis. Cf. Bailey (1971, chapter 9).

the market-clearing loci of figure 1.3 and illustrates the effect of this disturbance. The disturbance produces a leftward shift in the $l^d = l^s$ locus and a rightward shift in the $c^d + g^d = y^s$ locus. The dashed lines represent the new loci.

One effect of this disturbance, as illustrated in figure 1.6, is to raise $(W/P)^*$. This rise in the real wage rate is readily understandable since a higher value of W/P tends to reduce both the excess demand for

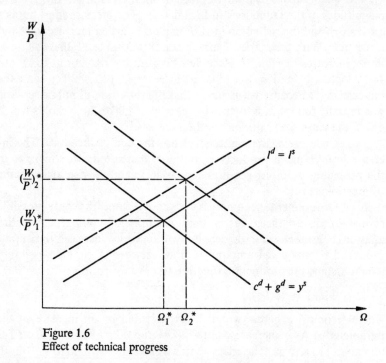

Figure 1.6
Effect of technical progress

labor services and the excess supply of commodities. In addition, figure 1.6 depicts an increase in Ω^*. To understand this result, suppose that Ω remained unchanged, while W/P rose sufficiently to clear the labor market. The increase in W/P would imply increases in c^d, l^s, and $(W/P)l^s$. On the one hand, assuming that the time path of c^d is constant until the planning horizon, the increase in c^d would be equal to (N'/N) times the increase in $(W/P)l^s$, which is less than the increase in $(W/P)l^s$. On the other hand, with the labor market clearing, l^d is equal to l^s, and the increase in l^d, together with the increase in α, would imply an increase in y^s. Moreover, the increase in y^s must be greater than the increase in $(W/P)l^d$, because the average product of labor exceeds the marginal product of labor. Thus, with Ω unchanged, c^d has increased by less than y^s, and the commodity market is not clearing. In order to clear the commodity market, while also keeping the labor market cleared, Ω must increase and W/P must increase further.

The increase in α also produces an increase in y^*. The proof of this result is that, under market-clearing conditions, y is equal to $c^d + g^d$ and the increases in Ω^* and $(W/P)^*$ imply an increase in c^d. However, the effect of an increase in α on l is generally ambiguous. Although we assume that the increase in $(W/P)^*$ would tend to raise l^s, a large enough increase in Ω^* could more than offset this effect. Finally, the increase in Ω^* implies that either $(M/P)^*$ or π^* must increase. The most likely result, the conditions for which we invite the reader to work out, is that both $(M/P)^*$ and π^* will increase.

Mathematical note

Any type of small exogenous disturbance in this model can be expressed in terms of small exogenous shifts in the l^s, l^d, y^s and $c^d + g^d$ functions. For example, in the last example in the text involving technical innovation, we have $\delta l^d > 0$, $\delta y^s > 0$ – that is, for any values of W/P and Ω, l^d and y^s are increased.

Using this method for describing exogenous disturbances, the impact of small disturbances on $(W/P)^*$ and Ω^* is determined from

$$
\begin{bmatrix} a_{11} & a_{12} \\ {\scriptstyle(-)} & {\scriptstyle(+)} \\ a_{21} & a_{22} \\ {\scriptstyle(+)} & {\scriptstyle(+)} \end{bmatrix}
\begin{bmatrix} d\left(\dfrac{W}{P}\right)^* \\ d\Omega^* \end{bmatrix}
=
\begin{bmatrix} \delta l^s - \delta l^d \\ \delta y^s - \delta c^d - \delta g^d \end{bmatrix}
$$

where

$$
a_{11} = \frac{\delta l^d}{\delta\left(\dfrac{W}{P}\right)} - \frac{\delta l^s}{\delta\left(\dfrac{W}{P}\right)},
$$

$$
a_{12} = -\frac{\delta l^s}{\delta\Omega},
$$

$$
a_{21} = \frac{\delta c^d}{\delta\left(\dfrac{W}{P}\right)} - \frac{\delta y^s}{\delta\left(\dfrac{W}{P}\right)}, \text{ and}
$$

$$
a_{22} = \frac{\delta c^d}{\delta\Omega}.
$$

By inverting the matrix

$$\begin{bmatrix} a_{11} & a_{12} \\ a_{21} & a_{22} \end{bmatrix},$$

we can calculate the change in $(W/P)^*$ and Ω^*
resulting from any small exogenous disturbance. The sign pattern of
the inverse matrix is

$$\begin{bmatrix} - & + \\ + & + \end{bmatrix}.$$

1.4 Dynamic analysis in the basic model

1.4.1 *The market process in the basic model*

As we have stressed in the preceding sections, the assumption that
exchange takes place only under market-clearing conditions is essential
for the formulation of the notional supply and demand functions of the
basic model. This section discusses how this assumption might be
rationalized. As we shall see, from an empirical standpoint, the rationalization which we are able to offer is, to say the least, strained. Consequently, we must conclude that the basic model, although a useful
starting point, may be seriously deficient as an analytical framework.

The usual rationalization of the assumption that exchange
takes place only under market-clearing conditions is the existence of a
recontracting mechanism as part of Walras' (1874) *tâtonnement* (groping)
process. As was explained in section 1.1 above, exchange in the basic
model takes place at two market places – a labor market, in which
labor services are exchanged for money, and a commodity market,
in which commodities are exchanged for money. Suppose that at each
market place there is a price-setting agent – it might be a man or a
suitably programmed computer – whose job it is to find the exchange
ratio between the goods being exchanged at that market place which is
consistent with the market-clearing conditions. The exchange ratios
which correspond to general market clearing are W^* for the labor
market and P^* for the commodity market. The price-setting agents
search for W^* and P^* through a trial-and-error process, which is the
Walrasian *tâtonnement*. They post trial values for W and P and observe
the quantities supplied and demanded. If these quantities are unequal,
they try other values for W and P.

Of course, the value of W for which l^d equals l^s depends on the
value of P, and the value of P for which $c^d + g^d$ equals y^s depends on

the value of W. Consequently, if either one of the price-setting agents hits on an equality between quantities demanded and supplied in his market, while the other price-setting agent is still changing his price in an attempt to find such an equality in his market, the first agent will find that the equality in his market is only momentary, and he will have to resume changing his price. Clearly, both of the price-setting agents will stop changing W and P only when they have hit on the combination W^* and P^* which is consistent with the market-clearing conditions of both markets. We may also refer to W^* and P^* as notional equilibrium values, since once W and P have achieved these values, they will have no tendency to change further in the absence of exogenous disturbances.[14]

To insure that no exchanges take place until the price-setting agents have hit on the combination of W^* and P^*, we must also suppose that any economic unit may renege on its offers to buy or sell at the trial values for W and P, if subsequently posted values of W and P are more favorable. For example, no household can be held to its offer to supply labor services at a previously posted wage which was lower than the currently posted wage. This arrangement, called the privilege of recontracting, derives from Edgeworth (1881). Recontracting insures that as long as W and P are changing, either buyers or sellers will renege on their previous offers to exchange. Only when the equilibrium values W^* and P^* are established will the incentive to recontract be eliminated and will exchange actually take place. If we take the recontracting privilege literally, it would seem that recontracting is applicable only to the finding of the market-clearing prices for the first and only time – that is, only to the act of creation of a static world.

In fact, of course, typical markets are not characterized either by a price-setting agent or by the privilege of recontracting. Prices, in the typical market, are actually posted by one of the economic units which engages in that market. Moreover, in the typical market, offers to buy or sell are binding, and perhaps the bulk of exchanges take place at non-market-clearing prices. We investigate this complication in chapter 2, where we shall see that the assumption of recontracting may seriously obscure understanding of the actual behavior of wages, prices, employment, and output.

[14] When, in chapters 4 and 5 below, we explicitly consider expectations, we shall adopt a more general concept of equilibrium as a situation in which relevant variables are changing at the rate at which they are expected to change. W^* and P^* are equilibrium values in this general sense, given the assumption of the basic model that neither W nor P are expected to change.

1.4.2 Wage and price adjustment relations

Despite the reservations noted above, the basic model provides an indispensable frame of reference for subsequent analysis. Therefore, let us complete our investigation of the determination of wages and prices in the context of the basic model.

We may presume that the price-setting agents know the signs of the partial derivatives of the demand and supply functions. That is to say, they know that, given P, an increase in W will lower l^d and raise l^s, and that, given W, an increase in P will decrease c^d and raise y^s. Consequently, we may presume that the price-setting agents will not post values of W and P at random. Rather, in their anxiety to find W^* and P^*, they will increase or decrease W according to whether they observe excess demand or supply for labor services, and will increase or decrease P according to whether they observe excess demand or supply for commodities. This behavior can be expressed in terms of the wage adjustment relation

$$\frac{1}{W}\frac{dW}{dt} = \lambda_W(l^d - l^s), \tag{1.16}$$

and the price adjustment relation

$$\frac{1}{P}\frac{dP}{dt} = \lambda_P(c^d + g^d - y^s), \tag{1.17}$$

where λ_W and λ_P are positive and may be regarded, for simplicity, as constants.

The implications of these wage and price adjustment relations can be seen with the aid of the market-clearing loci of figure 1.3. These loci are reproduced in figure 1.7. In order to summarize these implications, we specify the vector

$$\left[\frac{1}{P}\frac{dP}{dt}, \frac{1}{W}\frac{dW}{dt}, \frac{1}{W/P}\frac{d(W/P)}{dt}\right]$$

and indicate its sign pattern in each region of figure 1.7.

The price-adjustment relation implies that P will be rising whenever the posted combination of W/P and Ω is to the right of the $c^d + g^d = y^s$ locus – that is, in the regions labeled I and II – and that P will be falling whenever the posted combination of W/P and Ω is to the left of the $c^d + g^d = y^s$ locus – that is, in the regions labeled III and IV. The wage-adjustment relation implies that W will be rising whenever the posted combination of W/P and Ω is to the right of the $l^d = l^s$ locus – that is, in the regions labeled II and III – and that W will be falling whenever the posted combination of W/P and Ω is to the left of the $l^d = l^s$ locus – that is, in the regions labeled I and IV.

The movement of W/P cannot be immediately related to the market-clearing loci, because the wage and price adjustment relations relate the movements of W and P separately to these loci, whereas the movement of W/P depends on the relative movements of W and P. Consider the implications of the wage and price adjustment relations for the movement of W/P in the various regions labeled in figure 1.7.

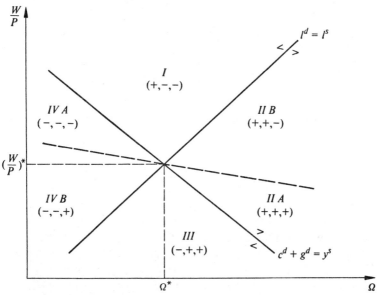

Figure 1.7
Wage and price dynamics in the basic model: sign patterns refer to

$$\left[\frac{1}{P} \frac{dP}{dt}, \frac{1}{W} \frac{dW}{dt}, \frac{1}{W/P} \frac{d(W/P)}{dt} \right]$$

In region I, W will be falling while P is rising, so that W/P will unambiguously be falling. In region III, W will be rising while P is falling, so that W/P will unambiguously be rising. However, in regions II and IV, W and P are moving in the same direction, so that the direction of movement of W/P depends on the relative rates of change of W and P. In region IV, W and P are both falling. We have divided this region, by the dashed line, into two subregions, labeled IVA and IVB. Points in subregion IVA are relatively distant from the $l^d = l^s$ locus and relatively close to the $c^d + g^d = y^s$ locus. Hence, in subregion

IVA, the excess supply of labor is relatively large and W is declining relatively rapidly, whereas the excess supply of commodities is relatively small and P is declining relatively slowly. Just the opposite is true of subregion IVB. Consequently, it should be possible, through appropriate placement of the dashed line, to identify subregion IVA with a falling W/P and subregion IVB with a rising W/P. The appropriate placement of the dashed line depends on the quantitative nature of the notional supply and demand functions and on the relative values of λ_W and λ_P in equations (1.16) and (1.17). Given the supply and demand functions, the larger is λ_W relative to λ_P, the closer the dashed line will be to the $l^d = l^s$ locus. A similar analysis applied to region II yields the dashed line which divides this region into subregions IIA and IIB. In figure 1.7, these dashed lines are shown as downward sloping, but in fact they could just as well.be upward sloping.[15] Our theory tells us only that the dashed lines go through regions II and IV.

1.4.3   The dynamics of exogenous disturbances

In section 1.3.3 above, we applied comparative-statics analysis to several examples of disturbances to the prevailing market-clearing situation. In each case, we saw that the initial effect of the disturbance was to make the prevailing combination of Ω and W/P inconsistent with equality between notional demand and notional supply in one or both of the markets. This inconsistency resulted either because the disturbance altered Ω with the market-clearing combination Ω^* and $(W/P)^*$ unchanged or because the disturbance altered either Ω^* or $(W/P)^*$ with Ω and W/P unchanged. The comparative-statics analysis revealed what changes, if any, were required in the various endogenous variables of the model in order to reestablish equality between Ω and Ω^* and between W/P and $(W/P)^*$. This section analyzes the time paths followed

---

[15] The equation for the dashed line is

$$\frac{1}{(W/P)} \frac{d(W/P)}{dt} = \lambda_W(l^d - l^s) - \lambda_P(c^d + g^d - y^s) = 0.$$

Thus, the slope of the dashed line is

$$\frac{-\left(\lambda_P \dfrac{\delta c^d}{\delta \Omega} + \lambda_W \dfrac{\delta l^s}{\delta \Omega}\right)}{\lambda_P \left(\dfrac{\delta c^d}{\delta(W/P)} - \dfrac{\partial y^s}{\partial(W/P)}\right) + \lambda_W \left(\dfrac{\delta l^s}{(\delta(W/P))} - \dfrac{\delta l^d}{\delta(W/P)}\right)}$$

The denominator of this expression is positive, so that the direction of the slope depends on the sign of the numerator.

in the basic model by these endogenous variables as these equalities are reestablished.

To focus this analysis, we consider a disturbance which alters Ω, but does not change Ω^* and $(W/P)^*$. The mathematical note at the end of this section sets out the general form of this analysis. Section 1.3.3 above discussed as an example of such a disturbance a change in government behavior in the form of an increase in m^s/P which is used to finance a reduction in τ. Figure 1.8 illustrates this disturbance. The regions of figure 1.8 are reproduced from figure 1 7. Point 0, which lies in region

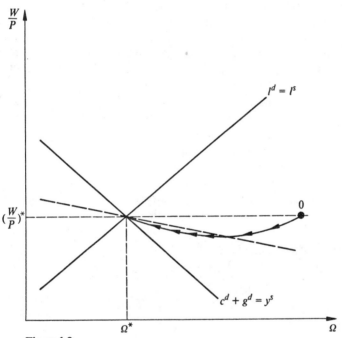

Figure 1.8
Convergence to the market-clearing conditions

IIB designates the combination of Ω and W/P initially resulting from the disturbance. At this point, Ω exceeds Ω^*, while W/P remains equal to $(W/P)^*$. The solid arrow depicts the implied time path for the actual values of Ω and W/P.

Starting at point 0, since l^d exceeds l^s and $c^d + g^d$ exceeds y^s, P and W are both increasing. Moreover, as we have assumed the dashed line to be downward sloping, P is initially rising proportionately faster than W so that W/P is falling. The increase in P reduces the real value of the money stock and thereby reduces Ω.[16] The reduction in Ω stimulates l^s and depresses c^d, thereby tending to reduce the excess demand in both markets and to slow the rates of increase of both P and W. The decrease in W/P reduces c^d and l^s and stimulates y^s and l^d. Thus, it also tends to reduce the excess demand for commodities and to slow the rate of increase of P, but it tends to increase the excess demand for labor and to quicken the rate of increase of W. Consequently, the initial rate of decrease of W/P moderates, and eventually when the dashed line is crossed W rises faster than P and W/P begins to increase. Asymptotically, the path approaches the point of intersection, at which Ω and W/P are again equal to Ω^* and $(W/P)^*$, with P and W having risen equiproportionately. Note that, had we assumed the dashed line to be upward sloping, W would have initially risen proportionately faster than P, so that W/P would have initially risen and then fallen back to $(W/P)^*$.[17]

In this example, as noted in section 1.3.3, Ω will continually tend to increase as long as m^s is positive. In that case, the posted values of W and P will be chasing continually moving targets and never actually reach $(W/P)^*$ and P^*. In the basic model, we must abstract from such a possibility. Otherwise, because of the recontracting privilege, exchange might never take place. This problem exemplifies the inadequacy of the basic model. In subsequent chapters, we shall see that this problem need not arise if we allow transactions to take place at non-market-clearing prices or if we introduce expectations regarding W^* and P^* into the wage and price adjustment relations.

Mathematical note

The following equations describe the dynamic system:

$$\frac{d(W/P)}{dt} = \frac{W}{P}\left[\lambda_W(l^d - l^s) - \lambda_P(c^d + g^d - y^s)\right] = G_1\left(\frac{W}{P}, P\right)$$

and

$$\frac{dP}{dt} = P\,\lambda_P(c^d + g^d - y^s) = G_2\left(\frac{W}{P}, P\right).$$

---

[16] This assertion assumes that profits are taken to remain equal to π^*. The basic problem is that, since the analysis assumes that actual transactions take place only under general-market-clearing conditions, the level of profits under non-market-clearing conditions remains undefined.

[17] With a downward sloping dashed line, the path of Ω and W/P from point 0 to $[\Omega^*, (W/P)^*]$ is confined to regions IIA and IIB. However, with an upward sloping dashed line, the path from point 0 to $[\Omega^*, (W/P)^*]$ could track a damped spiral through all four regions of $(\Omega, W/P)$ space.

The partial derivatives of G_1 and G_2 with respect to W/P and P, evaluated in the neighborhood of general market clearing, where $l^d \approx l^s$, $c^d + g^d \approx y^s$, and $\pi \approx \pi^*$, are

$$G_{11} = \frac{\delta G_1}{\delta(W/P)} = \frac{W}{P} \left\{ \lambda_W \left[\frac{\delta l^d}{\delta(W/P)} - \frac{\delta l^s}{\delta(W/P)} \right] \right.$$

$$\left. + \lambda_P \left[\frac{\delta y^s}{\delta(W/P)} - \frac{\delta c^d}{\delta(W/P)} \right] \right\},$$

$$G_{12} = \frac{\delta G_1}{\delta P} = \frac{W}{P} \frac{M}{P^2} \left(\lambda_P \frac{\delta c^d}{\delta \Omega} + \lambda_W \frac{\delta l^s}{\delta \Omega} \right),$$

$$G_{21} = \frac{\delta G_2}{\delta(W/P)} = P \lambda_P \left[\frac{\delta c^d}{\delta(W/P)} - \frac{\delta y^s}{\delta(W/P)} \right], \text{ and}$$

$$G_{22} = \frac{\delta G_2}{\delta P} = -P \frac{M}{P^2} \lambda_P \frac{\delta c^d}{\delta \Omega}.$$

Consider the Jacobian matrix of these partial derivatives,

$$\begin{bmatrix} G_{11} & G_{12} \\ G_{21} & G_{22} \end{bmatrix}.$$

The determinant of this matrix is positive and its trace is negative. These conditions are both necessary and sufficient for local dynamic stability of the basic model. In other words, if W/P and P are initially in the neighborhood of equilibrium, they will always converge to equilibrium. For a further discussion of these stability properties, see Samuelson (1947).

2 Output and employment under non-market-clearing conditions

This chapter develops a simple framework for analyzing the levels of output and employment when exchange takes place under non-market-clearing conditions. Section 2.1 outlines the essentials of this framework. Section 2.2 considers the case of general excess supply. Section 2.3 considers the case of general excess demand. Section 2.4 considers the general problem of determining the levels of output and employment corresponding to any given levels of wages and prices. Section 2.5 considers the dynamics of wage, price, output, and employment adjustments when exchange takes place under non-market-clearing conditions.

2.1 Exchange under non-market-clearing conditions

In chapter 1 we analyzed the determination of the quantities of the economic goods and their exchange ratios within two different contexts. First, we developed a comparative-statics analysis of the relations between the exogenous variables of the model and the values of the endogenous variables which satisfy the market-clearing conditions. Second, we developed a dynamic analysis of the endogenous variables as they moved over time in order to satisfy the market-clearing conditions. This analysis was based on the assumption of recontracting. In this analysis the nominal wage rate and the price of commodities adjusted gradually in response to notional excess supplies and demands in the markets for labor services and commodities. Meanwhile, because of the recontracting privilege, actual transactions remained suspended until the wage rate and price level were consistent with equality between the quantities supplied and demanded in both markets.

From an empirical standpoint, a major gap in the analysis of chapter 1 was the failure to consider quantity determination – in particular, the determination of output and employment – in situations that did not involve general market clearing. Recontracting does not characterize actual markets. In reality, offers to buy and to sell are usually binding, and the bulk of actual exchanges surely takes place at non-market-clearing prices. At the least, we must seriously consider the possibility that the recontracting paradigm, rather than being merely a convenient analytical device, may seriously obscure the understanding of essential features of the market process.

The auctioneer–recontracting model, which is historically associated with Walras (1874) and Edgeworth (1881), is not the only possible rationalization for neglecting quantity determination under non-market-clearing conditions. Alternatively, Marshall (1890) regarded all price adjustments as being nearly instantaneous responses to momentary discrepancies between quantities supplied and demanded. If all prices actually behaved in this manner, an explicit analysis of trading under non-market-clearing conditions would yield little empirically useful information. Actual quantities exchanged would, by and large, behave as if there were a recontracting mechanism. However, the Marshallian paradigm, like the Walrasian paradigm, does not account for such phenomena as the involuntary unemployment of depressions or the shortages which characterize suppressed inflations. Both of these phenomena seem to reflect the persistence of non-market-clearing prices, and their obvious empirical importance suggests that, in contrast to Marshall, we must view the process of adjustment to market-clearing prices as taking a significant amount of time. Not only must we reject recontracting in the literal sense, but we must also reject it as an 'as if' approach.

The analysis in this chapter evolves from this rejection of recontracting. It focuses on the determination of output and employment under non-market-clearing conditions. The general theoretical problem, however, concerns the nature of individual behavior and inter-market relations in a system of markets which are not generally cleared.[1]

The allowance for trading under non-market-clearing conditions has two essential implications for the determination of output and employment. First, these quantities cannot be determined simply by reference to market-clearing conditions. There is no automatic equivalence between actual transactions and the quantities supplied and demanded. In order to explain quantity determination under non-market-clearing conditions, we must consider the functioning of the actual trading process as well as the intentions of the individual economic units. The principle of voluntary exchange would seem to be crucial in this regard. Voluntary exchange is synonymous with the institution of free markets. Voluntary exchange means that no transactor can be forced to buy more than he demands or to sell more than

---

[1] Barro and Grossman (1971) contains a preliminary formulation of this analysis, which suppresses the essential intertemporal nature of the household utility maximization problem. Leijonhufvud (1968) argues that a focus on the interrelations between markets which may fail to clear was an essential distinguishing feature of Keynes' (1936) analysis. Grossman (1972*a*) offers a contrasting interpretation.

he supplies. Thus, voluntary exchange suggests that actual total transactions of any good will equal the smaller of the quantities supplied and demanded.[2] In particular, when there is excess supply of labor services, firms will be able to buy the quantity of labor services which they demand, but households will be unable to sell the quantity of labor services which they supply. The consequences of excess demand are the reverse. Similarly, when there is excess supply of commodities, firms will be unable to sell the quantity which they supply, but households will be able to buy the quantity which they demand, and, again, *vice versa* for excess demand.

The second essential implication of allowing for trading under non-market-clearing conditions is that every economic unit will not generally act as if it can buy or sell any amount which it supplies or demands at the existing wage-price vector. Any existing imbalance between demand and supply violates this presumption on the part of at least some units. The failure of a market to clear implies that actual quantities transacted diverge either from the quantities supplied or from the quantities demanded. From the standpoint of the individual, these divergences appear as constraints, to be taken into account when formulating behavior in other markets. Voluntary exchange, as we have just seen, determines the pattern of the constraints implied by excess supply or demand. As we shall see in the following sections, the notional demand and supply functions derived in the basic model of chapter 1 do not in general describe the behavior of firms and households. The existence of excess supply or demand in one market implies a divergence of the effective supply or demand from the notional supply or demand in the other market.

The main purpose of the present chapter is to understand the determination of effective supplies and demands and to analyze their implications for the determination of output and employment under non-market-clearing conditions. The discussion concentrates on the cases of general excess supply and general excess demand – that is, excess supply in both markets or excess demand in both markets. These cases would seem to be the most relevant, both from an empirical standpoint, and because they arise directly as a consequence of inappropriate monetary and fiscal policies.

[2] More rigorously, if x^d and x^s represent demand and supply of good x, voluntary exchange implies $x \leq \min [x^d, x^s]$. The equation of x to the smaller of demand and supply requires the additional condition that trade continues until all mutually advantageous transactions have occurred–that is, $x \geq \min [x^d, x^s]$. The combination of voluntary exchange with the exhaustion of all mutually advantageous trades guarantees $x = \min [x^d, x^s]$.

To facilitate the analysis, the basic approach takes a particular vector of the price level and real wage rate as given, and then works out the levels of output and employment implied by the trading which takes places at that vector. This procedure represents an extreme case, chosen for its simplicity. It may be contrasted with the alternative (Marshallian) extreme in which prices adjust rapidly and only general-market-clearing quantities are actually exchanged. The final section of this chapter discusses the implications for wage and price dynamics of allowing for trading at non-market-clearing prices.

2.2 The general excess supply case

This section analyzes the determination of output and employment when the values of W and P are such that excess supply exists in the markets for both labor services and commodities. In this situation the principle of voluntary exchange implies that employment and output are both demand-determined.[3] At first, we are tempted to assert that $l = l^d < l^s$ and $y = c^d + g^d < y^s$. However, quantities determined in this manner would be inconsistent with each other. In particular, if the firms were actually producing an output quantity less than y^s, their demand for labor services would not be given by the notional function l^d; while if household sales of labor services were actually less than l^s, their demand for commodities would not be given by the notional function c^d. The essential problem is that the notional demand functions fail to take account of the fact that the failure of one market to clear creates a constraint which will influence behavior in other markets. The formal analysis in this chapter is concerned with resolving this problem and with analyzing its implications.

2.2.1 *The behavior of firms under excess supply of commodities*[4]

In the basic model of chapter 1, the representative firm maximized $\pi = y^s - \dfrac{W}{P} l^d$, subject only to a given wage-price vector and to the constraint of the production function, $y^s = \Phi(l^d, g)$. This maximization implied the notional demand and supply functions l^d and y^s, as given

---

[3] Recall that, because commodities are assumed to be nonstorable, firms do not hold inventories, and they adjust output to be equal to sales at all times.

[4] For earlier development of analyses along these lines, see Patinkin (1956, chapter 13), Gogerty and Winston (1964), and Barro and Grossman (1971).

by equations (1.3–1.4). Underlying this formulation of the maximization problem was the assumption that the representative firm could sell all the output which it supplied and could buy all the labor which it demanded at the going wage-price vector. However, this assumption is appropriate only as long as the representative firm does not face either excess supply in the commodity market or excess demand in the labor market. In the present context, this assumption is inappropriate. In particular, excess supply in the commodity market means that the representative firm will be unable to sell its notional supply y^s.[5] Given excess supply, voluntary exchange implies that actual sales y will equal the quantity demanded and thus will be less than y^s.

Given $y < y^s$, the representative firm acts as a quantity taker with respect to its sales, in addition to acting as a wage and price taker.[6] In the basic model the level of sales was a choice variable. In sharp contrast the representative firm now sees the quantity, y, as a demand-determined constraint on its sales.[7] Given this constraint, profit maximization implies that the firm should produce exactly the quantity y. Producing less than y would not be optimal, since, at all quantities below y^s, the marginal product of labor exceeds the real wage rate. However, producing more than y would also not be optimal, since only the quantity y can be sold. Moreover, profit maximization implies that the quantity y should be produced with the minimum possible amount of labor services. We denote this minimum quantity as the effective demand for labor, and represent it by $l^{d'}$. Formally, the representative firm's problem is to choose $l^{d'}$ so as to maximize $\pi = y - (W/P)l^{d'}$, subject to $\Phi(l^{d'}, g) = y$. The solution is to select, for $y < y^s(W/P) g)$,

$$l^{d'} = l^{d'} \underset{(+)(-)}{(y, g)}, \tag{2.1}$$

[5] Voluntary exchange implies that firms are unaffected by excess supply in the labor market.

[6] We continue to focus on the representative firm, and we do not analyze the possible rationing processes which could determine the allocation of aggregate sales among the individual firms. Further, we do not consider any action by the firm which can alter its allocation. Similarly, in section 2.2.2 below, we do not consider the allocation of employment among the individual households. The implications of different rationing processes would be an interesting extension of the present analysis.

[7] As with prices and wages in the basic model, the determination of the actual value of y involves the market interaction of firm and household behavior. This interaction is analyzed is section 2.2.3 below. But, as with prices and wages in the basic model, the atomistic firm ignores its own contribution to the market process.

such that $\Phi[l^{d'}(y,g), g] = y$. The partial derivatives of the $l^{d'}$ function are $\delta l^{d'}/\delta y = 1/(\delta\Phi/\delta l)$ and $\delta l^{d'}/\delta g = -(\delta\Phi/\delta g)/(\delta\Phi/\delta l)$. The constraint of $y < y^s$ implies $l^{d'} < l^d$, with $l^{d'}$ approaching l^d as y approaches y^s.

In equation (1.3) derived in the basic model, notional labor demand was a function of the real wage rate, but was not a function of output. Output was maximized out as a separate choice variable. In contrast, in equation (2.1), effective labor demand is a function of output. The level of demand for commodities here imposes output, which equals sales, as a constraint on the effective demand for labor. The essential implication of equation (2.1) is that the effective demand for labor can vary even with the real wage rate fixed. Changes in the level of the constraint y influence effective labor demand independently of changes in W/P. In fact, as long as $y < y^s$, effective labor demand responds directly only to changes in y or g and not to changes in W/P.[8]

One way to interpret equation (2.1) is that the demand-imposed constraint on sales causes the representative firm to operate in a region where the marginal product of labor exceeds the real wage rate.[9] If the constraint on sales were relaxed, the representative firm would respond, at the existing wage-price vector, by raising output and employment. If possible, this process would continue until the marginal product fell sufficiently to equal the real wage rate – that is, until the representative firm was operating according to its notional supply of output and demand for labor functions.

---

[8] In the multi-input case, effective labor demand depends on relative wage rates as well as on y. In reducing output from y^s to y, the firm must choose among alternative input combinations – that is, it must choose the optimal point on a given isoquant. Formally, the multi-input problem may be illustrated as follows:

Maximize $\pi = y - \dfrac{W_1}{P} l_1^{d'} - \dfrac{W_2}{P} l_2^{d'},$

subject to the production function $y = \Phi(l_1^{d'}, l_2^{d'}, g)$, which has the usual convexity properties. The solution is to select

$l_1^{d'} = l_1^{d'} \underset{(-)(+)(-)}{(W_1/W_2, y, g)}$ and

$l_2^{d'} = l_2^{d'} \underset{(+)(+)(-)}{(W_1/W_2, y, g)},$

such that at output y, $\dfrac{\delta\Phi}{\delta l_1^{d'}} \Big/ \dfrac{\delta\Phi}{\delta l_2^{d'}} = W_1/W_2.$

[9] Given voluntary exchange, the firm will never operate in a region where the real wage exceeds marginal product, which would require $y > y^s (W/P)$.

Figure 2.1 depicts the preceding analysis of the representative firm's effective demand for labor. The l^d curve is reproduced from figure 1.1. The $l^{d'}$ curve depicts the effective demand for labor as given by equation (2.1). For a given value of y, $l^{d'}$ coincides with l^d when W/P is such that y is not an operative constraint – that is, when $y \geq y^s$.

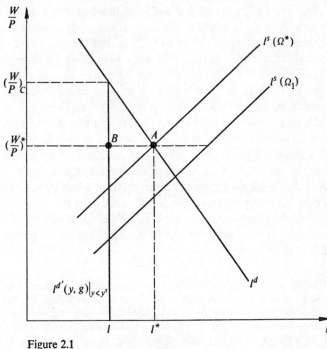

Figure 2.1
The labor market with excess supply of commodities

Alternatively, when W/P is such that y is an effective constraint – that is, when $y < y^s - l^{d'}$ is independent of the real wage rate and diverges from l^d. In the diagram the real wage rate $(W/P)_C$ is such that $y = y^s$ $[(W/P)_C, g]$. Therefore, at all real wage rates below $(W/P)_C$, the $l^{d'}$ curve is depicted as vertical and distinct from l^d.

The two l^s curves in figure 2.1 are also reproduced from figure 1.1. Since Ω^*, which equals $M/P^* + N(\pi^* - \tau)$, is the general-market-clearing value for nonwage wealth, the $l^s(\Omega^*)$ curve intersects the l^d curve at point A, at which the real wage rate is $(W/P)^*$ and employment is l^*. The $l^s(\Omega_1)$ curve corresponds to a smaller value of nonwage wealth, i.e., $\Omega_1 < \Omega^*$, which results from a price level higher than P^*. At the real wage rate $(W/P)^*$, the notional labor supply associated with Ω_1 exceeds the notional demand for labor services.

2.2.2 *The behavior of households under excess supply of labor services*

In the basic model of chapter 1, the representative working household maximized $U = \int_0^N u[c^d(t),\ l^s(t)]\ dt$, subject only to given constant values of W, P, π, and τ, the horizons N and N', and initial real asset holdings $M(0)/P$. This maximization implied the notional supply and demand functions l^s, c^d, and m^d/P, as given by equations (1.9–1.11). These functions satisfied the asset-exhaustion condition of equation (1.8) and the specification of saving given in equation (1.7).

Underlying this formulation of the maximization problem was the assumption that the representative working household could sell all the labor which it supplied and could buy all the commodities which it demanded. However, this assumption is appropriate only as long as the representative household does not face either excess supply in the labor market or excess demand in the commodity market. In the present context this assumption is inappropriate. In particular, excess supply in the labor market means that, at least currently, the representative working household will not be able to sell its notional supply l^s.[10] With excess supply, voluntary exchange implies that actual employment l will equal the quantity demanded and will be less than l^s.

Given $l < l^s$, the representative working household acts as a quantity taker with respect to employment, in addition to acting as a wage and price taker. In the basic model the level of employment and, hence, the amount of income were choice variables. In sharp contrast the representative working household now sees the quantity l as a demand-determined constraint on its employment and income.[11] Given this constraint, the household accepts employment quantity l and total disposable income of $(W/P)l + \pi - \tau$ as the maximum currently obtainable. The utility maximization problem reduces to the optimal division of this given disposable income between consumption and saving. We denote the optimal disposal pattern as the effective consumption demand and the effective demand for additions to money balances, and represent them by $c^{d'}$ and $m^{d'}/P$.

[10] Voluntary exchange implies that households are unaffected by excess supply in the commodity market.

[11] As with y, the determination of the actual value of l involves the market interaction of firm and household behavior, which is analyzed in section 2.2.3 below. But, like the atomistic firm, the atomistic household also ignores its own contribution to the market process.

Because money serves as a store of value, utility maximization in this context remains an intertemporal problem. The choice of the time paths of consumption and saving – $c^{d'}(t)$ and $m^{d'}(t)/P$ – depends not only on the current employment constraint l, which the representative working household directly perceives, but also on the entire expected future time path of this constraint. We attempt to treat these expectations in a manner which combines simplicity and generality. Specifically, we assume that the representative household expects to be effectively constrained to the current level of employment, l, until date $\hat{N}$, where $0 < \hat{N} < N'$, and expects to be unconstrained during the remaining $N' - \hat{N}$ working years. Given $l(t) = l$ for all $t \leq \hat{N}$, because $l^s(t)$ is also constant over time, $l < l^s(0)$ implies $l(t) < l^s(t)$ for all $t \leq \hat{N}$. We take $\hat{N}$ to be, like N' and N, exogenously determined. This treatment of expectations, although simple, does exhibit two important properties: First, the anticipated future shortfall of employment below the notional supply of labor services is larger the larger the present shortfall. Second, given $\hat{N} < N'$, the representative working household does not anticipate that this shortfall will persist indefinitely. The household expects to be unconstrained in its choice of employment at some time in the future.[12]

As in chapter 1, expectations regarding the future time paths of W, P, τ, and π are also relevant to the formulation of the household's plans. We continue to assume that the representative household takes W, P, and τ to be constant over time. Regarding profits, we assume that the representative household expects π to be constant at its current level until date $\hat{N}$ and then to rise to its general-market-clearing level, π^*. In other words, the representative household expects π to be below π^* for just as long as l is below l^s. This new assumption regarding profit expectations implies a revised specification of nonwage wealth, Ω. We now have

$$\Omega \equiv \frac{M}{P} + \hat{N}\pi + (N - \hat{N})\pi^* - N\tau.$$

Note, however, that the results derived below do not require that the representative household be able to predict π^* accurately. The only essential consideration is that the level of profits expected after date $\hat{N}$

[12] The present treatment also has the property, which may be overly restrictive, that the household expects a shortfall of employment in the future only if it experiences a current shortfall. More generally, expectations regarding effective future employment opportunities could depend on the entire past history of employment opportunities. Along these lines, chapter 6 below explores some implications of the possible distinction, developed by Friedman (1957), between current income and permanent income.

is independent of the current level of profits, which is associated with the situation of general excess supply.[13]

Given the above assumptions, the representative working household's formal problem is to maximize

$$U = \int_0^{\hat{N}} u[c^{d'}(t), l]dt + \int_{\hat{N}}^{N'} u[c^{d'}(t), l^{s'}(t)]dt$$

$$+ \int_{N'}^{N} u[c^{d'}(t), 0]dt,$$

subject to given values of W, P, π, τ, and l, the horizons $\hat{N}$, N', and N, and initial real asset holdings $M(0)/P$. The working household's life plan now involves three subperiods: the initial period from time 0 to time $\hat{N}$, during which employment is determined exogenously at the effective constraint level and during which consumption demand and saving demand are the only choice variables; a second period from time $\hat{N}$ to time N', during which consumption demand, labor supply, and saving demand are all choice variables; and the retirement period from time N' to time N, during which consumption demand and saving demand are choice variables and labor supply is set at zero.

The specification of saving for the three subperiods is

$$\frac{1}{P}\left(\frac{dM}{dt}\right)^{d'} \equiv \frac{m^{d'}}{P} = \begin{cases} \dfrac{W}{P}l + \pi - \tau - c^{d'} & \text{for } 0 \le t \le \hat{N}, \\[2mm] \dfrac{W}{P}l^{s'} + \pi^* - \tau - c^{d'} & \text{for } \hat{N} < t \le N' \text{ and} \\[2mm] \pi^* - \tau - c^{d'} & \text{for } N' < t \le N. \end{cases}$$

(2.2)

Optimal behavior again entails the exhaustion of asset holdings at date N. Therefore, the choice of $c^{d'}(t)$ and $l^{s'}(t)$ will satisfy

$$\frac{M(N)}{P} = \frac{M(0)}{P} + \hat{N}\pi + (N - \hat{N})\pi^* - N\tau + \hat{N}\frac{W}{P}l$$

$$+ \frac{W}{P}\int_{\hat{N}}^{N'} l^{s'}(t)dt - \int_0^N c^{d'}(t)dt = 0. \quad (2.3)$$

---

[13] If the representative household constrained its expectations to be consistent with a valid model of the economic system, it might expect the increases in l and π after date $\hat{N}$ to be associated with changes in W, P, or τ. However, the assumption that the representative household takes W, P, and τ to be constant over time yields a convenient simplification. The assumption that the representative household expects both Wl/P and π to remain at precisely their current levels until date $\hat{N}$ is also a convenient simplification.

The basic exogenous constraint on household behavior now equals nonwage wealth, as respecified above, plus anticipated wage income until date $\hat{N}$. We refer to this sum as the representative household's resource parameter and denote its value by Ω', where, given $\hat{N} < N'$,

$$\Omega' \equiv \Omega + \hat{N} \frac{W}{P} l \equiv \frac{M(0)}{P} + \hat{N} \left(\pi + \frac{W}{P} l \right) + (N - \hat{N})\pi^* - N\tau.$$

The maximization of U, subject to the asset-exhaustion condition,[14] yields a time path for $c^{d'}$ from date 0 to date N and a time path for $l^{s'}$ from date $\hat{N}$ to date N' which have the following properties: The time path for $l^{s'}$ is constant from date $\hat{N}$ to date N'. The time path for $c^{d'}$ is constant from date 0 to date $\hat{N}$, from date $\hat{N}$ to date N', and from date N' to date N, but generally at three different levels. However, if consumption and employment are independent influences on utility, the effective consumption demand at date t is independent of the level of employment at date t, and the time path for $c^{d'}$ is constant from date 0 to date N. In this case, the asset exhaustion condition of equation (2.3) simplifies to

$$\Omega' + (N' - \hat{N}) \frac{W}{P} l^{s'} - N c^{d'} = 0.$$

Given the saving specification of equation (2.2), these time paths for $c^{d'}$ and $l^{s'}$ also imply constant values for $m^{d'}/P$ from date 0 to date $\hat{N}$, from date $\hat{N}$ to date N', and from date N' to date N.

Let us compare, for given values of Ω and W/P, these time paths for $c^{d'}$, $l^{s'}$, and $m^{d'}/P$ chosen subject to the asset-exhaustion condition of equation (2.3), to the time paths of c^d, l^s, and m^d/P which were chosen in the basic model. Given that, from date 0 to date $\hat{N}$, l is constrained to be less than l^s, the representative working household's wage income during this time period is below the notional level which it would have chosen in the basic model. The representative working household absorbs this reduction in wage income in two ways: first, it reduces its total lifetime consumption; second, it reduces its leisure by increasing its effective labor supply during the unconstrained working years. Thus, from date 0 to date N, the average level of $c^{d'}$ is less than the average level of c^d, and, from date $\hat{N}$ to date N', $l^{s'}$ is larger than l^s.

---

[14] The maximization of U is also subject to the inequality constraints $[c^{d'}(t), l^{s'}(t), M(t)] \geq 0$. The present discussion assumes, as we did in chapter 1, that these constraints are ineffective, and therefore deals only with interior solutions for $c^{d'}$ and $l^{s'}$. However, section 2.2.4 below specifically analyzes the implications of the constraints $M(t) \geq 0$ and $c^{d'}(t) \geq 0$.

If consumption and employment are independent influences on utility, or at least if the enforced increase in leisure from date 0 to date $\hat{N}$ does not substantially affect the marginal utility of consumption during that period, the decrease in total lifetime consumption also implies that $c^{d'}$ is less than c^d during each of the three subperiods of the lifeplan. However, for the initial period from date 0 to date $\hat{N}$, even though $c^{d'}$ is less than c^d, the difference between c^d and $c^{d'}$ is less than the difference between $(W/P)l^s$ and $(W/P)l$ for two reasons: first, this shortfall of income from date 0 to date $\hat{N}$ can be spread over N years of reduced consumption; second, the excess of $l^{s'}$ over l^s from date $\hat{N}$ to date N' partially compensates for the shortfall of wage income during the preceding period.

These adjustments of effective consumption demand and effective labor supply imply a relation between $m^{d'}/P$ and m^d/P. Because $c^{d'}$ is less than c^d during the retired years from date N' to date N, the average level of $m^{d'}/P$ is less than m^d/P during the working years from date 0 to date N'. Moreover, from date $\hat{N}$ to date N', $l^{s'}$ exceeds l^s and $c^{d'}$ is less than c^d, so that $m^{d'}/P$ exceeds m^d/P. Consequently, from date 0 to date $\hat{N}$, $m^{d'}/P$ must be less than m^d/P.

In sum, the constraint on employment causes a reduction in both the current effective consumption demand and the current effective saving demand of working households. Specifically the maximization calculus implies interior solutions for the current values of $c^{d'}$ and $m^{d'}/P$ of the following form:

$$c^{d'} = c^{d'} \left(\Omega', \frac{W}{P} \right) \text{ and} \tag{2.4}$$
$$\underset{(+)\ (+)}{\phantom{c^{d'}}}$$

$$\frac{m^{d'}}{P} = \frac{m^{d'}}{P} \left(\Omega', \frac{W}{P}, \frac{W}{P} l + \pi - \tau \right). \tag{2.5}$$
$$\underset{(-)\ (-)\qquad\quad (+)}{}$$

The mathematical note at the end of this section spells out the derivation of these equations.

The form of the effective demand functions of equations (2.4) and (2.5) is similar to the form of the notional demand functions of equations (1.9) and (1.11). In these $c^{d'}$ and $m^{d'}/P$ functions, changes in Ω' have an effect which is analogous to the effect that changes in Ω had in the c^d and m^d/P functions. However, the notional demands were not functions of the level of employment. Employment was maximized out as a separate choice variable. In contrast, in equations (2.4) and (2.5), the effective demands for commodities and savings are functions, through Ω', of the level of employment. The level of demand for labor services here imposes employment as a constraint on the effective demand for commodities.[15] Total labor income during the constrained years, $\hat{N}(W/P)l$, enters as an additive component of Ω'.

Consider the case in which consumption and employment are independent influences on utility, so that planned consumption is constant until the planning horizon and, as noted above, the asset-exhaustion condition can be written as

$$\Omega' + (N' - \hat{N})\frac{W}{P}l^{s'} - Nc^{d'} = 0.$$

Differentiating this condition, given that $\delta l^{s'}/\delta\Omega'$ is negative, yields

$$\frac{\delta c^{d'}}{\delta\Omega'} = \frac{1}{N}\left[1 + (N' - \hat{N})\frac{W}{P}\frac{\delta l^{s'}}{\delta\Omega'}\right] < \frac{1}{N}.$$

In other words, the change in current effective consumption demand equals one-Nth of the change in Ω' less the induced change in planned wage income during the unconstrained years. This result is useful in the next section, which analyzes the determination of y and l under excess supply conditions.

Current wage income also enters the $m^{d'}/P$ function of equation (2.5) as a component of the term $(W/P)l + \pi - \tau$. Changes in this term have an effect which is analogous to the effect that changes in $\pi - \tau$ had in the m^d/P function. In addition, given Ω' and $(W/P)l + \pi - \tau$, an increase in W/P raises $l^{s'}$ and $(\hat{N} - N')(W/P)l^{s'}$ – that is, raises wage income from date $\hat{N}$ to date N' – and, in order to dispose of this increased income, raises $c^{d'}$ from date 0 to date N. This increase in current $c^{d'}$ implies a decrease in current $m^{d'}/P$.

It is also interesting to discuss the effect of a change in $\hat{N}$ on the effective demands and supplies. The principal effect of an increase in $\hat{N}$ would be to increase the number of working years during which the representative working household is constrained to employment level l, and correspondingly to decrease the number of working years during which the household is able to obtain the amount of employment $l^{s'}$. Thus, because l is less than $l^{s'}$, an increase in $\hat{N}$ causes a reduction in the household's lifetime resources.[16] Accordingly, the household would

---

[15] For an earlier, and seminal, interpretation of the effective consumption demand function along these lines, see Clower (1965). Barro and Grossman (1971) contains a further discussion.

[16] An additional effect of an increase in $\hat{N}$ is to increase the number of years during which anticipated profits are equal to π, and correspondingly to decrease the number of years during which anticipated profits are equal to the higher level π^*. This effect would cause a further reduction in the representative household's lifetime resources.

further reduce its total lifetime consumption, and this reduction would presumably involve a lower level of $c^{d'}$ during each of the three subperiods of the lifeplan. In addition, the household would raise the level of $l^{s'}$ planned for the reduced number of unconstrained years. The decline in current $c^{d'}$ implies an increase in current $m^{d'}/P$. The general result is that the larger is $\hat{N}$, the more the representative working household reacts to a given shortfall of current l below l^s by reducing effective consumption demand and the less by decreasing effective saving demand.[17]

Retired households differ from working households in that, for retired households, both the current and future level of l is zero and the existence of excess supply of labor services has no direct bearing. Their demands for commodities and additional money balances continue to depend only on Ω and $\pi - \tau$ as in the basic model of chapter 1, so that they can again be included without altering the form of the aggregate relationships. In the aggregate formulation in equations (2.3–2.5), N and $\hat{N}$ should be interpreted as the average planning horizon of all households and N' should be interpreted as the average value for working households.

Figure 2.2 depicts the preceding analysis of the representative household's effective demand for commodities. The y^s curve and the two $c^d + g^d$ curves are reproduced from figure 1.2. Since Ω^* is the general-market-clearing value for nonwage wealth, the $c^d(\Omega^*) + g^d$ curve intersects the y^s curve at point A, at which the real wage rate is $(W/P)^*$ and output and sales are y^*. The $c^d(\Omega_1) + g^d$ curve corresponds to a smaller value of nonwage wealth, i.e., $\Omega_1 < \Omega^*$, which results from a price level higher than P^*. At the real wage rate $(W/P)^*$, the notional

---

[17] The preceding discussion has assumed that $\hat{N}$ is less than N'. Alternatively, if $\hat{N}$ equals or exceeds N', the form of the asset-exhaustion condition is altered. Two cases must be considered. First, if $N' \leq \hat{N} < N$, the asset-exhaustion condition becomes

$$\frac{M(N)}{P} = \frac{M(0)}{P} + N'\frac{W}{P}l + \hat{N}\pi + (N - \hat{N})\pi^* - N\tau - \int_0^N c^{d'}(t)dt = 0.$$

Second, if $\hat{N} \geq N$, the asset-exhaustion condition becomes

$$\frac{M(N)}{P} = \frac{M(0)}{P} + N'\frac{W}{P}l + N(\pi - \tau) - \int_0^N c^{d'}(t)dt = 0.$$

Notice that in these cases the constraint on employment through retirement eliminates any choice of future wage income, rules out any substitution between leisure and consumption, and eliminates W/P as a separate argument of the $c^{d'}$ and $m^{d'}/P$ functions. We leave the derivation of $c^{d'}$ and $m^{d'}/P$ in these cases as an exercise for the reader.

supply of commodities exceeds the notional commodity demand associated with Ω_1.

The $c^{d'}(\Omega_1)|_l + g^d$ curve depicts the effective demand for commodities, for nonwage wealth Ω_1 and employment level l. For a given value of l, $c^{d'}(\Omega_1)|_l + g^d$ coincides with $c^d(\Omega_1) + g^d$ when l

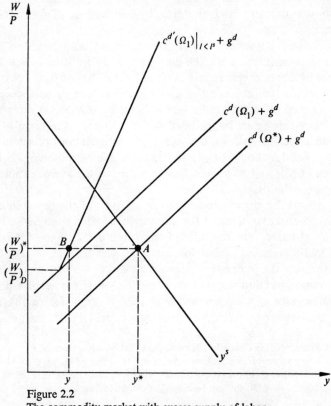

Figure 2.2
The commodity market with excess supply of labor

is not an effective constraint – that is, when $l \geq l^s(\Omega_1, W/P)$. Alternatively, when W/P is such that l is an effective constraint – that is, when $l < l^s(\Omega_1, W/P) - c^{d'} + g^d$ is to the left of $c^d + g^d$. In the diagram the real wage $(W/P)_D$ is such that $l = l^s[\Omega_1, (W/P)_D]$. Therefore, at all real wage rates above $(W/P)_D$, the $c^{d'} + g^d$ curve is depicted as distinct from $c^d + g^d$. The positive slope of the $c^{d'} + g^d$ curve involves two effects. First, given Ω_1 and l, an increase in W/P raises $\hat{N}(W/P)l$ and thereby raises Ω', which increases $c^{d'}$. Second, for a given value of Ω', an increase in W/P raises $(N' - \hat{N})(W/P)l^{s'}$, the planned wage income during the unconstrained years, and produces a corresponding increase in $c^{d'}$.

In figures 2.1 and 2.2, the effective demand schedules are juxtaposed with the notional supply schedules. This formulation assumes, as regards figure 2.1, that the representative working household continues to offer to sell labor services according to its notional supply schedule, despite the demand-imposed constraint on its employment. As regards figure 2.2, this formulation assumes that the representative firm continues to offer to produce and sell commodities according to its notional supply schedule, despite the demand-imposed constraint on its sales.[18] In these figures points A identify the general-market-clearing combination of real wage rate, price level, employment, and output. Points B identify the levels of employment and output associated with the real wage rate $(W/P)^*$ and nonwage wealth Ω_1, which is less than Ω^*. In the next section we explicitly analyze the determination of the characteristics of points such as B.

Mathematical note

The interior solution for optimal values of $c^{d'}(t)$ and $l^{s'}(t)$ satisfies the conditions

$$\frac{\delta u}{\delta c^{d'}(t)} = \lambda \qquad \text{for } 0 \leq t \leq N, \text{ and}$$

$$\frac{\delta u}{\delta l^{s'}(t)} = -\lambda \frac{W}{P} \qquad \text{for } \hat{N} < t \leq N',$$

[18] This formulation abstracts from three types of effects which might cause actual offers to sell to differ from notional supplies in this situation. First, the expectation of future constraints on employment could motivate households to seek more work currently to compensate for the anticipated shortfall of future income below desired levels. Second, if individual sellers of either labor services or commodities think that actual sales are directly related to the amount which they offer to sell they may communicate offers to sell in excess of their desired sales. Third, if there are costs associated with the expression of offers to sell, the representative household or firm may not bother to make offers which are not expected to be successful. This last effect would tend to reduce actual offers below notional supply and would tend to offset the first two effects. Grossman (1974) contains a more extensive discussion of these issues.

where λ is a constant determined so as to satisfy equation (2.3). These conditions imply that

$$c^{d'}(t) = \begin{cases} c^{d'}(0) & \text{for } 0 \leq t \leq \hat{N}, \\ c^{d'}(N') & \text{for } \hat{N} < t \leq N', \\ c^{d'}(N) & \text{for } N' < t \leq N, \end{cases}$$

and $l^{s'}(t) = l^{s'}(N')$ for $\hat{N} < t \leq N'$.

The effective consumption demand function for the current period has the form

$$c^{d'}(0) = c^{d'}(\Omega', W/P, l).$$
$$\quad \; (+) \quad (+) \quad (?)$$

If consumption and employment are independent influences on utility – that is, if $\delta^2 u/\delta c(t)\delta l(t) = 0$ – then l drops out as a separate argument of the $c^{d'}(0)$ function, as in equation (2.4), and $c^{d'}(t) = c^{d'}(0)$ for $0 \leq t \leq N$. Equation (2.4) is thus an approximation which abstracts from the effect of the level of employment on the marginal utility of consumption.

2.2.3 The determination of output and employment under general excess supply

Figures 2.1 and 2.2 both represent partial analyses. Figure 2.1 explains the effective demand for labor as a function of a given demand-imposed constraint on sales of commodities. To close this model, the effective demand for commodities must be explained. Figure 2.2 explains the effective demand for commodities as a function of a given demand-imposed constraint on sales of labor services. To close this model, the effective demand for labor services must be explained. Thus, these two partial analyses are essential complements. They can be combined to provide, for a given wage-price vector, a complete picture of the determination of output and employment under general excess supply conditions. Not surprisingly, the essence of this analytical exercise is the familiar Keynesian demand multiplier.

When a particular market is experiencing excess supply, voluntary exchange implies that the actual level of transactions will be demand determined. According to the analysis of the preceding two sections, when the commodity market and labor market are experiencing excess supply, an effective demand, which is less than the notional demand, prevails in the other market. Consequently, when both markets are experiencing excess supply, these effective demands for labor services and commodities determine both employment and output. Equations (2.1) and (2.4) give the effective demands for labor services and commodities, so that employment and output are determined by

$$l = l^{d'}(y, g) < l^s\left(\Omega, \frac{W}{P}\right) \text{ and} \tag{2.6}$$

$$y = c^{d'}\left(\Omega', \frac{W}{P}\right) + g^d < y^s\left(\frac{W}{P}, g\right). \tag{2.7}$$

Given that profits and wage income exhaust total output – that is, $y = \pi + (W/P)l$ – we can express the resource constraint Ω' as

$$\Omega' = \frac{M}{P} + \hat{N}y + (N - \hat{N})\pi^* - N\tau,$$

which depends on y, but does not depend separately on l or π. In order for conditions (2.6) and (2.7) to be relevant, the existing wage-price vector must imply the existence of excess supply in both markets. Section 2.4.1 below considers the general specification of such wage-price vectors.

Conditions (2.6) and (2.7) determine unique levels of output and employment. Given the exogenous variables – g^d, M, τ, N, N', $\hat{N}$, π^*, P, and W – condition (2.7) implies a current value for y. The essential relation is that the level of y determines the value $(W/P)l + \pi$ and, hence, the value of the resource parameter, Ω', which, in turn, determines $c^{d'}$. According to condition (2.7), the level of y must be such that the level of $c^{d'}$ so determined, plus g^d, is equal to y itself. With y so determined, given $g = g^d$, condition (2.6) relates l to y.

In order to illustrate the process by which y and l are determined, let us work through the mechanism of the demand multiplier which is implied by conditions (2.6) and (2.7). Consider the following thought experiment: Suppose that initially the wage-price vector was equal to (W^*, P^*) and thus was consistent with general market clearing. Now consider any permanent change in an exogenously determined variable such that W^* and P^* are reduced, while the actual wages and prices remain unchanged. Among the possibilities for the form of such a disturbance are an increase in τ or a decrease in M.[19]

---

[19] As we saw in section 1.3.3 above, the effect of an increase in τ, with g^d constant, or of a decrease in M would be to reduce W^* and P^* equiproportionately, leaving Ω^* and $(W/P)^*$ unchanged. A decrease in g^d would raise Ω^* and $(W/P)^*$, assuming that the marginal product of public services is less than unity.

The initial effect of such a disturbance would be a reduction in the notional demand for commodities below the notional supply and an increase in the notional supply of labor services above the notional demand. The disturbance thus creates excess supply in both markets. As an immediate consequence, the representative firm perceives a demand-imposed constraint on its sales, which both reduces its profits and causes it to reduce its effective demand for labor services below its notional demand. At the same time, the representative household perceives a demand-imposed constraint on its employment, which causes it to reduce its effective demand for commodities below its notional demand. However, these results are just the beginning of the story. The induced reduction in profits and effective labor demand implies a further reduction in the resource parameter of the households, which causes a further reduction in effective commodity demand. At the same time, the induced reduction in effective commodity demand implies a further constraint on sales, which causes a further reduction in profits and effective labor demand. This process cumulates until the actual levels of output and employment settle well below their general-market-clearing levels, with the point of convergence determined by the inter-action between the households' marginal propensity to consume out of current income and the marginal productivity of labor.

The outcome of the cumulative process can be determined analytically from condition (2.7). Differentiation of condition (2.7), holding π^* and $\hat{N}$ fixed, yields the following relationship between changes in government behavior and the level of output:

$$dy = \frac{1}{1 - \hat{N}\frac{\delta c^{d'}}{\delta\Omega'}}\left[dg^d - N\frac{\delta c^{d'}}{\delta\Omega'}\,d\tau + \frac{\delta c^{d'}}{\delta\Omega'}\,d\left(\frac{M}{P}\right) + \frac{\delta c^{d'}}{\delta(W/P)}\,d\left(\frac{W}{P}\right)\right].$$

$$(2.8)$$

For completeness and future reference, equation (2.8) also indicates the effect on output of an exogenous change in the real wage rate. According to equation (2.8), the ultimate negative effect on output of either a decrease in g^d, an increase in τ, a decrease in M/P, or a decrease in W/P results from two components. First, these shifts directly induce a decrease in effective commodity demand and output – reflecting the decrease in g^d or the initial decrease in $c^{d'}$ resulting from the decrease in M/P, the increase in τ, or the decrease in W/P. This effect is given by the bracketed term on the right side of equation (2.8). Second, this initial decrease in output means less employment and less profit, which lead to further decreases in effective consumption demand and output. This effect is given by the term preceding the brackets on the right side of equation (2.8). This term, $1/(1 - \hat{N} \, \delta c^{d'}/\delta \Omega')$, represents what is usually called the demand multiplier.

The term $\hat{N} \, \delta c^{d'}/\delta \Omega'$, which appears in the denominator of the demand multiplier expression, represents the marginal propensity to consume out of income, $\delta c^{d'}/\delta y$ – that is,

$$\hat{N} \frac{\partial c^{d'}}{\partial \Omega'} = \frac{\partial \Omega'}{\partial y} \frac{\partial c^{d'}}{\partial \Omega'} = \frac{\partial c^{d'}}{\partial y}.$$

The condition that the multiplier be finite but greater than unity requires that $\delta c^{d'}/\delta y$ be less than unity but greater than zero. Given that $\delta c^{d'}/\delta \Omega'$ is positive, $\delta c^{d'}/\delta y$ is also positive. The condition $\delta c^{d'}/\delta y$ less than unity is also easy to satisfy. For the case in which consumption and employment are independent influences on utility, we saw in the preceding section that $\delta c^{d'}/\delta \Omega'$ is less than $1/N$. Thus, $\delta c^{d'}/\delta y$ is less than $\hat{N}/N$, which is likely to be much less than unity, and the demand multiplier is less than $N/(N - \hat{N})$. The size of the demand multiplier increases with an increase in $\hat{N}$.[20]

The discussion of the determination of output and employment thus far has not considered the effective flow demand for money balances, which was specified by equation (2.5). In this regard, as in the analysis of chapter 1, the economy-wide budget constraint is again of interest. By combining the momentary household budget constraint,

$$c^{d'} + \frac{m^{d'}}{P} + \tau = \frac{W}{P} l + \pi,$$

the government budget constraint,

$$\tau = g^d - \frac{m^s}{P},$$

---

[20] The multiplier also would be larger if the marginal utility of consumption increased with an increase in the level of employment – that is, if u_{cl} were positive rather than zero. The formulation of this paragraph is valid only if $\hat{N}$ is less than N'. As was noted in the preceding section, if $\hat{N}$ equals or exceeds N', the form of the asset-exhaustion condition is altered. For the extreme of $\hat{N} = N$, given $u_{cl} = 0$, the multiplier is given by

$$\frac{N}{N - N'} \cdot \frac{1}{1 - \delta\pi/\delta y} = \frac{N}{N - N'} \cdot \frac{\delta\Phi/\delta l}{W/P},$$

which is still finite. We leave the verification of this result as an exercise for the reader.

and the specification of profits,

$$\pi = y - \frac{W}{P} l^{a'},$$

we obtain for the economy-wide budget constraint

$$(c^{a'} + g^a - y) + \frac{W}{P}(l^{a'} - l) + \frac{1}{P}(m^{a'} - m^s) = 0. \qquad (2.9)$$

Equation (2.9) implies that the combination of y and l which satisfies conditions (2.6) and (2.7) also satisfies

$$\frac{m^{a'}}{P}\left(\Omega', \frac{W}{P}, \frac{W}{P} l + \pi - \tau\right) = \frac{m^s}{P}. \qquad (2.10)$$

In other words, under general excess supply, equating output and employment to the effective demands for commodities and labor services also produces equality between the flow supply of money balances and the effective demand for money balances. This property is analogous to Walras' Law of Markets, which, as we saw in chapter 1, applies under general-market-clearing conditions.

   As we have formulated the analysis in this chapter, the convergence to output and employment levels y and l would be instantaneous. To create this result, we assumed, in effect, that firms instantaneously perceive the level of the demand-determined constraint on sales to be the value of y which satisfies condition (2.7). At the same time, households instantaneously perceive the levels of the demand-determined constraint on employment and the level of profits to be the values of l and π which satisfy conditions (2.6) and (2.7).

   This formulation involves two types of underlying dynamic assumption. First, it assumes a simultaneous determination of the actual transactions carried out in both markets by each economic unit and of the effective demands of each economic unit in both markets. Realistically however, households would not obtain information about actual transactions in the labor market until the firms had expressed their demands, while the firms would not obtain information about actual transactions in the commodity market until the household had expressed their demands. Furthermore, the profit income of households would not be determined until both y and l were determined. The actual effective demands which determine output and employment according to conditions (2.6) and (2.7) could only emerge in practice from a recursive interaction along the general lines of the above verbal sketch of the multiplier process

A second assumption is that the representative household acts instantaneously on the current level of income as its best estimate of the level of income up to date $\hat{N}$. Realistically, however, the presence of adjustment costs and nonstatic expectations would affect the formulation of demand and supply, and would, therefore, alter the magnitude and timing of the demand multiplier. Chapter 6 below considers these effects in some detail.

Figure 2.3 illustrates the determination of the levels of output and employment when there is excess supply in both markets. The

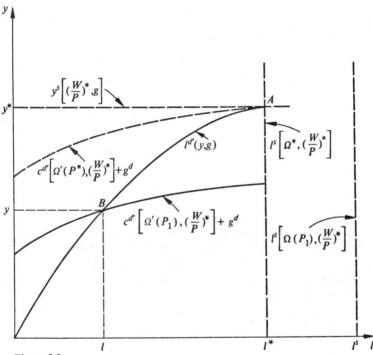

Figure 2.3
Output and employment with excess supply in both markets

diagram is drawn on the assumption that the existing real wage rate is equal to $(W/P)^*$ while the existing levels of wages and prices, W_1 and P_1, are equiproportionately higher than W^* and P^*. As was noted above, such a situation could result either from an increase in τ, with g^d constant, or from a decrease in M. We focus on such a situation because of its relative simplicity and because it illustrates an important lesson regarding the relation between real wage rates and employment.

In figure 2.3 the locus labeled $y^s[(W/P)^*,g]$ identifies both the general-market-clearing level of output, y^*, and the current notional supply of commodities. The locus labeled $l^s[\Omega^*, (W/P)^*]$ identifies the general-market-clearing level of employment l^*. These two loci intersect at point A, which corresponds to point A in figures 2.1 and 2.2. The locus labeled $l^s[\Omega(P_1), (W/P)^*]$ identifies the current notional supply of labor services.

In the present situation, however, the effective demand loci determine actual levels of y and l which fall short of these supply quantities. The locus labeled $l^{d'}(y,g)$ describes combinations of l and y which satisfy condition (2.6). This locus terminates at point A, and its slope is equal to the marginal product of labor, $\delta\Phi/\delta l$. The two loci labeled $c^{d'}[\Omega', (W/P)^*] + g^d$ describe combinations of l and y which satisfy condition (2.7), given that $y = \Phi(l,g)$. One locus corresponds to P^* and W^*, and also terminates at point A. The other locus corresponds to P_1 and W_1, which exceed P^* and W^*. The slope of these loci is equal to $(\delta c^{d'}/\delta y)(\delta\Phi/\delta l)$. Thus, if $\delta c^{d'}/\delta y$ is less than unity, these loci are flatter than the $l^{d'}(y,g)$ locus. The $c^{d'} + g^d$ locus corresponding to P_1 intersects the $l^{d'}(y,g)$ locus at point B, which identifies the levels of output and employment corresponding to the wage-price vector (W_1, P_1). Point B corresponds to point B in figures 2.1 and 2.2.

A shift from point B to point A would involve either a fall in the price level from P_1 to P^* with an equiproportionate fall in the nominal wage rate, or a restoration of τ or M to their original levels, at which (W_1, P_1) matches the general-market-clearing wage-price vector. Since, at point B, the real wage rate is consistent with general market clearing, no change in W/P is involved. In figure 2.3, an equiproportionate fall in the price and wage levels from P_1 to P^* and from W_1 to W^* implies an upward shift in the $c^{d'} + g^d$ locus to $c^{d'}[\Omega'(P^*), (W/P)^*] + g^d$, which intersects $l^{d'}(y,g)$ at point A. The demand multiplier is given graphically by the ratio of the difference between y^* and y to the vertical distance between the two $c^{d'} + g^d$ loci.

The gap between y^* and y, which is depicted in both figures 2.2 and 2.3, represents the shortfall of output, given the wage-price vector (W_1, P_1), below the full employment level associated with general market clearing. This gap also measures the existing amount of excess supply in the commodity market; hence, it may be referred to as involuntary underproduction. This shortfall of output reflects two components. First, with the price level above P^* and profit below π^*, the notional demand for commodities is less than y^*. Second, because of the employment constraint, the effective demand for commodities is less than the notional demand.

The gap between l^* and l, which is depicted in both figures 2.1 and 2.3, represents the shortfall of employment, given the wage-price vector (W_1, P_1), below the full employment level. This gap may be referred to as the amount of underemployment. The gap between l^s and l which is depicted in both figures 2.1 and 2.3, measures the existing amount of excess supply in the labor market. Because the current level of nonwage wealth is less than Ω^*, current l^s exceeds l^*, and this measure overstates the amount of underemployment.

A more important point, however, is that the real wage rate which is consistent with general market clearing is associated here with a positive amount of underemployment as well as a positive amount of excess supply in the labor market. Thus, we see that underemployment can occur without the real wage rate being 'too high'. Employment is below l^* in this case solely because the price level and nominal wage rate are 'too high' – that is, because P_1 and W_1 are equiproportionately higher than P^* and W^*. The wage-price vector (W_1, P_1) implies insufficient demand for commodities, which leads to cuts in output and, therefore, to cuts in the effective demand for labor services and in employment. Therefore, the existence of the real wage rate $(W/P)^*$ is not sufficient to insure the full employment level l^* despite the fact that the notional demand for labor services depends only on the real wage rate. With excess supply in the commodity market, the notional demand schedule does not represent the firms' effective offers of employment.

Given the wage-price vector (W_1, P_1), a fall in the real wage rate is not required to restore full employment. Rather, what is required is either an equiproportionate fall in the price level and nominal wage rate or an expansionary government action – for example, some combination of a decrease in taxes and an increase in the stock of money balances. Nevertheless, it is interesting to ask what, in fact, would be the consequence of the classical prescription for unemployment – that is, a fall in the real wage rate, in this situation. With P unchanged, a reduction in W/P would require a reduction in W. Given the values of the exogenous variables, such a reduction would motivate the representative working household to reduce both planned labor income during unconstrained working years and current consumption. As indicated by equation (2.8), this reduction in $c^{d'}$ would produce a multiple contraction of y and l. In this case, an excessive real wage rate is not the cause of the underemployment, and a reduction will not cure the problem. Real wage cuts would only reduce the effective demand for commodities and thereby worsen the problem.

Although a reduction in the real wage rate would depress the effective demand for labor services, such a reduction, according to equation (1.10), would also lower the notional supply of labor services. If l^s were sufficiently responsive to changes in W/P, reductions in W/P could reduce and eventually eliminate the excess supply of labor services. In this case, real wage cuts may appear superficially to be an effective remedy. However, in fact, real wage cuts would replace the reduced involuntary underemployment with more voluntary underemployment.[21]

The example of the wage-price vector (W_1, P_1) focuses attention on insufficient demand for commodities as a cause of underemployment and underproduction. However, our model is completely consistent with the classical result that an excessive real wage rate can lead to underemployment. In particular, if the real wage rate were above the general-market-clearing level $(W/P)^*$, no increase in demand for commodities could bring the economy to full employment. With the real wage above $(W/P)^*$, the representative firm will be unwilling to expand output and employment as far as (y^*, l^*). Therefore, a reduction in the real wage rate would be necessary to attain full employment. The essential point is that a real wage rate above $(W/P)^*$ is a sufficient condition, but not a necessary condition, for underemployment. The classical type of underemployment involving a real wage rate above $(W/P)^*$ must be distinguished from that underemployment which arises with the real wage rate at or below $(W/P)^*$, because of a deficiency of demand for commodities. Section 2.4 below considers the general problem of determining the levels of output and employment corresponding to any given levels of wages and prices.

2.2.4 The liquidity constraint

The asset-exhaustion condition, $M(N)/P = 0$, imposes on the household the lifetime budget constraint that its total expenditures may not exceed its initial asset holdings plus its total net receipts. However, the household's life plan is also subject to the condition that its pattern of expenditures and receipts should at no intermediate time between date 0 and date N overexhaust its real money balance. In other words, in addition to $M(N)/P = 0$, the life plan must satisfy the condition

$$\frac{M(t)}{P} = \frac{M(0)}{P} + \int_0^t \frac{m^{d\prime}(t)}{P}\, dt \geq 0 \text{ for } 0 \leq t < N.$$

---

[21] A reduction in the real wage rate is sometimes rejected as a remedy for underemployment on the grounds that the labor market might not have a stable equilibrium. One rationalization would be a 'backward bending' notional supply curve. Our analysis shows that a reduction in the real wage rate is an inadequate remedy even with a stable equilibrium.

We may denote this condition, that the real money balance must always be nonnegative, as the liquidity constraint.[22]

The analysis of the notional household supply and demand functions in chapter 1 did not deal explicitly with a liquidity constraint. In that context, the working households selected, as part of the life plan of employment and consumption, a constant value of notional saving demand for the working years and another constant value of notional saving demand for the retired years. Moreover, we may presume that working households would plan for their consumption after retirement to be at or at least near its preretirement level. Consequently, given the absence of wage income after retirement, the selected constant value of notional saving demand for the retired years would be negative, so that consumption after retirement could exceed $\pi - \tau$. To allow for this negative saving after retirement, the constant value of notional saving demand during the working years would have to produce a positive value for $M(N')/P$. Consequently, in practice, the liquidity constraint would be ineffective in the basic model.[23]

In the present context of general excess supply, the temporary shortfall of both employment and profits creates a new possibility for an effective liquidity constraint. The representative working household expects its income to remain below the general-market-clearing level until date $\hat{N}$. However, if $\hat{N}$ is small relative to N' and N, lifetime income prospects remain favorable, and the household may want to maintain consumption at a relatively high level during the period of temporarily depressed income. But, suppose that the current money balance is small. In that case, if the temporary shortfall of income is large, the household, if it ignored the liquidity constraint, might plan its consumption so as to cause its money balance to become negative sometime between date 0 and date $\hat{N}$. In that event, the liquidity constraint would become effective.[24]

---

[22] In a more general context in which fiat money was not the only asset, the liquidity problem would involve the costs of liquidating the various assets which might be owned as well as the costs of borrowing to finance expenditures. In the present context, assuming that fiat money is the only asset is equivalent to assuming that these costs are infinite. If, alternatively, these costs were finite, the analysis would be much more complicated, but its essential qualitative features would not seem to be changed. The literature contains some discussion of liquidity in this context. See, especially, Flemming (1973). Barro and Grossman (1974*b*) review this literature.

[23] This conclusion would be more tenuous if either W/P or π were expected to rise over time.

[24] The situation from date $\hat{N}$ to date N' is essentially the same as that of the basic model. Then, for the reasons given above, we may presume that the liquidity constraint would be ineffective during the second period.

For the initial period, from date 0 to date $\hat{N}$, and assuming $\hat{N} < N'$, the liquidity constraint requires

$$\frac{M(\hat{N})}{P} = \frac{M(0)}{P} + \hat{N}\frac{m^{d'}}{P} \geq 0,$$

where $m^{d'}/P$ is the constant value of effective saving demand during this period. This condition may also be expressed as

$$-\frac{m^{d'}}{P} \leq \frac{1}{\hat{N}}\frac{M(0)}{P}.$$

In other words, the liquidity constraint implies that during this initial period the rate of dissaving cannot exceed

$$\frac{1}{\hat{N}}\frac{M(0)}{P}.$$

By limiting the rate of dissaving, the liquidity constraint also limits the level of consumption. From equation (2.2), we see that the above conditions imply that $c^{d'}$ from date 0 to date $\hat{N}$ cannot exceed

$$\frac{W}{P}l + \pi - \tau + \frac{1}{\hat{N}}\frac{M(0)}{P}.$$

This discussion implies, in place of equation (2.4), the following more general specification for the current value of effective consumption demand:

$$c^{d'} = \min\left[c^{d'}\left(\Omega', \frac{W}{P}\right), \frac{W}{P}l + \pi - \tau + \frac{1}{\hat{N}}\frac{M}{P}\right], \qquad (2.11)$$

subject to $c^{d'} \geq 0$. In other words, the liquidity constraint is effective if $c^{d'}(\Omega', W/P)$ exceeds

$$\frac{W}{P}l + \pi - \tau + \frac{1}{\hat{N}}\frac{M}{P}.$$

If the liquidity constraint is effective, optimal behavior would involve adjusting $c^{d'}$ downward either until the liquidity constraint were just satisfied or until $c^{d'}$ reached zero.[25] Similarly, using equation (2.2), we have, in place of equation (2.5), the following more general specification for the current value of effective saving demand:

$$\frac{m^{d'}}{P} = \max\left[\frac{m^{d'}}{P}\left(\Omega', \frac{W}{P}, \frac{W}{P}l + \pi - \tau\right), -\frac{1}{\hat{N}}\frac{M}{P}\right], \qquad (2.12)$$

[25] In this case, the household must also appropriately revise its planned time paths for $c^{d'}$ from date $\hat{N}$ to date N and for $l^{s'}$ from date $\hat{N}$ to date N'.

subject to

$$\frac{m^{d'}}{P} \leq \frac{W}{P} l + \pi - \tau.$$

If the liquidity constraint were effective, the household would also set its rate of dissaving equal to its maximum permissible value.

The specification of effective consumption demand for the case of an effective liquidity constraint has two important implications. First, for given values of Ω' and W/P, an effective liquidity constraint implies a reduced value for $c^{d'}$. Second, if the liquidity constraint is satisfied for a positive value of $c^{d'}$, the marginal propensity to consume out of income is equal to unity, which is higher than the marginal propensity to consume when the liquidity constraint is ineffective. Consequently, if in the aggregate situation the liquidity constraint is effective for a positive fraction of the total of households, the average marginal propensity to consume and the demand multiplier would exceed the values determined in the preceding section where we abstracted from the liquidity constraint. Moreover, for given values of the exogenous variables, the levels of $c^{d'}$, y, and l would be lower than the values determined in the preceding section. However, as long as the liquidity constraint was not effective for all working households, the demand multiplier would still be finite.

In evaluating the significance of the liquidity constraint, the key question concerns the fraction of households for whom this constraint would be effective. To analyze this question, let us assume provisionally that all households are identical, so that the behavior of the representative household also represents the behavior of each household.[26] Under this assumption, we can move freely between individual and aggregate behavior. Given that profits and wages exhaust total output – that is, $y = (W/P)l + \pi$ – and the government budget constraint, $g^d - m^s/P = \tau$, the final term in equation (2.11) may be expressed as $y - g^d + m^s/P + (1/\hat{N})(M/P)$. Moreover, under conditions of general excess supply, output is determined to satisfy the condition, $y = c^{d'} + g^d$. Using this condition, the final term in equation (2.11) becomes $c^{d'} + m^s/P + (1/\hat{N})(M/P)$, and equation (2.11) can be written as

$$c^{d'} = \min \left[c^{d'}\left(\Omega', \frac{W}{P}\right), c^{d'} + \frac{m^s}{P} + \frac{1}{\hat{N}} \frac{M}{P} \right], \qquad (2.13)$$

[26] This assumption involves neglecting the distinction between working and retired households.

subject to $c^{d'} \geq 0$. According to equation (2.13), the liquidity constraint reduces to the condition

$$\frac{m^s}{P} + \frac{1}{\hat{N}} \frac{M}{P} \geq 0, \text{ or, equivalently, } -\hat{N} \frac{m^s}{P} \leq \frac{M}{P}. \tag{2.14}$$

Condition (2.14) restricts the rate of change of the money stock such that the money stock will not be exhausted before date $\hat{N}$.[27] If condition (2.14) is satisfied, the liquidity constraint is ineffective and $c^{d'}$ is equal to $c^{d'}(\Omega', W/P)$. In this case, the level of income turns out to be such that the representative household is able to determine its effective consumption demand without having to be concerned about exhausting its money holdings before date $\hat{N}$. Alternatively, if condition (2.14) is not satisfied, the liquidity constraint is effective and, moreover, $c^{d'}$ declines to zero.

Figure 2.4 illustrates the determination of consumption and output, taking account of the liquidity constraint, but assuming all households to be identical. In figure 2.4, the dashed 45° line through the origin depicts points of equality between $c^{d'} + g^d$ and y. The line labeled $c^{d'}(\Omega', W/P)$ represents, for given values of the exogenous variables, effective consumption demand as a function of income, ignoring the liquidity constraint. The 45° line labeled $y - g^d + m^s/P + (1/\hat{N})(M/P)$ with the positive intercept on the vertical axis represents effective consumption demand as determined by the liquidity constraint for the case in which $m^s/P + (1/\hat{N})(M/P)$ is positive. The solid locus composed of segments of the latter two lines depicts effective consumption demand, taking account of the liquidity constraint. Point B indicates the only point of equality between $c^{d'} + g^d$ and y. Notice that, because the liquidity constraint is a 45° line, point B must lie on $c^{d'}(\Omega', W/P)$. Thus, if $m^s/P + (1/\hat{N})(M/P)$ is positive and all households are identical, the level of y must be such that the liquidity constraint is ineffective. Finally, the 45° line labeled $y - g^d + m^s/P + (1/\hat{N})(M/P)$ with the positive intercept on the horizontal axis represents the liquidity constraint for the case in which $m^s/P + (1/\hat{N})(M/P)$ is negative. In this unlikely case, effective consumption demand follows the liquidity constraint to the horizontal axis and then, given that $c^{d'}$ cannot be negative, jumps to the origin. The only point of equality between $c^{d'} + g^d$ and y is at the origin.

[27] For moderate values of $\hat{N}$ – say, the two to three year period corresponding to half of the average business cycle – this condition restricts the rate of monetary contraction only to less than thirty to fifty per cent per annum. Historically, this restriction has certainly been met, except perhaps for short intervals.

The preceding analysis suggests that for the liquidity constraint to be effective for a positive fraction of households requires that all households not be identical. The size of this fraction would depend on the extent of specific distributional inequalities. Although our analytical framework is not adequate for a full analysis of distributional

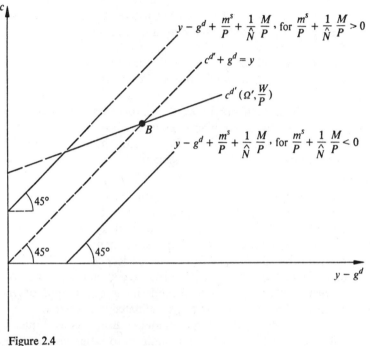

Figure 2.4
Liquidity, consumption and output

considerations, two general relationships are readily apparent. First, for a given aggregate shortfall of employment below notional labor supply, the fraction of working households for whom the liquidity constraint is effective will be larger the less evenly distributed is the amount of employment. Specifically, the greater the extent to which a reduction in aggregate employment involves layoffs, rather than equivalent reductions in man-hours worked, the greater would be the fraction of working households for whom the liquidity constraint is effective and, hence, the larger would be the demand multiplier and the lower would be the levels of output and employment. Second, the liquidity constraint is less likely to be effective for older households, which have already accumulated a large stock of M/P, than for younger households.

2.3   The general excess demand case

This section analyzes the determination of output and employment when the values of W and P are such that excess demand exists in the markets for both labor services and commodities. In this situation the principle of voluntary exchange implies that employment and output are both supply determined. Thus, we might be tempted to assert that $l = l^s < l^d$ and $y = y^s < c^d + g^d$. However, just as the notional demand functions were not relevant in the case of general excess supply, so the notional supply functions are not relevant in the case of general excess demand. The quantities determined according to the notional supplies would be inconsistent with each other. In particular, if the firms were actually employing a quantity of labor services less than l^d, their supply of commodities would not be given by the notional supply function y^s; while if household purchases of commodities were actually less than c^d, their supply of labor services would not be given by the notional supply function l^s. The following subsections analyze the intermarket interactions implied by excess demand.

2.3.1   *The behavior of the firms under excess demand for labor services*

Excess demand in the labor market means that the representative firm will not be able to purchase its notional demand l^d.[28] Given excess demand, voluntary exchange implies that actual purchases l will equal the quantity supplied and thus will be less than l^d. Therefore, excess demand in the labor market, like excess supply in the commodity market, violates an essential underlying assumption of the firm's profit maximization problem as formulated in chapter 1.

Given $l < l^d$, the representative firm acts as a quantity taker with respect to employment, in addition to acting as a wage and price taker.[29] In the basic model purchases of labor services were a choice variable. In contrast, the representative firm now sees the quantity l as a supply-determined constraint on its purchases.[30] Profit maximiza-

---

[28] Voluntary exchange implies that firms are unaffected by excess demand for commodities.

[29] We continue to focus on the representative firm and household, and, as in the analysis of the general excess supply case, we do not analyze the possible rationing processes which could determine the allocation of aggregate labor supply and aggregate commodity supply among the individual firms and households.

[30] As in the general excess supply case, the determination of the actual values of l and y involves the market interaction of firm and household behavior. This interaction is analyzed in section 2.3.3 below. But, again, the atomistic firm or household ignores its own contribution to the market process.

tion now implies producing as much output as possible with the available labor. We denote this maximum quantity as the effective supply of commodities, and represent it by $y^{s'}$. Formally, the representative firm's problem is to choose $y^{s'}$ so as to maximize $\pi = y^{s'} - \dfrac{W}{P} l$, subject to $y^{s'} = \Phi(l, g)$. The solution is to select

$$y^{s'} = \Phi(l, g) \equiv \underset{(+)(+)}{y^{s'}(l, g)} \text{ for } l < l^d \left(\frac{W}{P}\right). \tag{2.15}$$

The constraint of $l < l^d$ implies $y^s < y^s$, with $y^{s'}$ approaching y^s as l approaches l^d. Again, the representative firm is forced to operate in a region where the marginal product of labor exceeds the real wage rate.

In equation (1.4), derived in the basic model, the notional supply of commodities was a function of the real wage rate, but was not a function of employment. Employment was maximized out as a separate choice variable. In contrast, in equation (2.15), the effective supply of commodities is a function of the level of employment. The level of labor supply here imposes employment as a constraint on the effective supply of commodities. Equation (2.15) implies that the effective supply of commodities can vary even with the real wage rate fixed. Changes in the level of the constraint l determine effective commodity supply independently of changes in W/P.

Figure 2.5 depicts the preceding analysis of the representative firm's effective supply of commodities. The y^s curve is reproduced from figure 1.2. The $y^{s'}$ curve depicts the effective supply of commodities as given by equation (2.15). For a given value of l, $y^{s'}$ coincides with y^s when W/P is such that l is not an effective constraint – that is, when $l \geq l^d(W/P)$. Alternatively, when W/P is such that l is an effective constraint – that is, when $l < l^d(W/P) - y^{s'}$ is independent of the real wage rate and diverges from y^s. In the diagram the real wage rate $(W/P)_F$ is such that $l = l^d[(W/P)_F]$. Therefore, at all real wage rates below $(W/P)_F$, the $y^{s'}$ curve is depicted as vertical and distinct from y^s.

The two $c^d + g^d$ curves in figure 2.5 are also reproduced from figure 1.2. The $c^d(\Omega^*) + g^d$ curve intersects the y^s curve at point A. The $c^d(\Omega_2) + g^d$ curve corresponds to a higher value of nonwage wealth, i.e., $\Omega_2 > \Omega^*$, which results from a price level lower than P^*. At the real wage rate $(W/P)^*$, the notional commodity demand associated with Ω_2 exceeds the notional supply of commodities.

2.3.2 *The behavior of households under excess demand for commodities*

Given voluntary exchange, excess demand in the commodity market means that total purchases of commodities, y, will be less than total notional demand, $c^d + g^d$. For simplicity, we assume that government demand receives priority, so that g equals g^d as long as g^d does not exceed the total supply. This assumption is probably not grossly unrealistic. Consequently, the representative household is unable to purchase the quantity c^d.[31] Its actual purchases will be $c = y - g^d < c^d$. Thus,

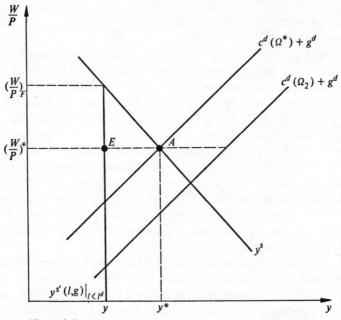

Figure 2.5
The commodity market with excess demand for labor services

excess demand in the commodity market, like excess supply in the labor market, violates an essential underlying assumption of the representative household's utility maximization problem, as formulated in chapter 1.

Given $c < c^d$, the representative household acts as a quantity taker with respect to consumption, in addition to acting as a wage and price taker. In the basic model consumption was a choice variable. In contrast, the representative household now sees the quantity c as a supply-determined constraint on its consumption. Given this constraint, the household must choose some combination of two options. First, it can continue to accept employment equal to its notional supply l^s, thereby maintaining its notional income, and then save, i.e., accumulate

[31] Voluntary exchange implies that households are unaffected by excess demand for labor services.

as money balances, the portion of this income which it would like to consume but cannot. Alternatively, it can accept less employment, substituting leisure for the consumption which it cannot obtain. We denote the optimal combination of these two options as the effective supply of labor services and the effective demand for additions to money balances, and represent them by $l^{s'}$ and $m^{d'}/P$. The effective savings demand $m^{d'}/P$ implies a planned effective future consumption demand, denoted by $c^{d'}$.

Utility maximization remains an intertemporal problem. The choice of time paths of employment and saving – $l^{s'}(t)$ and $m^{d'}(t)/P$ – depends not only on the current consumption constraint c, which the representative household directly perceives, but also on the entire expected future time path of this constraint. In the case of excess supply of labor discussed in Section 2.2.2, we assumed that the representative working household expected the current constraint on employment to prevail until date $\hat{N}$. In the present case, we assume similarly that the representative working household expects the current constraint on consumption to prevail until date $\hat{N}$, where $0 < \hat{N} < N'$, but expects to be unconstrained during the remaining $N - \hat{N}$ years until the planning horizon. Given $c(t) = c$ for all $t \leq \hat{N}$, because $c^d(t)$ is constant at least until date N', $c < c^d(0)$ implies $c(t) < c^d(t)$ for all $t \leq \hat{N}$. We again take $\hat{N}$ to be exogenously determined. Again, this treatment of expectations, although simple, does exhibit two important properties. First, the anticipated future shortfall of consumption below demand is larger the larger the present shortfall. Second, the representative household does not anticipate the shortages to persist indefinitely. The household expects to be unconstrained in its choice of consumption at some time in the future.[32]

We also retain the assumptions of the excess supply of labor case regarding expectations of the future time paths of W, P, τ, and π. Specifically, the representative household expects W, P, and τ to be constant over time and expects π to be constant until date $\hat{N}$ and then to rise to equal π^*.[33] Thus, the specification of nonwage wealth, Ω, is, as in the excess supply case,

$$\Omega \equiv \frac{M}{P} + \hat{N}\pi + (N - \hat{N})\pi^* - N\tau.$$

[32] This treatment also has the restrictive property that the household expects a shortfall of consumption in the future only if it experiences a current shortfall.

[33] Barro and Grossman (1974a) considers a variation on this analysis, in which the representative household expects π to be constant until date N.

Given the above assumptions, the representative working household's formal problem is to maximize

$$U = \int_0^{\hat{N}} u[c, l^{s'}(t)]dt + \int_{\hat{N}}^{N'} u[c^{d'}(t), l^{s'}(t)]dt + \int_{N'}^{N} u[c^{d'}(t), 0]dt,$$

subject to given values of W, P, π, τ, and c, the horizons $\hat{N}$, N, and N', and initial real asset holdings, $M(0)/P$. The working household's life plan now involves three subperiods: the initial period from 0 to $\hat{N}$, during which consumption is determined exogenously at the effective constraint level and during which labor supply and saving demand are the only choice variables; a second period from $\hat{N}$ to N', during which consumption demand, labor supply, and saving demand are all choice variables; and the retirement period from N' to N, during which consumption demand and saving demand are choice variables and labor supply is set at zero.

The specification of saving for the three subperiods is

$$\frac{1}{P}\left(\frac{dM}{dt}\right)^{d'} \equiv \frac{m^{d'}}{P} = \begin{cases} \dfrac{W}{P} l^{s'} + \pi - \tau - c \text{ for } 0 \le t \le \hat{N}, \\[2mm] \dfrac{W}{P} l^{s'} + \pi^* - \tau - c^{d'} \text{ for } \hat{N} < t \le N', \\[2mm] \pi^* - \tau - c^{d'} \text{ for } N' < t \le N. \end{cases}$$

(2.16)

Optimal behavior again entails the exhaustion of asset holdings at date N. Therefore, the choice of $l^{s'}(t)$ and $c^{d'}(t)$ will satisfy

$$\frac{M(N)}{P} = \frac{M(0)}{P} + \hat{N}(\pi - c) + (N - \hat{N})\pi^* - N\tau$$

$$+ \frac{W}{P}\int_0^{N'} l^{s'}(t)dt - \int_{\hat{N}}^{N} c^{d'}(t)dt = 0. \quad (2.17)$$

The basic exogenous constraint on household behavior now equals nonwage wealth, as respecified above, less anticipated consumption expenditure until date $\hat{N}$. This difference is now the resource parameter and we denote its value by Ω'', where

$$\Omega'' \equiv \Omega - \hat{N}c \equiv \frac{M(0)}{P} + \hat{N}(\pi - c) + (N - \hat{N})\pi^* - N\tau.$$

The maximization of U, subject to the asset-exhaustion condition,[34] yields an optimal time path for $l^{s'}$ from date 0 to date N' and an optimal time path of $c^{d'}$ from date $\hat{N}$ to date N. The optimal time path for $l^{s'}$ is constant from time 0 to time $\hat{N}$, and also constant, but generally at a different level, from time $\hat{N}$ to time N'. The effective consumption demand, $c^{d'}$, is constant from time $\hat{N}$ to time N', and also constant, but generally at a different level, from time N' to time N. However, if consumption and employment are independent influences on utility, $l^{s'}$ is constant from date 0 to date N', and $c^{d'}$ is constant from date $\hat{N}$ to date N. In this case, the asset exhaustion condition of equation (2.17) simplifies to

$$\Omega'' + N' \frac{W}{P} l^{s'} - (N - \hat{N})c^{d'} = 0.$$

Given the saving specification of equation (2.16), these time paths for $l^{s'}$ and $c^{d'}$ also imply constant values for $m^{d'}/P$ from date 0 to date $\hat{N}$, from date $\hat{N}$ to date N' and from date N', to date N.

Let us compare, for given values of Ω and W/P, these time paths for $c^{d'}$, $l^{s'}$, and $m^{d'}/P$, chosen subject to the asset-exhaustion condition of equation (2.17), to the time paths of c^d, l^s, and m^d/P which were chosen in the basic model. Given that, from date 0 to date $\hat{N}$, c is constrained to be less than c^d, the representative working household's expenditure, during this period, is below the notional level which it would have chosen in the basic model. The representative working household absorbs the reduction in expenditure in two ways. First, it reduces its total lifetime employment. Second, it increases its consumption during the future unconstrained years. Thus, from date 0 to date N', the average level of $l^{s'}$ is less than the average level of l^s, and, from date $\hat{N}$ to date N, the average level of $c^{d'}$ is larger than the average level of c^d.

If consumption and employment are independent influences on utility, or at least if the enforced decrease in consumption from date 0 to date $\hat{N}$ does not substantially affect the marginal disutility of work during that period, the decrease in total lifetime employment also implies that $l^{s'}$ is less than l^s during each of the first two subperiods of the life plan. However, for the initial period from date 0 to date $\hat{N}$, even though $l^{s'}$ is less than l^s, the difference between $(W/P)l^s$ and

$(W/P)l^{s'}$ is less than the difference between c^d and c. This result obtains for two reasons. First, the shortfall of expenditure from date 0 to date $\hat{N}$ can be spread over N' years of reduced wage income. Second, the excess of $c^{d'}$ over c^d from date $\hat{N}$ to date N partially compensates for the shortfall of expenditure during the preceding period.

These adjustments of effective labor supply and effective consumption demand imply a relation between $m^{d'}/P$ and m^d/P. Because $c^{d'}$ exceeds c^d from date N' to date N, the average level of $m^{d'}/P$ exceeds m^d/P from date 0 to date N'. Moreover, from date $\hat{N}$ to date N', $l^{s'}$ is less than l^s and $c^{d'}$ exceeds c^d, so that $m^{d'}/P$ is less than m^d/P. Thus, from date 0 to date $\hat{N}$, $m^{d'}/P$ must exceed m^d/P.

We should stress the fact that households respond to a constraint on current consumption by exercising two options – increase in future consumption and decrease in labor supply. The induced increase in future consumption, which is associated with an increase in current saving, corresponds to the classical concept of forced saving, or, more precisely, to what Robertson (1926) defined as 'automatic lacking'. In contrast to our conclusions, classical analysis implicitly assumed that households channel all frustrated consumption demand into forced saving, and did not consider the alternative possibility of a reduction in labor supply (increase in leisure). The inclusion in our analysis of the option of reducing labor supply is especially interesting, since, as the next section stresses, it has the apparently paradoxical implication that excess demand for commodities and labor services can result in decreased employment and output.

In sum, the constraint on consumption causes a reduction in the current effective labor supply and an increase in the current effective saving demand of working households. Specifically, the maximization calculus implies solutions for the current values of $l^{s'}$ and $m^{d'}/P$ of the following form:

$$l^{s'} = l^{s'} \left(\Omega'', \frac{W}{P} \right) \text{ and} \tag{2.18}$$
$$\phantom{l^{s'} = l^{s'} \left(} {\scriptstyle (-)} \; {\scriptstyle (+)}$$

$$\frac{m^{d'}}{P} = \frac{m^{d'}}{P} \left(\Omega'', \frac{W}{P}, \pi - \tau - c \right). \tag{2.19}$$
$$\phantom{\frac{m^{d'}}{P} = \frac{m^{d'}}{P} \left(} {\scriptstyle (-)} \; {\scriptstyle (+)} \quad\;\; {\scriptstyle (+)}$$

The mathematical note at the end of this section spells out the derivation of these effective demand functions.

The form of the effective supply and demand functions of equations (2.18) and (2.19) is similar to the form of the notional supply and demand functions of equations (1.10) and (1.11). In these $l^{s'}$ and

$m^{d'}/P$ functions, changes in Ω'' have an effect which is analogous to the effect that changes in Ω had in the l^s and m^d/P functions. However, the notional supply of labor and demand for savings were not functions of the level of consumption. Consumption was maximized out as a separate choice variable. In contrast, in equations (2.18) and (2.19), the effective supply of labor and demand for savings are functions, through Ω'', of the level of consumption. The level of supply of commodities net of government purchases here imposes consumption as a constraint on the effective supply of labor and demand for savings. Total consumption during the constrained years, $\hat{N}c$, enters as a negative component of Ω''.

Consider the case in which consumption and employment are independent influences on utility, so that, as noted above, the asset-exhaustion condition can be written as

$$\Omega'' + N' \frac{W}{P} l^{s'} - (N - \hat{N})c^{d'} = 0.$$

Differentiation of this condition, given that $\delta c^{d'}/\delta \Omega''$ is positive, yields

$$\frac{W}{P} \frac{\delta l^{s'}}{\delta \Omega''} = - \frac{1}{N'} \left[1 - (N - \hat{N}) \frac{\delta c^{d'}}{\delta \Omega''} \right] > - \frac{1}{N'}.$$

In other words, the change in current wage income corresponding to the change in current effective labor supply equals one-Nth of the change in Ω'' less the induced change in planned consumption during the unconstrained years. This result is useful in the next section, which analyzes the determination of y and l under excess demand conditions.

Current consumption also enters the $m^{d'}/P$ function of equation (2.19) as a component of the term $\pi - \tau - c$. Changes in this term have an effect which is analogous to the effect that changes in $\pi - \tau$ had in the m^d/P function. The effects of changes in W/P, given Ω'' and $\pi - \tau - c$, are more complicated, because, as in the basic model, offsetting income and substitution effects are involved. We assume here, as in chapter 1, that the substitution effect outweighs the income effect in the relevant range, so that the net effect of an increase in W/P is to raise $l^{s'}$. However, because substitution between consumption and leisure is now limited to increasing $c^{d'}$ during unconstrained years at the expense of leisure during working years, the substitution effect of W/P on $l^{s'}$ is weaker than the corresponding effect on l^s. Hence, our assumption that the substitution effect is dominant is more tenuous than it was in chapter 1. However, whether or not an increase in W/P causes $l^{s'}$ to increase, an increase in W/P does raise future $c^{d'}$ and, hence, must also raise current $(W/P)l^{s'}$.

This increase in labor income implies an increase in $m^{d'}/P$, which in turn allows for an increase in planned consumption after retirement.

It is also interesting to discuss the effect of a change in $\hat{N}$ on the effective demands and supplies. The principal effect of an increase in $\hat{N}$ would be to increase the number of years during which the representative working household is constrained to consumption level c and correspondingly to decrease the number of years during which the household is able to obtain the level of consumption $c^{d'}$. Thus, because c is less than $c^{d'}$, an increase in $\hat{N}$ causes an increase in the household's disposable lifetime resources.[35] Accordingly, the household would further reduce its total lifetime employment and this reduction would presumably involve a lower level of $l^{s'}$ from date 0 to date N'. In addition, the household would raise the level of $c^{d'}$ planned for the reduced number of unconstrained years. The decline in current $l^{s'}$ implies a decrease in current $m^{d'}/P$. The general result is that the larger is $\hat{N}$, the more the representative working household reacts to a given shortfall of current c below c^d by reducing effective labor supply and the less by increasing effective saving demand.[36]

Retired households differ from working households in that retired households have no possibility of substituting more leisure for the currently desired but unobtainable consumption. Retired households

[35] This increase in disposable lifetime resources results from an extension of the constraint on consumption and, thus, is associated with a decline in the household's maximum lifetime utility. Fischer (1972) presents a general analysis of the relation between wealth and welfare. An additional effect of an increase in $\hat{N}$ is to increase the number of years during which anticipated profit income is below π^*. This effect partially offsets the effect of the increase in the number of years during which consumption is at level c.

[36] The preceding discussion has assumed that $\hat{N}$ is less than N'. Alternatively, if $\hat{N}$ equals or exceeds N', and $c^d(t)$ exceeds $c(t)$ for $0 \leq t \leq \hat{N}$, the form of the problem is altered. Two cases must be considered: First, if $N' \leq \hat{N} < N$, the constraint on consumption extends beyond retirement and current $m^{d'}/P$ can be less than m^d/P, for given values of Ω and W/P. Also, $l^{s'}$ is constant from date 0 to date N' regardless of the sign of u_{cl}. Second, if $\hat{N} \geq N$, the constraint on commodity purchases is effectively permanent. Consequently, the household works only the minimum amount necessary to pay for the available lifetime consumption. The elasticity of $l^{s'}$ with respect to W/P reflects only an income effect and is equal to minus unity. Moreover, the asset-exhaustion condition becomes

$$\frac{M(N)}{P} = \frac{M(0)}{P} + N(\pi - c - \tau) + N'\frac{W}{P}l^{s'} = 0.$$

Also, current $m^{d'}/P$ is independent of W/P and is less than m^d/P.

can react to the shortfall of current c below c^d only by increasing current $m^{d'}/P$ and future $c^{d'}$. However, the directions of effect of Ω'' and $\pi - \tau - c$ upon $m^{d'}/P$ for retired households are the same as those for working households. Thus, assuming that the representative retired household also expects c and π to be constant at their current levels for $\hat{N}$ years, the aggregate $m^{d'}/P$ function has the same form as the function given in equation (2.19).

Figure 2.6 depicts the preceding analysis of the representative working household's effective supply of labor services. The l^d curve

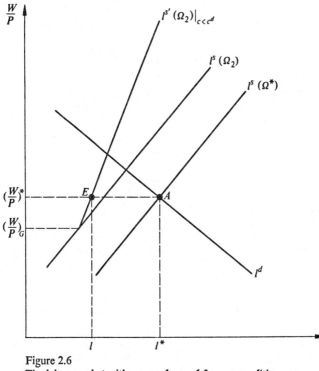

Figure 2.6
The labor market with excess demand for commodities

and the two l^s curves are reproduced from figure 1.1. The l^d curve again intersects the $l^s(\Omega^*)$ curve at point A. The $l^s(\Omega_2)$ curve corresponds to a larger value of nonwage wealth, $\Omega_2 > \Omega^*$, which results from a price level below P^*. At the real wage rate $(W/P)^*$, the notional demand for labor services exceeds the notional labor supply associated with Ω_2.

The $l^{s'}(\Omega_2)|_c$ curve depicts the effective supply of labor services, for nonwage wealth Ω_2 and consumption level c. For a given value of

c, which is equal to $y - g^d$, $l^{s'}(\Omega_2)|_c$ coincides with $l^s(\Omega_2)$ when c is not an effective constraint – that is, when $c \geq c^d(\Omega_2, W/P)$. Alternatively, when W/P is such that c is an effective constraint – that is, when $c < c^d(\Omega_2, W/P) - l^{s'}$ is to the left of l^s. In the diagram the real wage $(W/P)_G$ is such that $c = c^d[\Omega_2, (W/P)_G]$. Therefore, at all real wage rates above $(W/P)_G$, the $l^{s'}$ curve is depicted as distinct from l^s. The positive slope of the $l^{s'}$ curve reflects our assumption that $\delta l^{s'}/\delta(W/P)$ is positive.

In figures 2.5 and 2.6, the effective supply schedules are juxta-posed with the notional demand schedules. This formulation assumes, as regards figure 2.5, that the representative working household continues to offer to purchase commodities according to its notional demand schedule, despite the supply-imposed constraint on its consumption. As regards figure 2.6, the assumption is that the representative firm continues to offer to purchase labor services according to its notional demand schedule, despite the supply-imposed constraint on its employment of labor.[37] In these figures points A again identify the general-market-clearing combination of real wage rate, price level, employment, and output. Points E identify the levels of employment and production associated with the real wage rate $(W/P)^*$ and nonwage wealth Ω_2, which is above Ω^*. In the next section we explicitly analyze the deter-mination of the characteristics of points such as E.

Mathematical note

The interior solution for optimal values of $l^{s'}(t)$ and $c^{d'}(t)$ satisfies the conditions

$$\frac{\delta u}{\delta l^{s'}(t)} = -\lambda \frac{W}{P} \text{ for } 0 \leq t \leq N', \text{ and}$$

$$\frac{\delta u}{\delta c^{d'}(t)} = \lambda \text{ for } \hat{N} < t \leq N,$$

---

[37] Analogously to the general excess supply case, this formulation abstracts from three types of effects which might cause actual attempts to purchase to differ from notional demands. First, households may attempt, despite the constraint on current consumption, to substitute increased current consumption for future consumption which they do not expect to obtain. Second, if buyers think that actual purchases are directly related to the amount which they offer to buy, they may communicate offers to buy in excess of their desired purchases. Cf. Hansen (1951). Third, if there are costs associated with the expression of offers to purchase, the representative household or firm may not bother to make offers which are not expected to be successful. This last effect would tend to reduce actual orders below notional demand and would tend to offset the first two effects.

where λ is a positive constant determined so as to satisfy equation (2.17). These conditions imply

$$l^{s\prime}(t) = \begin{cases} l^{s\prime}(0) \text{ for } 0 \leq t \leq \hat{N}, \\ l^{s\prime}(N') \text{ for } \hat{N} < t \leq N', \end{cases}$$

and

$$c^{d\prime}(t) = \begin{cases} c^{d\prime}(N') \text{ for } \hat{N} < t \leq N', \\ c^{d\prime}(N) \text{ for } N' < t \leq N. \end{cases}$$

The effective labor supply function for the current period has the form

$$l^{s\prime}(0) = l^{s\prime}(\Omega'', W/P, c).$$
$$\phantom{l^{s\prime}(0) = l^{s\prime}(} (-) \quad (?) \quad (?)$$

If $\delta^2 u/\delta c(t)\delta l(t) = 0$, then c drops out as a separate argument of this function. Equation (2.18) is thus an approximation which abstracts from the effect of the level of consumption on the marginal disutility of work.

2.3.3 *The determination of output and employment under general excess demand*

Figures 2.5 and 2.6, like figures 2.1 and 2.2, both represent partial analyses. Figure 2.5 explains the effective supply of commodities as a function of a given supply-imposed constraint on purchases of labor services. To close this model, the effective supply of labor services must be explained. Figure 2.6 explains the effective supply of labor services as a function of a given supply-imposed constraint on household purchases of commodities. To close this model, the effective supply of commodities must be explained. Thus, these two partial analyses are essential complements. They may be combined to provide, for a given wage-price vector, a complete picture of the determination of output and employment under general-excess-demand conditions.

When a particular market is experiencing excess demand, voluntary exchange implies that the actual level of transactions will be supply determined. According to the analysis of the preceding two sections, when the commodity market and the labor market are experiencing excess demand, an effective supply, which is less than the notional supply, prevails in the other market. Consequently, when both markets are experiencing excess demand, these effective supplies of commodities and labor services determine both output and employment.

Equation (2.15) gives the effective supply of commodities, so that output is determined by

$$y = y^{s'}(l, g) < c^d\left(\Omega, \frac{W}{P}\right) + g^d, \qquad (2.20)$$

where $g = g^d$.

Similarly, equation (2.18) gives the effective supply of labor services, so that employment is determined by

$$l = l^{s'}\left(\Omega'', \frac{W}{P}\right) < l^d\left(\frac{W}{P}\right). \qquad (2.21)$$

Given the specification of profits, $\pi = y - (W/P)l$, and that consumption and government expenditures exhaust total output (that is, $c = y - g$) we can express the resource constraint Ω'' as

$$\Omega'' = \frac{M}{P} + \hat{N}\left(g - \frac{W}{P}l\right) + (N - \hat{N})\pi^* - N\tau,$$

which depends on l, but does not depend separately on y or π. In order for conditions (2.20) and (2.21) to be relevant, the existing wage-price vector must be such that excess demand exists in both markets. Section 2.4.1 below considers the general specification of the wage-price vectors which generate excess demand in both markets.

Conditions (2.20) and (2.21) determine unique levels of output and employment. Given the exogenous variables – g^d, M, τ, N, N', $\hat{N}$, π^*, P, and W – condition (2.21) implies a current value for l. The essential relation is that the level of l determines the value of $\pi - c$ and, hence, the value of the resource parameter, Ω'', which, in turn, determines $l^{s'}$. According to condition (2.21), the level of l must be such that the level of $l^{s'}$ so determined must be equal to l itself. With l so determined, given $g = g^d$, condition (2.20) relates y to l. The analogy should be obvious between the determination of y and l under general excess demand, as just discussed, and the determination of y and l under general excess supply, as discussed in section 2.2.3 above.

In order to emphasize this analogy and to illustrate more clearly the process by which y and l are determined under general excess demand, let us work through the mechanism of what we may denote the supply multiplier, which is implied by conditions (2.20) and (2.21). The analysis of the supply multiplier will be analogous to the analysis of the demand multiplier in section 2.2.3. Consider the following thought experiment: Suppose that initially the wage-price vector was equal to (W^*, P^*) and thus consistent with general market clearing. Now consider any permanent increase in an exogenously determined variable such that W^*

and P^* are increased, while the actual wages and prices remain unchanged. Among the possibilities for the form of such a disturbance are a decrease in τ or an increase in M.

The initial effect of such a disturbance would be an increase in the notional demand for commodities above the notional supply, and a decrease in the notional supply of labor services below the notional demand. The disturbance thus creates excess demand in both markets. As an immediate consequence, the representative working household perceives a supply-imposed constraint on its consumption, which causes it to reduce its effective supply of labor services below its notional supply. At the same time, the representative firm perceives a supply-imposed constraint on its employment, which both reduces its profits and causes it to reduce its effective supply of commodities below its notional supply. However, these initial effects are just the beginning of the story. The induced reduction in effective labor supply implies a further constraint on employment, which causes a further reduction in profits and effective commodity supply. At the same time, the induced reduction in effective commodity supply implies a further constraint on consumption, which induces a further reduction in effective labor supply, while the induced reduction in profits creates a partially offsetting stimulus to effective labor supply. This entire process cumulates until the actual levels of output and employment settle well below their general-market-clearing levels, with the point of convergence determined by the interaction between the household's marginal propensity to work given an increase in commodities available for purchase and the marginal productivity of labor.

The outcome of this cumulative process can be determined analytically from condition (2.21). Differentiation of condition (2.21), holding π^* and $\hat{N}$ fixed, yields the following relation between changes in exogenous government behavior and the level of employment:

$$
dl = \frac{1}{1 + \hat{N}\dfrac{W}{P}\dfrac{\delta l^{s'}}{\delta\Omega''}} \left\{ \hat{N}\frac{\delta l^{s'}}{\delta\Omega''}\,dg^d - \hat{N}\frac{\delta l^{s'}}{\delta\Omega''}\,d\tau \right.
$$

$$
\left. + \frac{\delta l^{s'}}{\delta\Omega''}\,d\left(\frac{M}{P}\right) - \left[\hat{N}l\frac{\delta l^{s'}}{\delta\Omega''} - \frac{\delta l^{s'}}{\delta(W/P)}\right]d\left(\frac{W}{P}\right)\right\}. \quad (2.22)
$$

For completeness and future reference, equation (2.22) also indicates the effect on employment of an exogenous change in the real wage rate. According to equation (2.22), the ultimate negative effect on employment of an increase in g^d, a decrease in τ, an increase in M/P, or a decrease in W/P results from two components. First, these shifts directly induce a decrease in effective labor supply and employment. This effect is given by the bracketed term on the right side of equation (2.22). Second, this decrease in employment means less output and hence less consumption, a constraint which induces further decreases in effective labor supply and employment. The reduction in employment also means less profit, which boosts effective labor supply and thereby offsets the effect of less consumption. The net effect is given by the term preceding the brackets on the right side of equation (2.22). This term, $1/[1 + \hat{N}(W/P)\delta l^{s'}/\delta\Omega'']$, represents what may be called the supply multiplier.

The term $\hat{N}(W/P)\delta l^{s'}/\delta\Omega''$, which appears in the denominator of the supply multiplier expression, represents the negative of the marginal effect of a change in employment on effective labor supply, $\delta l^{s'}/\delta l$ — that is,

$$- \hat{N} \frac{W}{P} \frac{\delta l^{s'}}{\delta\Omega''} = \frac{\delta\Omega''}{\delta l} \frac{\delta l^{s'}}{\delta\Omega''} = \frac{\delta l^{s'}}{\delta l}.$$

We can denote $\delta l^{s'}/\delta l$ as the marginal propensity to work. As with the demand multiplier, one would expect the supply multiplier to be finite but greater than unity. These bounds require that $\delta l^{s'}/\delta l$ be less than unity but greater than zero. Given that $\delta l^{s'}/\delta\Omega''$ is negative, $\delta l^{s'}/\delta l$ is positive. The condition $\delta l^{s'}/\delta l$ less than unity is also easy to satisfy. For the case in which consumption and employment are independent influences on utility, we saw in the preceding section that $(W/P)\delta l^{s'}/\delta\Omega''$ is greater than $- 1/N'$. Thus, $\delta l^{s'}/\delta l$ is less than $\hat{N}/N'$, which is likely to be much less than unity, and the supply multiplier is less than $N'/(N' - \hat{N})$. The size of the multiplier increases with an increase in $\hat{N}$.[38] As with the demand multiplier of the excess supply case, our formal analysis specifies the supply multiplier as an instantaneous interaction.

The discussion of the determination of output and employment again need not explicitly consider the effective flow demand for money balances, which was given by equation (2.19). Given $g = g^d$ and $y \equiv c + g$, by combining the momentary household budget constraint,

$$c + \frac{m^{d'}}{P} + \tau = \frac{W}{P} l^{s'} + \pi,$$

the government budget constraint,

$$\tau = g^d - \frac{m^s}{P},$$

---

[38] The supply multiplier also would be larger if the marginal disutility of employment increased with a decrease in the level of consumption – that is, if u_{cl} were positive rather than zero.

and the specification of profits,

$$\pi = y^{s'} - \frac{W}{P} l,$$

we obtain for the economy-wide budget constraint

$$(y - y^{s'}) + \frac{W}{P}(l - l^{s'}) + \frac{1}{P}(m^{d'} - m^{s}) = 0. \tag{2.23}$$

Equation (2.23) implies that the combination of y and l which satisfies conditions (2.20) and (2.21) also satisfies

$$\frac{m^{d'}}{P}\left(\Omega'', \frac{W}{P}, \pi - \tau - c\right) = \frac{m^{s}}{P}. \tag{2.24}$$

Figure 2.7 illustrates the determination of the levels of output and employment when there is excess demand in both markets. In order

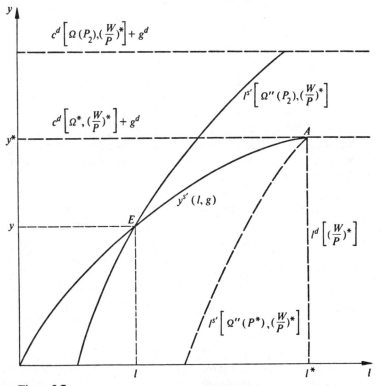

Figure 2.7
Output and employment with excess demand in both markets

to stress the analogy with the excess supply case depicted in figure 2.3, the diagram is drawn on the assumption that the existing real wage rate is still equal to $(W/P)^*$, while the existing levels of wages and prices, W_2 and P_2, are equiproportionately lower than W^* and P^*. As was noted above, such a situation could result either from a decrease in τ, with g^d constant, or from an increase in M.

In figure 2.7 the locus labeled $l^d[(W/P)^*]$ identifies both the general-market-clearing amount of employment, l^*, and the current notional demand for labor services. The locus labeled $c^d[\Omega^*,(W/P)^*] + g^d$ identifies the general-market-clearing level of output, y^*. These two loci intersect at point A, which corresponds to point A in the earlier figures. The locus labeled $c^d[\Omega(P_2), (W/P)^*] + g^d$ identifies the current notional demand for commodities.

In the present situation, however, the effective supply loci determine actual quantities of y and l, which fall short of these demand quantities. The locus labeled $y^{s'}(l,g)$ describes combinations of y and l which satisfy condition (2.20). This locus terminates at point A, and its slope is equal to the marginal product of labor, $\delta\Phi/\delta l$. The two loci labeled $l^{s'}[\Omega'', (W/P)^*]$ describe combinations of y and l which satisfy condition (2.21), given that $\pi = y - (W/P)l$ and that $c = y - g$. One curve corresponds to P^* and W^*, and also terminates at point A. The other curve corresponds to P_2 and W_2, which are below P^* and W^*. The slope of these curves is $(\delta\Phi/\delta l)/(\delta l^{s'}/\delta l)$. Hence, if $\delta l^{s'}/\delta l$ is less than unity, these curves are steeper than the $y^{s'}(l,g)$ locus. The $l^{s'}$ locus corresponding to P_2 and W_2 intersects the $y^{s'}(l,g)$ locus at point E, which identifies the levels of output and employment corresponding to the wage-price vector (W_2, P_2). Point E corresponds to point E in figures 2.5 and 2.6.

A shift from point E to point A would involve either a rise in the price level from P_2 to P^* with an equiproportionate rise in the nominal wage rate, or a restoration of τ or M to their original levels. Since, at point E, the real wage rate is consistent with general market clearing, no change in W/P is involved. In figure 2.7, an equiproportionate rise in the price and wage levels from P_2 to P^* and from W_2 to W^* implies a rightward shift in the $l^{s'}$ locus to $l^{s'}[\Omega''(P^*), (W/P)^*]$, which intersects $y^{s'}(l,g)$ at point A. The supply multiplier is given graphically by the ratio of the difference between l^* and l to the horizontal distance between the two $l^{s'}$ loci.

The gaps shown in figures 2.5–2.7 between y^* and y and between l^* and l represent shortfalls of output and employment below the levels associated with general market clearing. The gap between l^* and l also measures the existing amount of excess demand for labor. The gap between $c^d[\Omega\,(P_2),\,(W/P)^*] + g^d$ and y measures the existing amount of excess demand for commodities.

Two important implications of this analysis should be stressed. First, the real wage rate which is consistent with general market clearing may also be associated with a positive amount of excess demand for labor. Thus, 'too low' a level of the real wage rate is not a necessary condition for the existence of excess demand for labor. This observation parallels the earlier observation that excess supply of labor does not require a real wage rate above the level associated with general market clearing. Excess demand arises in the current case solely because the price level and nominal wage rate are 'too low' – that is, because P_2 and W_2 are lower than P^* and W^*.

The second important implication is that too low a price level and the consequent excess demand for commodities cause employment and output to be below full employment levels. This result obtains because households react to the frustration of their consumption plans by reducing their effective supply of labor services. Given voluntary exchange, employment cannot exceed the quantity supplied, and by the production function, the level of output is constrained by the level of employment. In section 2.2.3 above, we saw how too high a price level and deficient demand for commodities depress output and employment below the full employment level. Here, we see that too low a price level and excessive demand for commodities have the same effect. Thus, we must not conclude that if deficient demand is bad, excessive demand must be good. The fact is that any departure from general market clearing causes a shortfall of output and employment. Output and employment are maximized at the general-market-clearing wage-price vector.

Given the wage-price vector (W_2, P_2), a rise in the real wage rate is not required to restore full employment. The problem is a lack of incentive to work. However, what is needed to restore incentives is not a rise in the real wage rate, but rather an equiproportionate rise in the price level and nominal wage rate or a contractionary government action – for example, some combination of an increase in taxes and a decrease in the stock of money balances.

In the absence of either appropriate increases in P and W or appropriate monetary and fiscal action, an increase in the real wage rate, by inducing the representative working household to substitute an increase in planned consumption during future unconstrained years for current leisure, would improve the situation somewhat. With P unchanged, an increase in W/P would require an increase in W. Given the values of the exogenous variables, such an increase would produce, as indicated by equation (2.22), an increase in $l^{s'}$ and, hence, a multiple expansion of l and y.

An increase in W/P would also reduce notional labor demand. Suppose that, with P and all other exogenous variables remaining constant, W and hence W/P rose sufficiently to lower l^d and raise $l^{s'}$ so as to clear the labor market. At this point, however, the gaps between l^* and l and between y^* and y would not be eliminated. Because W/P would be above $(W/P)^*$, l^d and y^s, and hence l and y, would still be below l^* and y^*. Thus, a change in the real wage rate can be only a partial and superficial remedy for the economy's poor performance. The full restoration of employment incentives requires the elimination of excess demand in both markets through either a combination of contractionary monetary and fiscal policies or a rise in both nominal wages and prices.

In analyzing the case of general excess supply, we also considered, in section 2.2.4 above, the role of the liquidity constraint, $M(t) \geq 0$. The discussion showed that, whereas the analysis of the basic model could reasonably treat this constraint as ineffective, this constraint could be effective in the excess supply case for some positive fraction of households if the distribution of either money balances or the shortfall of income were sufficiently uneven. Before concluding the present section, consider briefly the role of the constraint $M(t) \geq 0$ in the present case of general excess demand. The main relevant consideration would seem to be that, in contrast to the effect of excess supply of labor services, excess demand for commodities enhances rather than threatens the liquidity of the individual household. In other words, in the excess demand situation, the representative household cannot spend as much as he would like to spend and, as a partial consequence, he sets $m^{d'}/P$ in excess of m^d/P, for given values of Ω and W/P. This factor suggests that the analysis of the case of general excess demand, like the analysis of the case of general market clearing, can reasonably treat the liquidity constraint as ineffective.[39] In this respect, the case of excess supply of labor services and the case of excess demand for commodities are asymmetrical.

[39] One possible distributional complication should be noted. In the basic model, the households expected profits to remain constant until date N. However, in the present case, the households expect profits to increase as of date $\hat{N}$. Suppose either that households had different expectations regarding the prospective increase in profits or that the shortfall of consumption below notional consumption demand were unevenly distributed among the households. In that case, a household which expected a relatively large increase in profits or which experienced a relatively small shortfall of consumption might confront an effective liquidity constraint.

2.4 Output and employment in general

This section is concerned with generalizing the analysis of the deter-mination of output and employment under non-market-clearing conditions. Any particular combination of wages and prices implies for each market either that the quantity demanded exceeds the quantity supplied, or that the quantity supplied exceeds the quantity demanded, or that these two quantities are equal. Given these three possible states in each market, combining the two markets yields a total of nine possible cases. Our analysis thus far has considered examples represent-ing three of these cases.

In chapter 1, we determined the unique combination of wages and prices associated with the general-market-clearing case. In sections 2.2 and 2.3 we suggested specific examples of wage-price vectors which would generate general excess supply and general excess demand. The subsection which follows considers the problem of associating each of the infinite combinations of wages and prices with one of the nine possible cases of market conditions. In other words, we investigate precisely which combinations of wages and prices produce general excess supply, and so forth. The next subsection considers the problem of associating each of the infinite combinations of wages and prices with particular levels of output and employment.

2.4.1 *Effective market-clearing loci*

In figure 1.3 the loci labeled $l^d = l^s$ and $c^d + g^d = y^s$ depicted com-binations of values of W/P and Ω which were consistent with equality between the notional demands and supplies for labor services and commodities. In chapter 1, households regarded profits as always equal to π^*, the general-market-clearing level. Consequently, changes in Ω, where $\Omega \equiv M/P + N(\pi - \tau)$, corresponded to changes in M/P, which in turn reflected solely changes in P. Therefore, $(\Omega, W/P)$ space corresponded to $(M/P, W/P)$ space. For reference, figure 2.8 reproduces these notional market-clearing loci in vestigial form in $(M/P, W/P)$ space.

An implication of the analysis in the present chapter is that these loci describe market-clearing wage-price vectors only under the assumption of recontracting. Section 2.2 showed that, when actual trading is taking place with excess supply in either one of the markets, the notional demand function in the other market becomes irrelevant and is replaced by the effective demand function. Analogously, section 2.3 showed that, when actual trading is taking place with excess demand in either one of the markets, the notional supply function in the other

market becomes irrelevant and is replaced by the effective supply
schedule. Thus, all four notional demand and supply functions are
relevant only when both markets are simultaneously clearing – that is,
only at point A in figure 2.8.

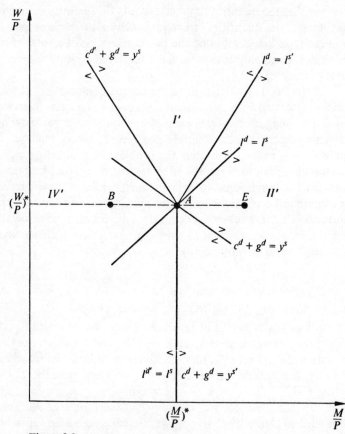

Figure 2.8
Effective market-clearing loci

Figure 2.8 also depicts the effective market-clearing loci, which
identify the regions of excess supply and excess demand when trading is
permitted at non-market-clearing prices. The positioning of these
loci is implicit in the analysis of the preceding sections. All the loci, of
course, must pass through point A, which corresponds to the points A
in the earlier figures, since general market clearing is still uniquely
associated with the combination $[(M/P)^*, (W/P)^*]$. However, at all

other combinations of M/P and W/P, the effective market-clearing loci diverge from the notional market-clearing loci. The other points specified in figure 2.8 also correspond to the same points specified in the figures above: B to B in figures 2.1–2.3 and E to E in figures 2.5–2.7. We depict all the loci as linear for convenience only.

Consider first the effective market-clearing loci for the commodity market. With the commodity market clearing, the notional demand and supply will be relevant in the labor market. In the region to the left of the $l^d = l^s$ locus, l^s exceeds l^d. Excess supply of labor services constrains the households, and the effective demand for commodities is less than the notional demand. Neglecting the liquidity constraint, effective clearing of the commodity market will be specified by

$$y = c^{d'} \left(\Omega', \frac{W}{P} \right) + g^d = y^s \left(\frac{W}{P}, g \right), \tag{2.25}$$

$$\text{with } l = l^d \left(\frac{W}{P} \right) < l^s \left(\Omega, \frac{W}{P} \right),$$

$$\text{where } \Omega' \equiv \frac{M}{P} + \hat{N}y + (N - \hat{N})\pi^* - N\tau.$$

The equating of $c^{d'} + g^d$ to y^s requires for any given real wage rate a level of real money balances above the level which would equate $c^d + g^d$ to y^s. Consequently, the locus $c^{d'} + g^d = y^s$ originates at point A and lies everywhere to the right of the locus $c^d + g^d = y^s$. Thus, the existence of excess supply in the labor market enlarges the region of excess supply in the commodity market. The negative slope of the $c^{d'} + g^d = y^s$ locus can be confirmed by observing that, with excess supply in both markets, if W/P were steadily increased while M/P were held fixed, $c^{d'}$ would rise and y^s would fall until eventually the two were equated. Thus, a vertical line through a point such as B must intersect the $c^{d'} + g^d = y^s$ locus.[40] The mathematical note at the end of

[40] Condition (2.25) describes the model developed by Keynes (1936) and discussed in standard macro-economic texts. Specifically, in Keynes' analysis, the price level always adjusts to clear the commodity market. Firms are always able to sell their notional supply of commodities, and so always express their notional demand for labor services. However, the nominal wage rate is fixed, and the ratio of this fixed W to the level of P necessary to clear the commodity market implies a real wage rate above $(W/P)^*$. Consequently, l^d is below both l^s and l^*, implying both underemployment and excess supply of labor services. This excess labor supply generates the Keynesian consumption function, which corresponds to our effective consumption demand function. In this context, all exogenous

this chapter specifies analytically the slopes of all the notional and effective market-clearing loci.

In the region to the right of the $l^d = l^s$ locus, l^d exceeds l^s. Excess demand for labor services constrains the firms, and the effective supply of commodities is less than the notional supply. Effective clearing of the commodity market will be specified by

$$y = c^d \left(\Omega, \frac{W}{P}\right) + g^d = y^{s'}(l,g), \tag{2.26}$$

$$\text{with } l = l^s \left(\Omega, \frac{W}{P}\right) < l^d \left(\frac{W}{P}\right),$$

$$\text{where } \Omega \equiv \frac{M}{P} + \hat{N}\pi + (N - \hat{N})\pi^* - N\tau \text{ and}$$

$$\pi = y - (W/P)l.$$

Equating $c^d + g^d$ to $y^{s'}$ requires for any given real wage rate a level of real money balances below the level which would equate $c^d + g^d$ to y^s. Consequently, the locus $c^d + g^d = y^{s'}$ originates at point A and lies everywhere to the left of the locus $c^d + g^d = y^s$. The dual nature of this locus will be explained presently. The main point to be stressed here is that the existence of excess demand in the labor market enlarges the region of excess demand in the commodity market. Figure 2.8 depicts the locus $c^d + g^d = y^{s'}$ as vertical, because the sign of its slope is ambiguous. With excess demand in both markets, a decrease in W/P, with M/P fixed, would reduce both c^d and $y^{s'}$. Hence, it is unclear whether a vertical line through a point such as E would intersect the $c^d + g^d = y^{s'}$ locus. An analytical expression for the slope of this locus appears in the mathematical note at the end of this chapter.

Consider now the effective market-clearing loci for the labor market. With the labor market clearing, the notional demand and supply will be relevant in the commodity market. In the region to the right of the $c^d + g^d = y^s$ locus, $c^d + g^d$ exceeds y^s. Excess demand for commodities constrains the households, and the effective supply of labor services is less than the notional supply. Effective clearing of the labor market will be specified by

$$l = l^d \left(\frac{W}{P}\right) = l^{s'} \left(\Omega'', \frac{W}{P}\right), \tag{2.27}$$

---

disturbances produce only movements along the $c^{d'} + g^d = y^s$ locus. These movements imply both the inverse Keynesian relation between l and W/P and, with W fixed, the direct Keynesian relation between l and P.

with $y = y^s \left(\dfrac{W}{P}, g \right) < c^d \left(\Omega, \dfrac{W}{P} \right) + g^d,$

where $\Omega'' \equiv \dfrac{M}{P} + \hat{N} \left(g - \dfrac{W}{P} l \right) + (N - \hat{N})\pi^* - N\tau.$

The equating of l^d to $l^{s'}$ requires for any given real wage rate a level of real money balances below the level which would equate l^d to l^s. Hence, the locus $l^d = l^{s'}$ originates at point A and lies everywhere to the left of the locus $l^d = l^s$. The causal relations between the two markets are analogous; the existence of excess demand for commodities enlarges the region of excess demand in the labor market. The positive slope of the $l^d = l^{s'}$ locus can be confirmed by observing that, with excess demand in both markets, if W/P were steadily increased, while M/P was held fixed, l^d would fall and $l^{s'}$ would rise until eventually the two were equated. Thus, a vertical line through a point such as E must intersect the $l^d = l^{s'}$ locus.

Finally, in the region to the left of the $c^d + g^d = y^s$ locus, y^s exceeds $c^d + g^d$. Excess supply of commodities constrains the firms, and the effective demand for labor services is less than the notional demand. Effective clearing of the labor market will be specified by

$$l = l^{d'}(y, g) = l^s \left(\Omega, \dfrac{W}{P} \right), \tag{2.28}$$

with $y = c^d \left(\Omega, \dfrac{W}{P} \right) + g^d < y^s \left(\dfrac{W}{P}, g \right),$

where $\Omega \equiv \dfrac{M}{P} + \hat{N}\pi + (N - \hat{N})\pi^* - N\tau$ and

$$\pi = y - (W/P)l.$$

Equating $l^{d'}$ to l^s requires for any given real wage rate a level of real money balances above the level which would equate l^d to l^s. Hence, the locus $l^{d'} = l^s$ originates at point A and lies everywhere to the right of the $l^d = l^s$ locus. The existence of excess supply in the commodity market enlarges the region of excess supply in the labor market. More interestingly, notice that, because $\delta l^{d'}/\delta y = (\delta y^{s'}/\delta l)^{-1}$, the same combinations of W/P and M/P which satisfy condition (2.26) also satisfy condition (2.28). Thus, the locus $l^{d'} = l^s$ is coincident with the locus $c^d + g^d = y^{s'}$. The reason for this coincidence is that the production function implies a unique relation between y and l. Consequently, the conditions $l = l^s < l^{d'}$, in which household behavior determines l, and $y = c^d + g^d < y^{s'}$, in which household and government behavior determine y, cannot obtain simultaneously. Firms cannot be simultaneously constrained in both markets.[41]

Again, the sign of the slope of the coincident locus is ambiguous. With excess supply in both markets, a decline in W/P would reduce both l^s and $l^{d'}$. Hence, it is unclear whether a vertical line through a point such as B would intersect the $l^{d'} = l^s$ locus.

2.4.2   Iso-employment loci

The effective market-clearing loci of figure 2.8 divide $(M/P, W/P)$ space into seven subspaces. At point A, both markets are clearing. Along each effective market-clearing locus, one market is clearing while the other market is not clearing. As just noted, one of these loci covers two of these four cases. In the regions between these loci, both markets are not clearing. As noted, the region corresponding to one of these four cases is empty. The three non-empty regions are labeled I', II', and IV' to correspond to the labeling of the regions in figure 1.7 of chapter 1.

We now want to associate each point in $(M/P, W/P)$ space with a particular level of output and employment. Consider each of the three regions in turn. In region I' M/P and W/P are such that there is excess demand for commodities and excess supply of labor services. Thus, households are constrained in both markets, and the notional supplies and demands of the firms determine both employment and output – that is,

$$
\text{I'} \quad
\begin{cases}
l = l^d \left(\dfrac{W}{P} \right) < l^{s'} \left(\Omega'', \dfrac{W}{P} \right) \text{ and} \\[3mm]
y = y^s \left(\dfrac{W}{P}, g \right) < c^{d'} \left(\Omega', \dfrac{W}{P} \right) + g^d.
\end{cases}
$$

In region II' M/P and W/P are such that there is excess demand in both markets, so that, as was indicated in section 2.3.3 above by conditions

---

[41] An analogous coincidence does not apply to the $c^{d'} + g^d = y^s$ and $l^d = l^{s'}$ loci because the possibility of saving prevents a unique relation between consumption demand and labor supply. Similarly, the coincidence between the $l^{d'} = l^s$ and $c^d + g^d = y^{s'}$ loci would disappear if firms were permitted another frontier of choice, such an inventory holding.

(2.20) and (2.21), employment and output are given by

$$
\text{II}' \quad
\begin{cases}
l = l^{s'}\left(\Omega'', \dfrac{W}{P}\right) < l^{d}\left(\dfrac{W}{P}\right) \text{ and} \\[3mm]
y = y^{s'}(l, g) < c^{d}\left(\Omega, \dfrac{W}{P}\right) + g^{d}.
\end{cases}
$$

Finally, in region IV′, M/P and W/P are such that there is excess supply in both markets, so that, as was indicated in section 2.2.3 above by conditions (2.6) and (2.7), employment and output are given by

$$
\text{IV}' \quad
\begin{cases}
l = l^{d'}(y, g) < l^{s}\left(\Omega, \dfrac{W}{P}\right) \text{ and} \\[3mm]
y = c^{d'}\left(\Omega', \dfrac{W}{P}\right) + g^{d} < y^{s}\left(\dfrac{W}{P}, g\right).
\end{cases}
$$

The above conditions which determine l and y imply that in each region various combinations of M/P and W/P will be associated with the same level of l and, hence, through the production function, the same level of y. We may denote a locus of such combinations of M/P and W/P as an iso-employment locus. An iso-employment locus is also an iso-output locus. Figure 2.9 illustrates two iso-employment loci, labeled l_1 and l_2. The l_1 locus indicates all combinations of M/P and W/P which imply level l_1, and similarly for the l_2 locus. The relative magnitudes of l_1 and l_2 are $l^* > l_1 > l_2$. As we know, l^*, which is associated with the general-market-clearing combination, $(M/P)^*$ and $(W/P)^*$, is the maximum voluntarily attainable level of employment. The level of employment steadily declines on any ray emanating from point A. In the preceding sections, we analyzed the determination of employment and output for particular combinations of M/P and W/P. The present analysis of iso-employment loci represents a generalization of the analysis of the determination of l and y to the entire $(M/P, W/P)$ space.

Consider the form of the iso-employment loci in the three regions. In region I′, l is equal to l^d, which depends only on W/P and not on M/P. Consequently, the iso-employment loci are horizontal, and a higher real wage rate implies a lower level of employment. In region II′, l is equal to $l^{s'}$. For a given W/P, an increase in M/P would raise Ω'' and reduce $l^{s'}$. Constancy of $l^{s'}$ would then require an increase in W/P. Consequently, in region II′ the slopes of the iso-employment loci are positive. Finally, in region IV′ l depends on y, which is equal to $c^{d'} + g^d$. For a given W/P, an increase in M/P would raise Ω' and increase $c^{d'}$. Constancy of $c^{d'}$ would then require a decrease in W/P. Consequently, in region IV′ the iso-employment loci are downward sloping. The mathematical note at the end of this chapter spells out analytically the slopes of all the iso-employment loci. We depict these loci as linear for convenience only.

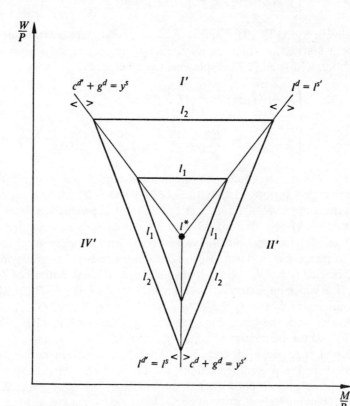

Figure 2.9
Iso-employment loci

2.5   Dynamic analysis in the absence of recontracting

In the basic model of chapter 1, given the assumption of recontracting, dynamic analysis was concerned simply with the convergence of wages and prices to their general-market-clearing levels. In contrast, in the present chapter, where the recontracting assumption has not been employed, not only must the analysis of wage and price dynamics be revised, but the scope of dynamic analysis must also be broadened to include the behavior of quantities.

2.5.1   *Wage and price adjustment relations*

In chapter 1 we proposed the concept of price-setting agents for each market place whose job it was to find the general-market-clearing wage-price vector. Section 1.4.2 assumed that these price-setting agents knew the signs of the partial derivatives of the demand and supply functions, and that they consequently would increase or decrease W according to whether they observed excess demand or supply for labor services, and would increase or decrease P according to whether they observed excess demand or supply for commodities. The discussion of chapter 2 makes this formulation neither more nor less plausible.

The analysis in the present chapter does, however, call for a reconsideration of the appropriate specification of the concepts of excess supply and demand which are relevant in this context. Section 1.4.2 assumed that the price-setting agents responded to differences between the notional supplies and demands. This assumption is no longer tenable when exchange can take place under non-market-clearing conditions. In these circumstances, as we have seen, firms and households will express effective demands which will differ from certain of the notional demands. The price-setting agents will observe these effective demands and not the notional demands which they have replaced. The appropriate specification of wage and price adjustment relations, therefore, would seem to be

$$\frac{1}{W}\frac{dW}{dt} = \lambda_W (l^{d'} - l^{s'}) \text{ and} \tag{2.29}$$

$$\frac{1}{P}\frac{dP}{dt} = \lambda_P (c^{d'} + g^d - y^{s'}), \tag{2.30}$$

where λ_W and λ_P may still be regarded as positive constants. Relations (2.29) and (2.30) replace relations (1.16) and (1.17) of chapter 1, in the absence of recontracting. Relations (2.29) and (2.30) specify that whenever an effective supply or demand does not coincide with the corresponding notional supply or demand, the effective supply or demand is the relevant magnitude influencing the speed of wage or price adjustment. In the model which we are considering the effective supply or demand, when relevant, is less than the corresponding notional supply or demand.

The implications of relations (2.29) and (2.30) can be seen in terms of the three regions of (M/P), (W/P) space created by the effective market-clearing loci. Figure 2.10 reproduces these loci and indicates the sign pattern of

$$\left[\frac{1}{P}\frac{dP}{dt}, \frac{1}{W}\frac{dW}{dt}, \frac{1}{W/P}\frac{d(W/P)}{dt}\right]$$

in each of the three regions. In regions II′ and IV′, W and P will be changing in the same direction, so that a dashed line is again necessary to identify subregions in which W/P is either rising or falling. The most striking contrast between figure 2.10 and its counterpart figure 1.7 is that, because regions II′ and IV′ are each larger than regions II and IV,

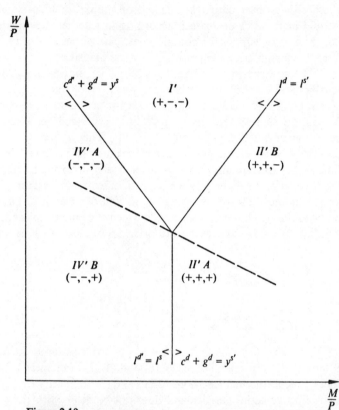

Figure 2.10
Wage and price dynamics without recontracting: sign patterns refer to

$$\left[\frac{1}{P}\frac{dP}{dt},\ \frac{1}{W}\frac{dW}{dt},\ \frac{1}{W/P}\frac{d(W,P)}{dt}\right]$$

respectively, the absence of recontracting, and the implied replacement of notional demands and supplies by effective demands and supplies, creates a presumption that wages and prices are more likely to be moving in the same direction. The region in which P rises while W falls has shrunk, and the region in which P falls while W rises no longer exists.

2.5.1 *The dynamics of exogenous disturbances*

Section 1.4.3 analyzed the time paths of wages and prices resulting from an exogenous disturbance under the assumption of recontracting. We considered in particular a disturbance which left W/P equal to $(W/P)^*$, but which caused M/P and Ω to be above $(M/P)^*$ and Ω^*. An example of such a disturbance was an increase in the flow supply of money, m^s/P, which was used to reduce taxes, τ.

This section considers the dynamic response of the economy without recontracting. As we have seen, in the absence of recontracting, a disturbance which causes W and P to differ from W^* and P^* will affect the actual levels of employment and output. Consequently, the reestablishment of general-market-clearing conditions would involve changes in l and y, as well as in W and P.

To facilitate comparability, this section analyzes the same disturbance which was considered in section 1.4.3. Figure 2.11 reproduces

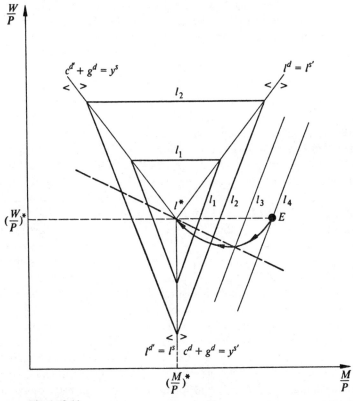

Figure 2.11
Convergence to market-clearing conditions

the effective market-clearing loci and the iso-employment loci. Point E indicates the combination of W/P, M/P and l initially resulting from the disturbance. Point E corresponds to points E in the earlier figures. In addition to causing M/P to be above $(M/P)^*$, creating excess demand in both markets, this disturbance also causes l to be below l^*. The solid arrow from point E depicts the time paths for W/P, M/P, and l, implied by our assumptions regarding wage and price adjustment and our analysis of quantity determination.

Starting at point E, since l^d exceeds $l^{s'}$ and $c^d + g^d$ exceeds $y^{s'}$, P and W are both increasing. Moreover, as we have assumed the dashed line to be downward sloping, P is initially rising proportionately faster than W, and W/P is falling. The rise in P means that M/P is declining, which would tend to reduce Ω''. A reduction in Ω'' would stimulate $l^{s'}$. However, the decline in W/P would tend to raise Ω'' and also to depress $l^{s'}$ directly. Because the effect of the rising P in depressing W/P is offset by the rising W, the solid arrow assumes that the effect of the rising P in depressing M/P is dominant, so that both $l^{s'}$ and l initially increase. The decline in W/P also raises l^d, so that the initial direction of change in the excess demand for labor services and in the rate of increase of W is ambiguous.

Turning to the commodity market, the rise in l enables $y^{s'}$ to increase, while the decline in both W/P and M/P causes c^d to decline. Thus, the excess demand for commodities diminishes, and the rate of increase of P declines. Gradually, the initial rate of decrease in W/P moderates, and eventually, when the dashed line is crossed, W rises faster than P, and W/P begins to increase. Moreover, l continues to rise, and the path asymptotically approaches the point of general market clearing at which l equals l^*, W/P equals $(W/P)^*$, and M/P equals $(M/P)^*$.

A few additional complications may be noted. First, had we assumed the dashed line to be upward sloping, W would have initially risen proportionately faster than P, so that W/P would have initially risen, before falling back to $(W/P)^*$. Second, as was noted in section 1.4.3, M and hence P^* also, will be increasing as long as m^s is positive. In that case P and W will be chasing continually moving targets, and nothing in the present analysis insures that P and W would actually be getting closer to P^* and W^*. In chapter 4 we shall see that this potential problem is readily avoided by introducing expectations regarding rates of change of P^* and W^* into the wage and price adjustment relations. Finally, recall that our formal analyses of the determination of output and employment, which underlie the iso-employment loci, specify both the demand and supply multipliers to be instantaneous interactions. Consequently, the adjustment path depicted by the solid arrow in

Figure 2.11 supposes that, while W and P gradually converge to W^* and P^*, the level of employment associated with each transient combination of W and P is that level implied by the full multiplier effect. This assumption represents a good approximation to reality only if the recursive interaction which actually generates the multiplier is very rapid relative to the adjustment of wages and prices.

Mathematical note

Figures 2.8–2.11 are based on the following input:

1. Slopes of the notional market-clearing loci in figure 2.8:

$$c^d + g^d = y^s: \dfrac{-\dfrac{\delta c^d}{\delta \Omega}}{\dfrac{\delta c^d}{\delta(W/P)} - \dfrac{\delta y^s}{\delta(W/P)}}$$

This slope is unambiguously negative.

$$l^d = l^s: \dfrac{\dfrac{\delta l^s}{\delta \Omega}}{\dfrac{\delta l^d}{\delta(W/P)} - \dfrac{\delta l^s}{\delta(W/P)}}$$

This slope is positive if $\dfrac{\delta l^d}{\delta(W/P)}$ is less than $\dfrac{\delta l^s}{\delta(W/P)}$.

2. Slopes of the effective market-clearing loci:

$$c^{d'} + g^d = y^s: \dfrac{\dfrac{\delta c^{d'}}{\delta \Omega'}}{\dfrac{W}{P}\dfrac{\delta l^d}{\delta(W/P)}\left(1 - \hat{N}\dfrac{\delta c^{d'}}{\delta \Omega'}\right) - \dfrac{\delta c^{d'}}{\delta(W/P)}}.$$

Given $\hat{N}\,\delta c^{d'}/\delta \Omega' < 1$, this slope is unambiguously negative.

$c^d + g^d = y^{s'}$ and $l^{d'} = l^s$:

$$-\dfrac{\dfrac{\delta c^d}{\delta \Omega} - \dfrac{\delta \Phi}{\delta l}\dfrac{\delta l^s}{\delta \Omega}}{\begin{vmatrix} \dfrac{\delta c^d}{\delta \Omega} - \dfrac{\delta \Phi}{\delta l}\dfrac{\delta l^s}{\delta \Omega} & \dfrac{\delta c^d}{\delta(W/P)} - \dfrac{\delta \Phi}{\delta l}\dfrac{\delta l^s}{\delta(W/P)} \\ \hat{N}\left(\dfrac{\delta \Phi}{\delta l} - \dfrac{W}{P}\right)\dfrac{\delta l^s}{\delta \Omega} - 1 & \hat{N}\left[\left(\dfrac{\delta \Phi}{\delta l} - \dfrac{W}{P}\right)\dfrac{\delta l^s}{\delta(W/P)} - l\right] \end{vmatrix}}.$$

The sign of this slope is ambiguous.

$$l^d = l^{s'}: \frac{\dfrac{\delta l^{s'}}{\delta \Omega''}}{\dfrac{\delta l^d}{\delta(W/P)}\left[1 + \hat{N}\dfrac{W}{P}\dfrac{\delta l^{s'}}{\delta \Omega''}\right] + \hat{N}l\dfrac{\delta l^{s'}}{\delta \Omega''} - \dfrac{\delta l^{s'}}{\delta(W/P)}}$$

Given $\hat{N}\dfrac{W}{P}\dfrac{\delta l^{s'}}{\delta \Omega''} > - 1$, this slope is unambiguously positive.

3.   Slopes of iso-employment loci:

Region II′: $\dfrac{-\dfrac{\delta l^{s'}}{\delta \Omega''}}{\dfrac{\delta l^{s'}}{\delta(W/P)} - \hat{N}l\dfrac{\delta l^{s'}}{\delta \Omega''}}.$

Given $\delta l^{s'}/\delta(W/P) > 0$, this slope is unambiguously positive.

Region IV′: $\dfrac{-\dfrac{\delta c^{d'}}{\delta \Omega'}}{\dfrac{\delta c^{d'}}{\delta(W/P)}}.$

The slope is unambiguously negative.

3 Capital, financial assets, and the rate of return

This chapter introduces capital goods, equity shares, and
government bonds into the analytical framework. Section
3.1 explains the changes necessary to accommodate these
modifications. Section 3.2 analyzes, within this revised
framework, the behavior of the individual economic units under
market-clearing conditions. Section 3.3 analyzes, in
comparative-statics terms, the effects of some exogenous
disturbances on the market-clearing conditions implied by this
behavior. Section 3.4 analyzes, also within this revised
framework, the implications of excess supply in the markets
for labor services and current output.

3.1 The framework for analyzing capital and financial assets

Chapters 1 and 2 involved a number of simplifying assumptions about
the nature of the production process and the distribution of profits. In
these chapters labor services and public services were the only variable
inputs and consumable commodities and public services were the only
forms of output. The discussion abstracted completely from capital
goods, capital services, and investment. Profits were distributed according to an arbitrary and predetermined pattern.

Chapters 1 and 2 also assumed a very simplified framework of
public finance. In these chapters, the government could accommodate
a difference between its expenditures and tax receipts only by changing
the outstanding stock of money. An excess of expenditures over taxes
implied a positive flow supply of money, whereas an excess of taxes over
expenditures implied a negative flow supply of money.

The analysis in this chapter is concerned with the implications
of removing these abstractions. To get at these implications, we introduce three new and related considerations into the analytical framework.
First, we explicitly consider the accumulation of capital goods by firms,
called investment, and we include the services generated by capital goods
as an additional input to the production process. Second, we explicitly
consider the ownership of marketable claims to the profits of the firms.
Firms issue these claims, called equity shares, to finance their investment.
For households, these claims represent an alternative to money as a
store of value. We continue to assume that all profits of firms are paid
out as dividends to stockholders – that is, we abstract from direct

business taxes and retained earnings. Finally, we now assume that the government can issue a form of interest-bearing debt, which we assume to be a perpetual bond which pays a fixed nominal coupon. Issue of new debt is now an alternative to issue of new money as a means of balancing the difference between government expenditure, which now includes the interest payments on the outstanding stock of bonds, and tax receipts. For households, government bonds represent an additional store of value. Because our analysis excludes uncertainty, we assume that households regard government bonds and equity shares issued by firms as perfect substitutes.

The introduction of capital goods means that demand for current output now has an additional source – investment demand by firms, which must be added to the consumption demand by households and government demand for public services – and that current output can now take an additional form – capital goods as well as consumable commodities and public services. To keep the discussion as simple as possible, we continue to assume that all output is produced by the same technology, and only assumes its specific identity according to the identity of its purchaser. Capital goods and other commodities are perfectly substitutable on the supply side. However, we assume that, once produced and sold, capital goods and other commodities are not interchangeable. In particular, as before, consumables and public services are not storable, and, once in place, capital goods cannot be converted into either consumables or public services.

The introduction of equity shares and government bonds means that, in addition to the labor and commodity markets, exchange now takes place in the equity market, in which shares are exchanged for money, and in the bond market, in which bonds are exchanged for money. Accordingly, there now exist two new independent exchange ratios, the number of dollars per equity share, P_e, and the number of dollars per bond, P_b. Given the nominal profit per share, $P\pi/E$, where E is the number of outstanding shares, the price of equity shares, P_e, implies an anticipated rate of return on equity shares, denoted by r_e. Specifically, the variable r_e represents the implied discount rate at which the present value of the expected future stream of dividend payments per share equals the current share price. Thus, given that the total profit flow is paid out to share owners, and assuming that the representative household expects $P\pi/E$ and r_e to be constant over time, r_e satisfies the following relation:

$$P_e(0) \equiv \frac{P\pi}{E} \int_0^\infty exp\,(-r_e t)\mathrm{d}t,$$

which implies

$$r_e \equiv P\pi/P_e E.$$

Similarly, given the nominal coupon on each bond, i/B, where i is the government's total nominal interest payments and B is the number of outstanding bonds, the price of bonds, P_b, implies an anticipated rate of return on bonds, denoted by r_b.[1] Specifically, the variable r_b represents the implied discount rate at which the present value of the expected future stream of nominal interest payments per bond equals the current bond price. Thus, assuming that the representative household expects r_b to be constant over time, r_b satisfies the following relation:

$$P_b(0) \equiv \frac{i}{B} \int_0^\infty exp(-r_b t) \, \mathrm{d}t,$$

which implies

$$r_b \equiv i/P_b B.[2]$$

Abstracting from any transactions costs involved in portfolio rearrangement, the assumption that households regard equity shares and bonds as perfect substitutes implies that, if finite quantities of both assets are in existence, the rates of return on the two assets must be equal. That is, $r_e = r_b = r$, where r denotes the common rate of return.[3] Further, we may view the equity and bond markets as a single market, which we call the financial asset market.

We continue to focus on the representative household and the representative firm, so that individual firms are not distinguished and equity is a homogeneous asset in terms of rate of return. Both the representative firm and the representative household act as price takers in the financial asset market, and both believe that they can buy or sell any

---

[1] The bulk of the following discussion assumes that bonds have fixed nominal coupons. However, in section 3.3.4 below, we note the possibility of varying the nominal coupon with the price level in such a way that the real value of bond coupons is fixed.

[2] Because, at this stage, we are assuming that the representative household expects P to be constant over time, anticipated real and nominal rates of return are identical. We introduce the distinction between real and nominal rates of return in chapter 4.

[3] Equality between r_e and r_b implies that

$$\frac{P_e}{P_b} = \frac{P\pi/E}{i/B}.$$

The ratio of share price to bond price equals the ratio of profit per share to coupon per bond.

quantity of financial assets without affecting the rate of return. By implication, we shall assume throughout the discussion that exchange takes place in the financial asset market only under market-clearing conditions.

The introduction of equity shares and bonds means that households can now accumulate their savings and store their wealth in the form of earning assets. If equity shares and bonds earn a positive rate of return, while money earns no return, if transactions involving money are costless, and if equity earnings and interest payments are predictable with certainty, households would seem to have no motivation to hold money. In that case receipts of money, from either income sources or sales of financial assets, would be perfectly synchronized with expenditures, on either commodities or financial assets, and all wealth would be stored in the form of equity and bonds. In order to rationalize the holding of money and the diversification of wealth between money and earning assets, we must introduce into the analysis transactions costs or uncertainty.

Our approach will be to assume that transactions costs are incurred by households in buying and selling financial assets.[4] These costs involve financial services which must be purchased by households in order to effect exchanges between money and earning assets. For simplicity, we assume that each such exchange requires a certain amount of financial services. Consequently, the total amount of transactions costs incurred depends on the number of such exchanges, and households are motivated to economize on this number. This economizing implies that the act of saving or dissaving generally will not be perfectly synchronized with purchases or sales of earning assets. The lack of synchronization generates a positive average amount of accumulated savings which are held as money.[5]

[4] We do not introduce uncertainty explicitly for two reasons. First, a consistent treatment of uncertainty would introduce complications throughout the analysis of both firm and household behavior, which, at this stage, are best deferred in the interest of clearer development of more essential points. Second, transactions costs seem essential to the holding of the medium of exchange (money), whereas uncertainty does not.

[5] We continue to abstract from transactions costs in the purchase of commodities and in the rendering of payments from firms to households, since, given the alternative of earning-asset holding, such costs alone could not explain the holding of money. For simplicity, we also assume that firms incur no transactions costs, and so still have no motive for holding money. For recent and more general discussions of the relation between transactions costs and money holding, see Feige and Parkin (1971) and Barro and Santomero (1974).

The introduction of financial services means that demand for current output now includes household demand for these services along with investment demand by firms, consumption demand by households, and government demand for public services. On the supply side, financial services are another form of output by firms. As in the case of capital goods, we simplify the analysis by assuming that financial services are also produced according to the production function which governs the production of consumables and public services. Hence, the four forms of output – consumables, public services, capital goods, and financial services – are perfectly substitutable on the supply side. Under this simplification we can continue to speak unambiguously of aggregate commodity supply, aggregate commodity demand, and aggregate commodity production and sales.

The new considerations introduced in this chapter involve the following new variables, the notation for some of which has already been mentioned:

K: stock of capital goods owned by firms, measured in physical units,

k: flow accumulation of capital goods (investment), measured in physical units per year, $k \equiv dK/dt$,

E: stock of equity shares, measured in number of shares,

e: flow of equity shares, measured in shares per year, $e \equiv dE/dt$,

B: stock of bonds, measured in number of bonds,

b: flow of bonds, measured in bonds per year, $b \equiv dB/dt$,

π: flow of profits, measured in units of commodities per year,

i: flow of interest payments, measured in dollars per year,

P_e: price of shares, which is the number of dollars per share,

P_b: price of bonds, which is the number of dollars per bond,

r: rate of return on financial assets,

$$r \equiv \frac{P\pi}{P_e E} = \frac{i}{P_b B},$$

F: total nominal stock of financial earning assets, $F \equiv P_e E + P_b B$,

f: nominal flow of financial earning assets, $f \equiv P_e e + P_b b$ – which implies, if P_e and P_b are constant, $f = dF/dt$,

A: total nominal stock of assets, $A \equiv M + F$,

a: nominal flow accumulation of assets (saving), $a \equiv m + f$ – which implies, if P_e and P_b are constant, $a = dA/dt$,

v: frequency of exchanges in the financial asset market, measured in exchanges per year,

γ: real cost per financial market exchange, measured in units of commodities per exchange, and

y: flow of current output, measured in units of commodities per year, $y = c + g + k + \gamma v$.

The discussion in this chapter focuses on two of the cases which were developed in chapters 1 and 2. Section 3.2 introduces capital, equity, and bonds into the framework of the basic model, developed in chapter 1, in which all exchanges take place only under market-clearing conditions. This section first revises the analysis of the behavior of firms, households, and government to take account of the existence of capital, equity, and bonds. Second, the section works out the comparative-statics analysis of the determination of wages, prices, and the rate of return under market-clearing conditions. Section 3.3 introduces capital, equity, and bonds into the nonrecontracting framework developed in chapter 2. In the interest of brevity we consider only the case in which the wage-price vector implies excess supply in the markets for both commodities and labor services. Within this context, this section revises the analysis of the behaviour of firms, households, and government and the determination of income and employment to take account of the existence of capital, equity, and bonds. The analysis of the general excess supply case should enable the reader to work out the implications for other non-market-clearing circumstances.[6]

3.2 Capital, financial assets, and the behavior of firms, households, and government

This section revives the spirit of the basic model of chapter 1 by assuming that exchange takes place only under market-clearing conditions. There are now three markets – labor services, commodities, and financial assets – and at each of these each economic unit is able either to buy that quantity which it demands or to sell that quantity which it supplies. We analyze in turn the behavior of firms, households, and government in the three markets under these conditions.

3.2.1 *The behavior of firms*

We continue to view firms as separate decision-making units from households. However, we now assume that households, as stockholders, impose on the firms the objective of maximizing the market price of

---

[6] Space considerations do not permit us to spell out a dynamic analysis for the framework developed in this chapter. Using the dynamic analysis in chapters 1 and 2 as a guide, the reader should be able to carry out this exercise independently. The reader may also wish to refer to Grossman (1971).

equity shares. Given the definition of r, maximizing P_e is equivalent to maximizing $P\pi/Er$. Because the representative firm regards P and r as exogenous, maximizing P_e then amounts to maximizing real profit per share, π/E. Real profit, all of which is paid out as dividends to shareholders, is again defined as $\pi = y - (W/P)l$.

Following traditional practice, we assume that, in the short run, labor services are a variable factor and capital services are a fixed factor, whereas, in the long run, both are variable factors. More precisely, changes in the employment of capital involve a penalty cost, whereas changes in the employment of labor do not.[7] Consequently, at every point in time (the short run) the firm demands and employs labor and produces, supplies, and sells output so as to maximize current profit subject to a given stock of capital and equity outstanding. However, over time (the long run) the firm issues equity and invests (purchases additional capital) so as to achieve the optimal (target) quantity of capital, which is that quantity which maximizes profit per share subject to a variable capital stock.

With the introduction of capital services as an input, the production function is now

$$y = \Phi(l, g, K),$$

where Φ exhibits positive and diminishing marginal product with respect to each input, as well as decreasing returns to scale. The employment of capital services is proportional to K, with the constant of proportionality normalized to unity. We also assume, for simplicity, that capital does not depreciate and that its employment involves no user cost. Finally, we assume, also for simplicity, that the marginal product of capital, like the marginal product of labor, is independent of the level of g, and that the marginal product of labor is independent of the level of K.[8]

Since all three markets are assumed to be clearing, the firm is able to buy that quantity of labour services which it demands and sell that quantity of output which it supplies. Consequently, the maximization of short-run profit – with K and E fixed – requires, as in chapter 1, the equating of the marginal product of labor to the real wage rate. Thus, the firm fixes its notional labor demand and its notional commodity

---

[7] The introduction of penalty costs for changes in the employment of labor would suggest interesting dynamic modifications to the labor demand function derived in our analysis. See, for example, Oi (1962) and Parsons (1972).

[8] None of these simplifying assumptions is essential for our main conclusions. The signs of the partial derivatives of Φ are

$$[\Phi_l, \Phi_g, \Phi_K] > 0, [\Phi_{ll}, \Phi_{gg}, \Phi_{KK}] < 0, \text{ and } \Phi_{lg} = \Phi_{lK} = \Phi_{gk} = 0.$$

supply according to

$$l^d = l^d \left(\frac{W}{P}\right) \text{ and}^9 \tag{3.1}$$

$$\underset{(-)}{}$$

$$y^s = \Phi\left[l^d\left(\frac{W}{P}\right), g, K\right] \equiv y^s\left(\frac{W}{P}, g, K\right) \tag{3.2}$$

$$\underset{(+)}{} \quad \underset{(+)(+)}{} \qquad \underset{(-)(+)(+)}{}$$

such that $\dfrac{\delta\Phi}{\delta l}(l^d) = \dfrac{W}{P}$.

In the long-run, the firm can also choose K. However, investments must be financed through the issue of equity.[10] Since the firm's objective is to maximize profit per share, a decision to issue new equity and to invest involves a weighing of the increased profit flow resulting from the additional capital against the dilution of earnings per share resulting from the increase in the number of shares outstanding. Profit is given by

$$\pi = \Phi\left[l^d\left(\frac{W}{P}\right), g, K\right] - \frac{W}{P} l^d\left(\frac{W}{P}\right),$$

and profit per share is π/E. The financing constraint is

$$\frac{P_e}{P} dE = dK.^{11}$$

Abstracting from adjustment costs, the firm would choose K so as to maximize π/E, subject to the financing constraint. We denote this value of K as the notional target capital stock, and designate it by K°. The solution for K° involves equating the marginal product of capital to the rate of return on equity shares. Thus, assuming that the firm regards r as constant over time, it selects

---

[9] Because we have assumed $\Phi_{lK} = 0$, l^d is independent of K. However, if Φ_{lK} were positive (complementarity between capital and labor in production), l^d would increase with an increase in K. Alternatively, if Φ_{lK} were negative (substitutability between capital and labor in production), l^d would decrease with an increase in K.

[10] If investment were paid for out of retained profits, we could proceed within the same framework by assuming that the firm issues new equity shares of equivalent value to its stockholders.

[11] This financing constraint applies to marginal units of K and E. When considering a discrete change in K and E, the firm also takes into account implied shifts in P_e, assuming that $r \equiv P\pi/P_eE$ is fixed.

[12] Because we have assumed that $\Phi_{lK} = \Phi_{gK} = 0$, K° is independent of W/P and g. More generally, K° would satisfy

$$\frac{\delta\Phi}{\delta K}\left[l^d\left(\frac{W}{P}, g, K^\circ\right), g, K^\circ\right] = r.$$

$$K^\circ = K^\circ(r),^{12}$$
$$\underset{(-)}{}$$

such that $\dfrac{\delta\Phi}{\delta K}(K^\circ) = \dfrac{P\pi}{P_e E} \equiv r.$

Given that changes in K involve costs of adjustment, maintaining K continually equal to K° is unlikely to be optimal. The firm's optimal adjustment policy must weigh the costs of adjusting K against the profits foregone by allowing K to be unequal to K°. We assume that the solution to this dynamic optimization problem relates notional investment demand to K° by a simple gradual-adjustment relation of the form

$$k^d = \lambda_k[K^\circ(r) - K] \equiv k^d(r, K), \tag{3.3}$$
$$\underset{(-)(-)}{}$$

where λ_k is positive and, for simplicity, is treated as a constant.[13] According to equation (3.3), notional investment demand depends linearly on the gap between K° and the actual stock of capital K. Thus, notional investment demand is such that, so long as K° does not change, this gap is continually reduced and K approaches K° asymptotically over time. This notional investment demand function implies that the notional flow supply of equity is

$$\frac{P_e}{P} e^s = k^d(r, K). \tag{3.4}$$
$$\underset{(-)(-)}{}$$

We also assume for simplicity that for each individual firm, K° is at least as large as K, so that k^d and e^s are nonnegative.[14]

3.2.2 The behavior of households: optimal transactions frequency and money holding

The objective of households, as in chapter 1, is to maximize utility over the planning horizon,

$$U = \int_0^N u[c^d(t), l^s(t)]dt.$$
$$\underset{(+)\quad(-)}{}$$

---

[13] For a detailed derivation of such an investment demand function, under the assumption that the costs of investing, e.g., installation costs, increase with the rate of investment, see Lucas (1967). An alternative derivation of equation (3.3) as an aggregate relation would assume that installation costs are lump sum and independent of the speed of adjustment, but that K° is stochastic rather than permanently fixed. For an example of such an adjustment model, see Barro (1972).

[14] The introduction of the possibility of disinvestment would require consideration of a market for used capital goods and of depreciation.

The representative household's disposable income now consists of its wage income, $(W/P)l^s$, plus its profit (dividend) income, $\pi = rP_eE/P$,[15] plus its interest income, $i/P = rP_bB/P$, less its tax liabilities, τ. Saving is the difference between disposable income and expenditure on consumption and financial services. Thus, for working households, assuming P_e and P_b to be constant,

$$\frac{1}{P}\left(\frac{dA}{dt}\right)^d = \frac{a^d}{P} = \frac{W}{P}l^s + \pi + \frac{i}{P} - \tau - c^d - \gamma v$$

$$= \frac{W}{P}l^s + r\left(\frac{A}{P} - \frac{M}{P}\right) - \tau - c^d - \gamma v. \quad (3.5)$$

Equation (3.5) also applies to retired households, but with l^s set at zero. Saving may now be used to accumulate either shares, bonds, or money balances. Thus,

$$\frac{1}{P}\left(\frac{dA}{dt}\right)^d = \frac{a^d}{P} = \frac{P_e}{P}e^d + \frac{P_b}{P}b^d + \frac{m^d}{P} \equiv \frac{f^d}{P} + \frac{m^d}{P}. \quad (3.6)$$

As in chapter 1, working households will typically engage in positive saving in order to provide for consumption during retirement. The positive rate of return on equity and bonds now provides an inducement to use these earning assets, rather than money balances, as a store for these savings. However, income is received in the form of money, and the costs involved in exchanging money for equity and bonds induce households to economize on the number of such exchanges. Suppose that the representative working household adopts the time interval $1/v$ between exchanges in the financial-asset market. Because v measures the number of exchanges per year, $1/v$ measures the fraction of a year between exchanges. During this interval $1/v$, saving accumulates as money, and at the end of the interval the accumulated real savings, of amount $(a^d/P)/v$, are used to purchase earning assets. Given this pattern, the representative working household's average real money balance equals $(a^d/P)/2v$. An increase in v would reduce its average money holding and would correspondingly increase its average real holding of earning assets. The household's expenditure on financial services is γv. Thus, an increase in v increases transactions costs, but,

[15] The preceding section assumed that if K° exceeds K, the firms will be investing to increase K. Such a steady increase in K will cause a steady increase in π/E and, if P and r are constant, a steady increase also in P_e. The present section assumes that the representative household does not anticipate these capital gains, which is a satisfactory approximation if K is within a small neighborhood of K°.

given a^d/P, it also decreases the income foregone by holding money rather than earning assets.[16]

The choice of a target value for v involves a trade-off between these two considerations. Specifically, given a^d/P, the target value, v°, will be chosen to minimize the sum of dividend and interest income foregone and transactions costs incurred,

$$\frac{ra^d/P}{2v} + \gamma v.\text{[17]}$$

Minimizing this sum requires setting

$$v^{\circ} = \left(\frac{ra^d/P}{2\gamma}\right)^{1/2}. \tag{3.7}$$

The target average real money balance is then

$$\left(\frac{M}{P}\right)^{\circ} = \frac{a^d/P}{2v^{\circ}} = \left(\frac{\gamma a^d/P}{2r}\right)^{1/2}. \tag{3.8}$$

In equation (3.7), the target transactions frequency increases with r and a^d/P and decreases with γ. The corresponding target average real money balance, in equation (3.8), increases with γ and a^d/P and decreases with r.

Retired households have no wage income and must dissave out of their accumulated savings to finance their consumption. In order to purchase commodities, they convert their holdings of equity and bonds into money, but again transaction costs induce them to economize on the number of such exchanges. However, the positive rate of return provides an inducement not to sell equity and bonds in advance of consumption needs. The weighing of these considerations is analogous to the problem faced by working households. Specifically, for the representative retired household (more generally, for households whose

---

[16] This analysis does not take account of variations over time in a^d/P. Specifically, if the household expected a^d/P to change in the near future from positive to negative, as would typically be the case near the retirement date, it would have less incentive to acquire earning assets which would soon be liquidated. However, if the average holding period for earning assets were long relative to the time between trips to the financial-asset market, this consideration would seem to be of second-order significance. In the interest of simplicity, we have neglected this type of effect.

[17] The use of $ra^d/2vP$ to measure the income foregone represents an approximation which neglects the compounding of interest over the interval $1/v$ between exchanges in the financial-asset market. This approximation is satisfactory if $r/v \ll 1$, as seems reasonable.

current saving is negative), the target frequency of sales in the financial-asset market and the target average money balance will also satisfy equations (3.7) and (3.8), but with a^d/P, which is negative, replaced by its absolute value.

Taking working and retired households together, the relevant determinant of the average target transactions frequency and aggregate target money holding is the absolute magnitude of saving flow. The average target transactions frequency and aggregate target money holding functions, which combine both working and retired households, have the forms

$$v^\circ = v^\circ(\underset{(+)}{|a^d/P|}, \underset{(+)(-)}{r, \gamma}), \quad \text{and} \tag{3.9}$$

$$\left(\frac{M}{P}\right)^\circ = \left(\frac{M}{P}\right)^\circ (\underset{(+)}{|a^d/P|}, \underset{(-)(+)}{r, \gamma}), \tag{3.10}$$

where $|a^d/P|$ represents the aggregate of absolute saving flow.

Equation (3.9) would determine optimal transactions frequency under the assumption that changes in v involve no adjustment costs. However, if such changes do involve adjustment costs, optimal behavior must weigh these costs against the costs of allowing v to be unequal to v°. As in the case of capital stock adjustment by the firm, we assume here that, if the average value of v differs from the average value of v°, desired adjustment of average v conforms to the simple gradual-adjustment relation

$$\frac{dv}{dt} = \lambda_v (v^\circ - v), \tag{3.11}$$

where λ_v is positive and is treated, for simplicity, as a constant.[18]

Similarly, equation (3.10) would determine optimal real money holding under the assumption that changes in average real money holding involve no adjustment costs. However, given that such changes do involve adjustment costs, optimal behavior must also weigh these costs against the cost of allowing M/P to be unequal to $(M/P)^\circ$. A difference between M/P and $(M/P)^\circ$ would reflect the net effect of two components. First, M/P might not correspond to the existing predetermined value of v – that is, M/P might not be equal to

$$\frac{|a^d/P|}{2v}.$$

[18] The rationalization of equation (3.11) would be similar to the rationalization of equation (3.3) above, except that lump-sum adjustment costs seem more plausible in the present case.

Such a discrepancy could result from a change in either $|a^d/P|$ or P. In this case, the desired adjustment of average money holding would involve bringing M/P into accord with the predetermined value of v. Second, as indicated above, v might not be equal to $v°$. In this case, the desired adjustment of money holdings would correspond to the desired adjustment of v described by equation (3.11). In the interest of simplicity, we assume here that, if M/P differs from $(M/P)°$ for either reason, desired aggregate adjustment of money holdings conforms to the simple gradual adjustment relation

$$\frac{1}{P}\left(\frac{dM}{dt}\right)^d \equiv \frac{m^d}{P} = \lambda_m\left[\left(\frac{M}{P}\right)° - \frac{M}{P}\right] = \frac{m^d}{P}\left(\underset{(+)}{|a^d/P|}, \underset{(-)(+)(-)}{r, \gamma, \frac{M}{P}}\right),$$

$$(3.12)$$

where λ_m is positive and is treated, for simplicity, as a constant.

3.2.3 *The behavior of households: labor supply, consumption demand, and saving*

Having considered the subsidiary and separable problem of the optimal disposition of the household's given saving flow, we now turn to the central problem of determining the optimal flows of labor services, consumption, and saving. As in chapter 1, the household's optimal intertemporal plan entails the exhaustion of asset holdings at date N. The specification of saving in equation (3.5) represents a first-order differential equation in A/P. The solution of this equation determines the planned amount of real asset holding at any point in time. Specifically, assuming that the household takes r, W, P, and τ to be constant over time, that it also treats $(M/P)°$ and $v°$ as constant over time, and that it treats M/P and v as equal to $(M/P)°$ and $v°$ at all future times, the solution for real asset holdings at date N is[19]

$$\frac{A(N)}{P} = \frac{A(0)}{P}e^{rN} + \frac{W}{P}\int_0^{N'} l^s(t)e^{r(N-t)}dt$$

$$- \int_0^N\left[\tau + c^d(t) + r\left(\frac{M}{P}\right)° + \gamma v°\right]e^{r(N-t)}dt.$$

[19] With r and γ treated as constant, treating $(M/P)°$ and $v°$ as constant amounts to neglecting planned variations over time in $|a^d/P|$, insofar as these variations affect $v°$ and $(M/P)°$. We are also neglecting here the effect on asset accumulation of the adjustment costs associated with any anticipated changes in v and average M/P. Equations (3.7) and (3.8) imply that $\gamma v° = r(M/P)°$ – that is, at the target values $v°$ and

The first term in this expression describes the effect of continuous compounding at rate r of the initial real asset holding, $A(0)/P$, until date N. The second term describes the effect of continuous compounding at rate r of wage income from the date t at which it is received until date N. The final term describes the effect of continuous compounding at rate r of all expenditures from the date t at which they are incurred until date N. Note that the income foregone from holding money, $r(M/P)^\circ$, enters into this term as a positive expenditure.

The asset-exhaustion condition, $A(N)/P = 0$, may be expressed in present value terms by multiplying through the above expression for $A(N)/P$ by e^{-rN}. After rearranging terms, we obtain

$$\Omega_0 \equiv \frac{A(0)}{P} - \left[r \left(\frac{M}{P} \right)^\circ + \gamma v^\circ + \tau \right] \int_0^N e^{-rt} dt$$

$$= \int_0^N c^d(t) e^{-rt} dt - \frac{W}{P} \int_0^{N'} l^s(t) e^{-rt} dt, \qquad (3.13)$$

where

$$\frac{A(0)}{P} \equiv \frac{M(0)}{P} + \frac{P_e}{P} E(0) + \frac{P_b}{P} B(0)$$

$$\equiv \frac{M(0)}{P} + \frac{\pi(0) + i(0)/P}{r}.$$

This condition says that the present value of lifetime nonwage resources, denoted by Ω_0, must equal the present value of consumption until the planning horizon minus the present value of real wage income earned until retirement. Equation (3.13) also applies to retired households, but with wage income set at zero.

The maximization of U, given the values of N' and N and the asset-exhaustion condition of equation (3.13), implies that the current levels of c^d and l^s are determined by functions of the following form:[20]

$$c^d = c^d \underset{(+) \quad (+) \quad (?)}{(\Omega_0, W/P, r)} \quad \text{and} \qquad (3.14)$$

$$l^s = l^s \underset{(-) \quad (+) \quad (?)}{(\Omega_0, W/P, r)}. \qquad (3.15)$$

$(M/P)^\circ$, the transaction costs incurred equal the earnings foregone by holding money. We have retained the separation of these two terms for expositional purposes.

[20] The maximization of U is also subject to the inequality constraints $[c^d(t), l^s(t), M(t), E(t), B(t)] \geq 0$. We assume these constraints to be ineffective, and we deal only with interior solutions for c^d and l^s, subject to equation (3.13).

The mathematical note at the end of the section spells out the derivation of these functions. However, we can readily explain their form intuitively.

The effects of changes in Ω_0 and W/P in equations (3.14) and (3.15) are similar to the effects of changes in Ω and W/P in the notional consumption demand and labor supply functions of chapter 1. Specifically, an increase in Ω_0, given W/P and r, involves a pure wealth effect and thereby raises c^d and lowers l^s. An increase in W/P, given Ω_0 and r, involves both income and substitution effects, both of which tend to raise c^d, but which are offsetting influences on l^s. As in chapter 1, we assume here that the substitution effect outweighs the income effect in the relevant range.

The new consideration which enters in equations (3.14) and (3.15) is the rate of return, r. An increase in r, given Ω_0 and W/P, also involves both substitution and wealth effects. In the substitution effect, a higher value of r means a lower implicit price of future expenditure relative to current expenditure. In other words, a higher rate of return on saving transforms a unit of foregone current expenditure into a larger amount of possible future expenditure. From this standpoint, an increase in r motivates a substitution of future consumption and future leisure for current consumption and current leisure. In other words, an increase in r tends to reduce current c^d and to raise current l^s. Moreover, with a positive rate of return, the lifetime consumption plan has a positive inclination and the lifetime employment plan has a negative inclination, in contrast to the constant levels of c^d and l^s in chapter 2.[21]

Consider now the wealth effect of a change in r, given Ω_0 and W/P. According to equation (3.13), the lifetime plans for $c^d(t)$ and $l^s(t)$ are such that the present value of planned consumption less the present value of planned wage income is equal to Ω_0. Given the planned time paths of $c^d(t)$ and $l^s(t)$, an increase in r will reduce the present values of both consumption and wage income. However, the reduction in the present value of planned consumption will be larger than the reduction in the present value of planned wage income for two reasons. First, because the lifetime consumption plan has a positive inclination whereas the lifetime employment plan has a negative inclination, and because planned consumption is positive until date N whereas planned employment is positive only until date N', the planned time path of consumption

---

[21] If the household expected W/P to increase over its lifetime or if it applied a discount factor to future utility flows, the lifetime consumption and employment plans might not be inclined in this manner. For example, if the discount factor were equal to r, the planned levels of c^d and l^s would again be constant. Moreover, with W/P not expected to be constant, the household's lifetime plan would depend on the nature of its access to borrowing facilities.

is relatively more concentrated in the distant future and, therefore, its present value is the more sensitive to changes in r. Second, if Ω_0 is positive, the present value of planned consumption is larger than the present value of planned wage income, and, also on this account, would be more sensitive to changes in r. Because an increase in r depresses the present value of planned consumption more than the present value of planned wage income, it follows from equation (3.13) for a given value of Ω_0 that the household would be able both to increase planned consumption and to reduce planned employment at all points in time. Accordingly, the wealth effect of an increase in r tends to raise current c^d and to reduce current l^s. Thus, with regard to both c^d and l^s, the substitution and wealth effects of a change in r, given Ω_0 and W/P, are offsetting, and we have specified the net effect as ambiguous.

We may also consider, at this point, a separate wealth effect of a change in r, which arises through the effect of the rate of return on Ω_0. As equations (3.14) and (3.15) are written, this effect is not explicitly specified. Given M/P, π, i/P, τ, and γ, if Ω_0 is positive, an increase in r implies a decrease in Ω_0.[22] This change in Ω_0 would tend to offset the wealth effect of a change in r for a given Ω_0, which was discussed above. The analysis of market-clearing conditions in section 3.2.5 below assumes that the substitution effect of a change in r dominates over the net ambiguous impact of the two types of wealth effects.

Substitution of the optimal values of current c^d and l^s from equations (3.14) and (3.15) into equation (3.5) yields for working households the following expression for current notional saving demand:

$$\frac{a^d}{P} = \frac{a^d}{P}\left(\underset{(-)}{\Omega_0}, \underset{(+)}{\frac{W}{P}}, \underset{(?)}{r}, \underset{(+)}{\pi + \frac{i}{P} - \tau - \gamma v}\right). \tag{3.16}$$

An increase in Ω_0 raises current c^d and lowers current l^s, and so, given W/P, r, and $\pi + i/P - \tau - \gamma v$, lowers saving. An increase in W/P raises planned consumption after retirement and so, given Ω_0, r, and $\pi + i/P - \tau - \gamma v$, raises saving. An increase in r has ambiguous effects on current c^d and l^s, and so, given Ω_0, W/P, and $\pi + i/P - \tau - \gamma v$, also has an ambiguous effect on saving. Given Ω_0, W/P, and r, which determine current c^d and l^s, an increase in $\pi + i/P - \tau - \gamma v$ increases current disposable income and raises saving.

Retired households differ from working households in that, for retired households, l^s is zero and no possibility exists for substitution

[22] Given that N is finite, a positive value of Ω_0 is sufficient but not necessary for this result. If N were infinite and if $M(0)/P$ equalled $(M/P)^\circ$, we would have $\delta\Omega_0/\delta r = -\Omega_0/r$. A finite value of N implies $\delta\Omega_0/\delta r < -\Omega_0/r$.

between consumption and leisure. Consequently, as in chapter 1, the real wage rate has no effect on the optimal behavior of retired households. However, the direction of effect of Ω_0, r, and $\pi + i/P - \tau - \gamma v$ on c^d and a^d/P for retired households is the same as that for working households. Thus, as in chapter 1, the aggregate c^d, l^s, and a^d/P functions, combining both working and retired households, have the same form as the functions given in equations (3.14–3.16), where Ω_0 and $\pi + i/P - \tau - \gamma v$ are interpreted as aggregate quantities.

Some special interest attaches to the effect on Ω_0 of a change in i/P. Given r, an increase in i/P involves an increase in the real value of the government debt, $P_b B/P$. Suppose that the increase in i/P is financed by an equal increase in τ. (The next section discusses the government budget constraint in detail.) Differentiating equation (3.13) with respect to i/P yields, holding all other variables except τ fixed,

$$\left. \frac{d\Omega_0}{d(i/P)} \right|_{d\tau = d(i/P)} = \frac{1}{r} - \int_0^N e^{-rt} dt = \frac{e^{-rN}}{r} > 0.$$

Such an increase in i/P, financed by an increase in τ, raises lifetime nonwage wealth. This result obtains because the household capitalizes the increase in i/P over an infinite horizon, which is appropriate because the financial asset market places this capitalized value on its bond holdings, whereas it capitalizes the increase in τ only over the finite planning horizon N.[23] Because an increase in i/P raises Ω_0, it follows from equations (3.14–3.16) that it also raises current c^d and lowers current l^s and a^d/P.

Having considered aggregate notional saving demand, we can now utilize the earlier analysis of money demand from section 3.2.2 to determine the allocation of the flow of saving between accumulation of money balances and accumulation of earning assets. Equation (3.12) specifies the notional flow demand for money balances as a function of the aggregate absolute saving flow, as well as r, γ, and M/P. What does the a^d/P function of equation (3.16) imply about $|a^d/P|$? Consider, for example, the effect of an increase in Ω_0, with the other independent variables fixed. The induced algebraic reduction in a^d/P comes partly

[23] This result depends on our assumptions that tax liabilities do not depend on profit or interest income and that the planning horizon is finite. Alternatively, if either tax liabilities were proportionate to profit or interest income or the planning horizon extended into the lifetimes of the representative household's descendants, the representative household would also capitalize the increase in τ over an infinite horizon. In that case, the net effect on Ω_0 of an increase in i/P, financed by an increase in τ, would be nil. See Barro (1974) for an analysis of these issues.

from households for whom a^d/P is positive, typically working households, and partly from households for whom a^d/P is negative, typically retired households. However, in the latter case, the reduction in a^d/P means that a^d/P becomes more negative, so that the absolute saving flow increases. Therefore, the net effect of a change in Ω_0 on $|a^d/P|$ is ambiguous. Similarly, the net effects of changes in r and $\pi + i/P - \tau - \gamma v$ on $|a^d/P|$ are also ambiguous. To simplify the subsequent analysis, we assume that these ambiguous effects can be neglected.[24]

In contrast, the effect on $|a^d/P|$ of an increase in W/P, with the other independent variables fixed, is not ambiguous. An increase in W/P is relevant only for working households, and because working households typically do positive saving, the effect of increasing a^d/P will carry over to $|a^d/P|$. Substituting this direct relation between $|a^d/P|$ and W/P into equation (3.12), we obtain

$$\frac{m^d}{P} = \frac{m^d}{P} \underset{(+)\ (-)(+)\ (-)}{(W/P, r, \gamma, M/P)}. \tag{3.17}$$

Finally, as indicated by equation (3.6), the real notional flow demand for earning assets, f^d/P, is the difference between a^d/P and m^d/P. Therefore, by subtracting equation (3.17) from equation (3.16), we obtain

$$\frac{f^d}{P} = \frac{f^d}{P} \underset{(-)\ (?)\ (+)\ (+)\ \ \ (+)\ \ \ \ (-)}{(\Omega_0, W/P, r, M/P, \pi + i/P - \tau - \gamma v, \gamma)}. \tag{3.18}$$

The direction of effect of Ω_0, M/P, $\pi + i/P - \tau - \gamma v$, and γ are readily apparent. An increase in Ω_0 lowers a^d/P and hence lowers f^d/P. An increase in M/P lowers m^d/P and hence raises f^d/P. An increase in $\pi + i/P - \tau - \gamma v$ raises a^d/P and hence raises f^d/P. An increase in γ raises m^d/P and hence lowers f^d/P. In contrast, an increase in W/P raises both a^d/P and m^d/P, so that the net effect is ambiguous. Finally, an increase in r lowers m^d/P, and we assume that this effect outweighs the ambiguous effect of an increase in r on a^d/P, so that an increase in r raises f^d/P.

Mathematical note

The interior solution for optimal values of $c^d(t)$ and $l^s(t)$ satisfies the following conditions:

$$\frac{\delta u}{\delta c^d(t)} = \frac{\lambda(t)}{1 + r/2v^\circ(t)} \quad \text{for } 0 \leq t \leq N',$$

---

[24] In the basic model of chapter 1, the net effects of Ω and $\pi - \tau$ on $|a^d/P|$ will be exactly zero if $a^d/P = 0$. However, the introduction of a positive rate of return or of $a^d/P \neq 0$ makes these effects ambiguous.

$$\frac{\delta u}{\delta c^d(t)} = \frac{\lambda(t)}{1 - r/2v^\circ(t)} \quad \text{for } N' < t \leq N,$$

$$\frac{\delta u}{\delta l^s(t)} = \frac{-\lambda(t)}{1 + r/2v^\circ(t)} \cdot \frac{W}{P} \quad \text{for } 0 \leq t \leq N',$$

$$l^s(t) = 0 \quad \text{for } N' < t \leq N,$$

$$\frac{d\lambda}{dt} = \frac{-\lambda(t)}{1 + r/2v^\circ(t)} \cdot r \text{ for } 0 \leq t \leq N', \quad \text{and}$$

$$\frac{d\lambda}{dt} = \frac{-\lambda(t)}{1 - r/2v^\circ(t)} \cdot r \text{ for } N' < t \leq N,$$

assuming $a^d(t) \geq 0$ for $0 \leq t \leq N'$ and $a^d(t) \leq 0$ for $N' < t \leq N$. The constant $\lambda(0)$ is determined so as to satisfy equation (3.13). The expression for $d\lambda/dt$ implies that $\lambda(t) \approx \lambda(0)e^{-rt}$. Therefore, as a first approximation, a positive value of r causes λ, which measures the marginal utility of income, to decline over time and causes the lifetime plan to tilt towards relatively more work in early years and relatively more consumption in later years.

3.2.4 *The behavior of government*

As in chapters 1 and 2, government here demands commodities, collects taxes (net of transfers), and supplies money balances. The new element of government behavior in this chapter is that the government can now issue an interest-bearing liability, bonds. The government's budget constraint now is

$$g^d + i/P = \tau + \frac{P_b}{P} b^s + \frac{m^s}{P}. \tag{3.19}$$

The total of the government's demands for commodities plus interest payments must equal the sum of tax receipts plus the flow supply of bonds and money. The amount of current real interest payments, i/P, depends on the existing stock of outstanding bonds, B, the coupons attached to these bonds when they were issued, and the current price level, P. Thus, i/P is independent of current government policy. The government does have currently at its disposal four policy variables – g^d, τ, m^s/P, and $P_b b^s/P$. The budget constraint implies that three of these may be chosen independently.

Since the government can now participate in the financial asset market separately from the commodity market, the government is able to carry out open-market operations and to account for differences between expenditures on current output and receipts by the sale or purchase of earning assets. Consequently, we can now distinguish between what is conventionally called monetary policy and what is conventionally called fiscal policy. An active monetary policy, in the form of open-market operations, by itself involves nonzero and offsetting values for m^s/P and $P_b b^s/P$, with implied equality between τ and $g^d + i/P$. If m^s is positive, monetary policy is denoted as expansionary; otherwise, it is contractionary. An active fiscal policy by itself involves a difference between $g^d + i/P$ and τ equal to the value of $P_b b^s/P$, with the implication that m^s/P is zero. An active fiscal policy could be instituted either by a change in τ (tax policy) or by a change in g^d (expenditure policy) or by a change in both. If $g^d + i/P$ exceeds τ, a current budget deficit, fiscal policy is denoted as expansionary; otherwise, it is contractionary. Of course, at any time, the government may pursue a mixture of active monetary policy and active fiscal policy, with either both expansionary, or both contractionary, or one expansionary and the other contractionary.

3.3   Investment and the rate of return under market-clearing conditions

This section considers the nature of the market-clearing conditions implied by the behavior of households, firms, and government, and analyzes the effects of some exogenous disturbances on these market-clearing conditions.

3.3.1   *Market-clearing conditions*

In the present context exchange takes place at three market places – the labor market, the commodity market, and the financial asset market. Consequently, the harmonization of the behavior of firms, households, and government now involves three independent market-clearing conditions:

in the labor market,

$$l^d \left(\frac{W}{P}\right) = l^s \left(\Omega_0, \frac{W}{P}, r\right) = l; \tag{3.20}$$

$$\underset{(-)}{} \qquad \underset{(-)\,(+)\,(?)}{}$$

in the commodity market,

$$k^d (r, K) + c^d \left(\Omega_0, \frac{W}{P}, r\right) + \gamma v + g^d = y^s \left(\frac{W}{P}, g, K\right) = y;$$

$$\underset{(-)(-)}{} \qquad \underset{(+)\,(+)\,(?)}{} \qquad \qquad \underset{(-)\,(+)(+)}{}$$

$$\tag{3.21}$$

and, in the financial asset market,

$$\frac{f^d}{P}\left(\Omega_0, \frac{W}{P}, r, \frac{M}{P}, \pi + i/P - \tau - \gamma v, \gamma\right) = k^d(r, K) + \frac{P_b}{P}\, b^s = \frac{f}{P}.$$
$$\quad\ \ (-)\ \ (?)\,(+)(+)\qquad\ \ (+)\qquad\qquad (-)\qquad\ \ (-)(-)$$

$$(3.22)$$

To simplify the subsequent notation, we denote aggregate notional commodity demand by y^d – that is, $y^d \equiv k^d + c^d + \gamma v + g^d$ – and we denote aggregate notional earning asset supply by f^s/P – that is, $f^s/P \equiv k^d + P_b b^s/P$.

The variables which appear in these market-clearing conditions fall, as usual, into three groups. First, g^d, τ, and $P_b b^s/P$ represent government behavior, and, by assumption, are exogenously determined. Second, the stocks K, E, M, and B and nominal interest payments, i are predetermined, the result of the past history of firm, household, and government behavior.[25] We are also treating expenditures on financial transactions, γv, as predetermined, since γ is exogenous and v adjusts only gradually to changes in v^0. Third, the three exchange ratios – represented by the real wage rate, the price level, and the rate of return – and the levels of employment, output, and accumulation of financial assets are endogenous. Given the values of the exogenous and predetermined variables, these endogenous variables have unique values which satisfy the market-clearing conditions. As in chapter 1, we denote these as general-market-clearing values and indicate them by a star.[26]

In order to facilitate the analysis of the implications of the market-clearing conditions, it will be helpful to rewrite these conditions in terms of the three exchange ratios – W/P, P, and r – by substituting for Ω_0 from equation (3.13) and for π from the relation $\pi = y^s - (W/P)l^d$.[27,28] Making these substitutions, and suppressing the exogenous

[25] The discussion below considers how monetary and fiscal policy change M and B over time. The discussion also considers the effect of changes in K and E, which occur over time when $k \neq 0$.

[26] Note that the model involves only six independent endogenous variables. The remaining variables are defined in terms of these six. Specifically, given the values of the exogenous and predetermined variables, and the values of $(W/P)^*$, P^*, r^*, l^*, y^*, and f^* implied by the three market-clearing conditions, the calculation of the market-clearing value for any other variable – e.g., π^*, Ω_0^*, k^*, c^*, P_e^*, etc – is simply a matter of working through the appropriate definitions.

[27] In chapter 1, because M/P and π entered into the relevant market-clearing conditions only through Ω, it was relatively simple to analyze the market-clearing conditions in terms of Ω^* and $(W/P)^*$ and then

and predetermined variables, we obtain

$$l^d\left(\frac{W}{P}\right) = l^s\left(\underset{(+)}{\frac{W}{P}}, \underset{(+)}{P}, \underset{(+)}{r}\right) = l, \tag{3.23}$$

where the first argument has sign $(-)$.

$$y^d\left(\underset{(+)}{\frac{W}{P}}, \underset{(-)}{P}, \underset{(-)}{r}\right) = y^s\left(\underset{(-)}{\frac{W}{P}}\right) = y, \text{ and} \tag{3.24}$$

$$\frac{f^d}{P}\left(\underset{(?)}{\frac{W}{P}}, \underset{(-)}{P}, \underset{(+)}{r}\right) = \frac{f^s}{P}\left(\underset{(-)}{r}\right) = \frac{f}{P}. \tag{3.25}$$

The functional forms specified in equations (3.23 – 3.25) require some explanation. Given P and r, the direction of the effects of changes in W/P on l^s, c^d, and f^d/P involve both the direct effects indicated in equations (3.20 – 3.23) and the indirect effects operating through Ω_0 and the inverse relation between π and W/P. Taking account of these indirect effects, given P and r, an increase in W/P involves a negative net wealth effect.[29] Consequently, given P and r, an increase in W/P (1) unambiguously raises l^s, because the net wealth effect reinforces the substitution effect, (2) raises c^d and y^d, if the substitution effect outweighs the net wealth effect, but (3) still has an ambiguous effect on f^d/P.

Given W/P and r, the direction of the effects of changes in P on l^s and c^d, and hence y^d, involves simply the inverse relation between

---

to infer P^*. In the present context, an analogous procedure would not be so simple. Firstly, Ω_0 and M/P appear as separate arguments in equation (3.22). This separation occurs because the household must now make a choice regarding the division of saving between accumulation of money balances and accumulation of earning assets in addition to its choice regarding the division of disposable income between consumption and saving. Secondly, Ω_0 involves r as well as P and π, and so is rather more difficult to sort into its components than Ω was.

[28] This specification of π is appropriate because the market-clearing conditions, which are assumed to be satisfied, imply that $y^s = y^*$ and that $l^d = l^*$.

[29] From equation (3.13), the net wealth effect, given P and r, of a change in W/P is

$$\int_0^{N'} l^s(t)e^{-rt}dt + \frac{1}{r}\frac{d\pi}{d(W/P)} - \left(r\frac{\delta(M/P)^\circ}{\delta|a^d/P|} + \gamma\frac{\delta v^\circ}{\delta|a^d/P|}\right)\frac{\delta|a^d/P|}{\delta(W/P)}\int_0^N e^{-rt}dt,$$

where $\dfrac{d\pi}{d(W/P)} = \dfrac{\delta y^s}{\delta(W/P)} - \dfrac{W}{P}\dfrac{\delta l^d}{\delta(W/P)} - l^d = -l^d.$

Given $l^d(0) = l^s(0)$, the discounting of $l^s(t)$ only until N', and the tendency for $l^s(t)$ to decline over time, the sum of the first two terms is negative. The third term is also negative.

Ω_0 and P, based on the inclusion of M/P and i/P in Ω_0. However, the direction of the effect on f^d/P involves the direct effect of M/P indicated in equation (3.22), in addition to the indirect effect involving Ω_0.[30] Recall that $f^d/P = a^d/P - m^d/P$. An increase in P reduces Ω_0 and hence, according to equation (3.16), raises a^d/P. However, an increase in P also reduces M/P and hence, according to equations (3.12) and (3.17), also raises m^d/P. We assume that the coefficient λ_m in equation (3.12) is sufficiently large that the latter effect is dominant. This desired rapid adjustment to the target money balance means that an increase in P, given W/P and r, produces a decrease in f^d/P even though a^d/P rises.[31]

Finally, given W/P and P, the direction of the effects of changes in r on l^d, c^d, and f^d/P involve both the substitution and wealth effects for a given Ω_0 indicated in equations (3.20–3.23) and the additional wealth effect involving the inverse relation between Ω_0 and r. The discussion in section 3.2.3 above pointed out how these two wealth effects tend to be offsetting. We assume here that the unambiguous substitution effect dominates the ambiguous net result of these wealth effects. Consequently, given W/P and P, an increase in r reduces c^d and raises both l^s and a^d. Because an increase in r also reduces k^d, such an increase unambiguously reduces y^d. Moreover, because an increase in r also reduces m^d/P, such an increase, given W/P and P, unambiguously raises f^d/P.

As in chapter 1, the specification of general-market-clearing conditions does not require a separate statement of the equality between the notional flow demand and flow supply of money balances. Walras' Law of Markets again applies. We can verify this result by combining the momentary household budget constraint,

$$c^d + \gamma v + \frac{f^d}{P} + \frac{m^d}{P} + \tau = \frac{W}{P} l^s + \pi + \frac{i}{P},$$

the firm financing contraint,

$$k^d = \frac{P_e}{P} e^s,$$

[30] An increase in P also reduces i/P, which appears as part of the separate term $\pi + i/P - \tau - \gamma v$ in the f^d/P function. However, we assume that the government varies τ so as to keep the difference $i/P - \tau$ constant, which keeps the term $\pi + i/P - \tau - \gamma v$ unchanged.

[31] Suppose λ_m were *extremely* large. Then, $(M/P)^\circ > M/P$ would imply $m^d/P \gg 0$, $f^d/P \ll 0$, and $f^d/P \ll f^s/P$. Alternatively, $(M/P)^\circ < M/P$ would imply $m^d/P \ll 0$, $f^d/P \gg 0$, and $f^d/P \gg f^s/P$. Consequently, if λ_m were extremely large, desired adjustment of money balances would dominate the notional demand for earning assets, and the market-clearing condition $f^d/P = f^s/P$ would require $M/P \approx (M/P)^\circ$.

the government budget constraint,

$$\tau = g^d + \frac{i}{P} - \frac{P_b}{P} b^s - \frac{m^s}{P},$$

and the definition of profits,

$$\pi = y^s - \frac{W}{P} l^d,$$

to obtain the economy-wide budget constraint,

$$(y^d - y^s) + \frac{W}{P}(l^d - l^s) + \frac{1}{P}(f^d - f^s) + \frac{1}{P}(m^d - m^s) = 0.$$

(3.26)

Equation (3.26) implies that the combination $(W/P)^*$, P^*, and r^* which satisfies equations (3.23–3.25) also satisfies

$$\underset{(+)(+)(-)}{\frac{m^d}{P}\left(\frac{W}{P}, P, r\right)} = \frac{m^s}{P} = \frac{m}{P}.$$

(3.27)

3.3.2   Comparative-statics analysis under market-clearing conditions

As in chapter 1, comparative-statics analysis here is concerned with the effects of exogenous disturbances on the values of the endogenous variables which satisfy the market-clearing conditions. General possibilities of exogenous disturbances include changes in predetermined variables or changes in the current production function, household tastes, or government behavior. The present discussion analyzes explicitly the effects of shifts in government behavior and of growth in the stock of capital.

The general form of this analysis corresponds to the procedure described in the mathematical note to section 1.3, with the modification that the present context would require inversion of a three-by-three matrix, corresponding to the three independent market-clearing conditions. However, in order to gain more insight into the workings of the model, we will again find it useful to discuss the comparative-statics analysis in diagrammatic form. Unfortunately, diagrammatic analysis of the implications of the market-clearing conditions involves more complexity here than in chapter 1, because three dimensions would be required to depict the interaction of the market-clearing conditions in a single diagram.

In order to avoid this difficulty, we provisionally assume that notional labor supply, l^s, is equal to a constant l, rather than determined by the l^s functions of equations (3.15, 3.20, 3.23). Because l^d depends only on W/P, this assumption implies that $(W/P)^*$, the value of W/P consistent with general market clearing, follows immediately from the labor-market clearing condition, $l^d(W/P) = \bar{l}$. Given $(W/P)^*$, we can analyze the interaction of the commodity-market and financial-asset-market clearing conditions to determine P^*, r^*, and the other endogenous variables. This method of simplifying the analysis seems reasonable in that the new considerations on which we want to focus in the present chapter involve the roles of investment, the financial asset market, and the rate of return. Chapter 1 has already considered in some detail the interaction between the labor and commodity markets.

Figures 3.1 depicts, for a given value of W/P, the interaction of the commodity-market and financial-asset-market clearing conditions

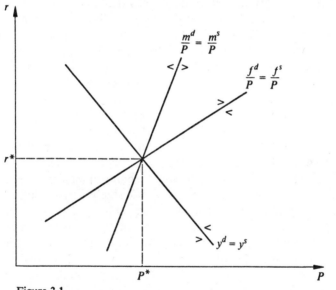

Figure 3.1
Market-clearing loci for commodity and financial-asset markets

as specified by equations (3.24–3.25). The locus labeled $y^d = y^s$ depicts the combinations of values of r and P which are consistent with commodity market clearing. To determine the slope of this locus, consider the following thought experiment: Suppose that the commodity-market clearing condition were initially satisfied, but that, given W/P, P then increased. As a result, c^d, and hence y^d, would decline, and y^s would exceed y^d. What change in r would be required to reestablish the commodity-market clearing condition? Clearly, r would have to decline, to cause k^d and c^d, and hence y^d, to rise. The commodity-market clearing locus is thus downward sloping. The ($>$, $<$) signs bordering this locus indicate that combinations of P and r below and to the left imply excess demand for commodities, whereas combinations above and to the right imply excess supply.

Similarly, the locus labeled $f^d/P = f^s/P$ depicts the combinations of values of r and P which are consistent with financial-asset market clearing. To determine the slope of this locus, consider a similar thought experiment: suppose that the financial-asset-market clearing conditions were initially satisfied, but again that P then increased. As a result, f^d/P would decline, and f^s/P would exceed f^d/P. What change in r would be required to reestablish the financial-asset-market clearing condition? Clearly, r would have to rise, to cause f^d/P to rise and f^s/P to decline. The financial-asset-market clearing locus is thus upward sloping. The ($>$, $<$) signs here indicate that the locus separates the region of excess demand, above and to the left of the locus, from the region of excess supply, below and to the right of the locus. The intersection of these two market-clearing loci at r^* and P^* identifies this combination of the rate of return and the price level as the only one consistent with general market clearing, given $l^d = l^s = l$ and the implied value of $(W/P)^*$.

To facilitate the comparative-statics analysis, figure 3.1 also includes the locus labeled $m^d/P = m^s/P$, which depicts combinations of values of r and P which are consistent with equality between the notional flow demand and supply of money balances. This locus is upward sloping because an increase in r would require an increase in P in order to keep m^d/P unchanged. The economy-wide budget constraint, equation (3.26), also implies that, at points other than (P^*, r^*), the locus $m^d/P = m^s/P$ must be either in the region where there is notional excess supply in the commodity market and notional excess demand in the financial-asset market, or in the region where there is notional excess demand in the commodity market and notional excess supply in the financial-asset market. In other words, given that the labor market is clearing, if m^d/P is to equal m^s/P, the differences between notional demand and notional supply in the commodity and financial asset markets must be exactly offsetting. Consequently, the locus $m^d/P = m^s/P$ must be more steeply sloped than the locus $f^d/P = f^s/P$.[32]

---

[32] An analytical proof of the relative positions of these loci would be as follows. From equation (3.25), the slope of the $f^d/P = f^s/P$ locus is given by

$$- \frac{d(f^d/P)}{\delta P} \bigg/ \left[\frac{\delta(f^d/P)}{\delta r} - \frac{\delta(f^s/P)}{\delta r} \right],$$

3.3.3 The effects of fiscal policy

As a first example of comparative-statics analysis, consider a shift toward a more expansionary fiscal policy, involving a reduction in tax receipts, τ, financed by an increased bond issue, $P_b b^s / P$. As with the comparative-statics analysis of government policy in chapter 1, we first analyze the initial effects associated with the changes in the flows, τ and b^s, and then we analyze the effects associated with the accumulated change over time in stocks, in this case the stock of bonds, B.

To analyze the initial effects, consider first the $y^d = y^s$ locus, as described by equation (3.21). The reduction in τ increases Ω_0, thereby raising y^d and shifting this locus to the right. Next, consider the $m^d/P = m^s/P$ locus. Because neither the reduction in τ nor the increase in $P_b b^s / P$ affect either m^s/P or m^d/P, as given by equation (3.17), this locus does not shift. Finally, consider the $f^d/P = f^s/P$ locus as described by equation (3.22). The reduction in τ increases both Ω_0 and $\pi + i/P - \tau - \gamma v$, and so has offsetting effects on f^d/P. The increase in $P_b b^s / P$ raises f^s/P. However, because the reduction in τ raises c^d but does not affect m^d/P, f^d/P cannot increase by as much as the reduction in τ. Therefore, on net, the $f^d/P = f^s/P$ locus must shift to the left, where it

---

which has a positive numerator and denominator. From equation (3.27), the slope of the $m^d/P = m^s/P$ locus is given by

$$\frac{\delta(m^d/P)}{\delta P} \bigg/ -\frac{\delta(m^d/P)}{\delta r},$$

which also has a positive numerator and denominator. Differentiating equation (3.26), neglecting l^d and l^s, yields

$$\frac{\delta y^d}{\delta r} + \frac{\delta(f^d/P)}{\delta r} - \frac{\delta(f^s/P)}{\delta r} + \frac{\delta(m^d/P)}{\delta r} = 0$$

and

$$\frac{\delta y^d}{\delta P} + \frac{\delta(f^d/P)}{\delta P} + \frac{\delta(m^d/P)}{\delta P} = 0.$$

Thus, equation (3.26) implies

$$\frac{\delta(f^d/P)}{\delta r} - \frac{\delta(f^s/P)}{\delta r} > -\frac{\delta(m^d/P)}{\delta r} \quad \text{and} \quad -\frac{\delta(f^d/P)}{\delta P} < \frac{\delta(m^d/P)}{\delta P},$$

which confirms the relative magnitudes of the two positive slopes. Note also that, from equation (3.24), the slope of the $y^d = y^s$ locus is given by $-(\delta y^d/\delta P)/(\delta y^d/\delta r)$, which has a positive numerator and a negative denominator.

passes through the new intersection of the $y^d = y^s$ and $m^d/P = m^s/P$ loci.[33]

Figure 3.2 depicts the initial effects of a more expansionary fiscal policy. The dashed lines represent the new market-clearing loci. The new general-market-clearing situation involves higher values for both the price level and the rate of return. A simple rationalization for this result would be the following. An increase in $P_b b^s/P$ suggests that r should rise to clear the financial asset market. A higher r, in turn, means that P must rise to reduce M/P and keep m^d/P equal to the unchanged value of m^s/P. The higher P and r offset the decrease in τ and clear the commodity market. Regarding the composition of output, the increase in r depresses investment demand, so that on net consumption rises and investment falls. Total output itself is unchanged because of our working assumption that labor supply is constant.[34]

[33] As in chapter 1, the effect of the reduction in τ in increasing Ω_0 involves the assumption that the representative household regards this reduction as permanent. Alternatively, if the representative household regarded the reduction in τ as purely transitory, Ω_0 would not change initially, and an increase in f^d/P would absorb the entire decrease in τ and increase in $P_b b^s/P$. In that case, the market-clearing conditions would not be disturbed initially, and the expansionary fiscal policy would have effects on the economy only through the accumulated change over time in B, which is discussed below. In assuming that the representative household expects τ to remain permanently at precisely its current reduced level, we are assuming that the representative household does not take account of the effect of the current increase in borrowing on the government's budget constraint in the future. Specifically, the representative household ignores the fact that an increase in current $P_b b^s/P$ implies higher levels of B/P and i/P in the future, and that, given g^d, m^s/P, and $P_b b^s/P$, higher future levels of i/P would imply higher future levels of τ. If the representative household took the full implications of future taxes into account, the expansionary fiscal policy would affect Ω_0 and, hence, aggregate demand, only because future taxes beyond the planning horizon, N, are not capitalized into Ω_0. If the representative household also had a bequest motive, so that the effective horizon for taxes became infinite, then the full effect of this fiscal policy on Ω_0 would be nil. In that situation, 'expansionary' fiscal policy, with g^d fixed, would have no effects at all on aggregate demand, and, hence, no effect on r^* and P^*. For more on this issue, see Barro (1974).

[34] As indicated above, allowing l^s to vary according to the function in equation (3.20) would make the analysis more complicated. The initial decrease in τ and the induced increases in P and r would all affect l^s. Because the net effect of these changes was to increase c^d, and because W/P, the relative price of leisure and consumption, has been held fixed, it is reasonable to suppose that desired leisure would also increase on net. In that case, l^s would decrease on net. Accordingly,

The above analysis of expansionary fiscal policy deals only with the initial effects. Over time, two further considerations become relevant. First, if b^s was initially zero, the shift to an expansionary fiscal policy would make b^s positive, and thereby cause B and i to increase over time. As was pointed out in section 3.2.3 above, an increase

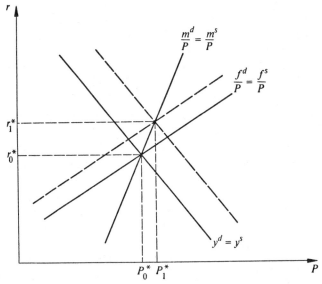

Figure 3.2
Initial effect of expansionary fiscal policy under general-market-clearing conditions

in i, even if financed by an increase in τ, raises Ω_0 because tax liabilities are capitalized only up to date N. In this context, the increase in i over time will continually shift the $y^d = y^s$ locus, as described by equation (3.21), further to the right, and will continually shift the $f^d/P = f^s/P$ locus, as described by equation (3.22), further to the left. Consequently, the initial increases in r^* and P^* will tend to be followed by further steady increases, so long as the expansionary fiscal policy is in effect. Moreover, these further increases in r^* will involve further shifting in the composition of output towards more consumption and less investment.[35]

---

in a fuller analysis, l and y would decline and W/P would rise to maintain clearing of the labor market.

[35] This decline in current k implies a smaller capital stock, K, in the future. Section 3.3.5 below considers the repercussions of a relatively smaller K. The effect of an increase in $P_b b^s/P$ in reducing k is a process

Second, the initial and subsequent increases in r^* motivate households to increase the frequency of financial-asset-market transactions – that is, v° rises. Initially, the actual transactions frequency was predetermined. However, over time, as households adjust v towards the higher v°, they also increase their demand for financial services, γv. This increase in γv over time directly increases y^d and induces an equivalent decrease in f^d/P, through the term $\pi + i/P - \tau - \gamma v$.[36] Consequently, the $y^d = y^s$ locus shifts still further to the right and the $f^d/P = f^s/P$ locus shifts still further to the left. These shifts further reinforce the tendency for r^* and P^* to steadily increase. Moreover, the increases in r^* and P^* caused by the increases in γv involve decreases in c^* as well as further decreases in k^*. By raising r^*, the expansionary fiscal policy induces households to engage in a larger number of costly transactions in order to economize on money holdings. Consequently, a larger amount of current output consists of financial services and a smaller amount is available for consumption and investment.

Finally, suppose that after some finite interval, the expansionary fiscal policy is terminated. Specifically, $P_b b^s/P$ returns to its original level, and τ rises to a level consistent with the original levels of $P_b b^s/P$ and g^d and with the existing level of i/P. This reversal would imply immediate declines in P^* and r^*. It would also return all the exogenous and predetermined variables to their original values, except for the accumulated increases in B, i, and v.[37] Because of the accumulated changes in B and i, P^* and r^* would remain permanently above their original values and k^* would remain below its original value.[38] Figure 3.3 depicts the time paths of $P_b b^s/P$, P^* and r^* in this example.

3.3.4 *The effects of monetary policy*

As a second example of comparative-statics analysis, consider a shift toward a more expansionary monetary policy, involving an increase in m^s/P and a corresponding decrease in $P_b b^s/P$. Again, we first analyze the

---

by which the incurring of public debt may be considered to impose a relative burden on future generations. For more on this issue, see Ferguson (1964), Tobin (1965), and Barro (1974).

[36] Households reduce only f^d/P to pay for the increase in γv. We have assumed that households calculate Ω_0 and choose c^d and m^d/P on the basis of v° rather than v.

[37] We again neglect for the moment the accumulated change in K.

[38] We may note that much of conventional macro-economic analysis is concerned only with comparing this final situation with the original situation. See, for example Patinkin (1965).

initial effects associated with the changes in the flows, m^s and b^s, and then we analyze the effects associated with the accumulated changes over time in stocks, in this case, M and B.

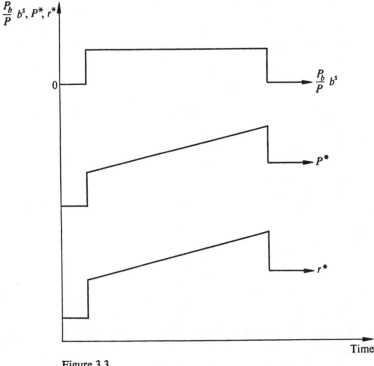

Figure 3.3

Time paths of $\frac{P_b}{P} b^s$, P^* and r^*

Considering the initial effects, the decrease in $P_b b^s/P$ reduces f^s/P and shifts the $f^d/P = f^s/P$ locus to the right. The increase in m^s/P also shifts the $m^d/P = m^s/P$ locus to the right. The $y^d = y^s$ locus does not shift.[39] Figure 3.4 depicts the initial effects of a more expansionary monetary policy. The dashed lines represent the new market-clearing loci. The new general-market-clearing situation involves a higher price level and a lower rate of return.

[39] This result is again based on the assumption that the representative household does not take account of the implications of a change in $P_b b^s/P$ for future values of τ. If the representative household did adjust Ω_0 to take account of expected future changes in τ, the initial effect of expansionary monetary policy on r^* would be ambiguous.

A simple rationalization for this result would be the follow-ing. The decrease in $P_b b^s/P$ suggests that r should fall to clear the financial-asset market. A lower r, in turn, means that P must rise to clear the commodity market. The higher P also helps to clear the financial-asset market. Regarding the composition of output, the decrease in r implies that investment has increased at the expense of consumption. The decline in r and increase in P also induce households to increase m^d/P to equal the new higher level of m^s/P. The contrast between the effects of

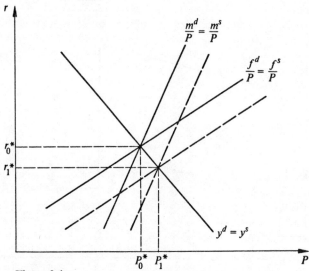

Figure 3.4
Initial effect of expansionary monetary policy under general-market-clearing conditons

expansionary fiscal policy and expansionary monetary policy is interest-ing. In both cases, P^* increases. However, expansionary fiscal policy raises r^*, whereas expansionary monetary policy lowers r^*.

The above analysis of expansionary monetary policy again deals only with the initial effects. Over time, two further considerations, analogous to those discussed with regard to fiscal policy, become relevant. The first of these longer-run effects involves changes in asset stocks. If m^s and b^s were both initially zero, the shift to an expansionary mone-tary policy would make m^s positive and b^s negative, and thereby cause M to increase over time and B and i to decrease over time. The increase in M raises Ω_0, while the decrease in i/P, assumed to be matched by a decrease in τ, only partially offsets this rise in Ω_0. Consequently, the

$y^d = y^s$ locus shifts continually to the right. The increase in M also depresses m^d/P and so also shifts the $m^d/P = m^s/P$ locus to the right. The increases in Ω_0 and in M have offsetting effects on f^d/P. However, the f^d/P function, as specified in equation (3.25), assumed that λ_m is sufficiently large that the change in M is dominant. Consequently, f^d/P increases and the $f^d/P = f^s/P$ locus also shifts to the right.

Because all three loci continue to shift to the right, it is clear that the initial increase in P^* will tend to be followed by further steady increases, as long as the expansionary monetary policy is in effect. However, this geometric analysis does not directly reveal the effect on r^*. Suppose that the further increase in P^* were equiproportional to the increase in M, but that there were no further change in r^*. These movements would satisfy the condition $m^d/P = m^s/P$. However, although M/P would be unchanged, the reduction in i and increase in P would reduce i/P. This reduction in i/P, even if matched by a reduction in τ, would reduce Ω_0 when taxes are capitalized only up to date N. Consequently, r^* would have to decline steadily in order to prevent y^d from falling and to satisfy the condition $y^d = y^s$. Moreover, the decline in r^* implies that in order actually to satisfy the condition $m^d/P = m^s/P$, the increase in P^* would have to be less than equiproportional to the increase in M.

The second longer-run effect involves a decrease in v° induced by the initial and subsequent decreases in r^*. This effect is precisely the reverse of the effect of the higher v° associated with the more expansionary fiscal policy. The decrease in v° induces a decrease in v over time. This decrease in v tends to reinforce the steady decrease in r^*, tends to moderate the steady increase in P^*, and permits an increase in c^* and k^*. Here again, our assumption that households do not anticipate the continual increase in the price level should be stressed. As chapter 4 explains, this assumption is necessary for the result that a more expansionary monetary policy induces a decrease in transactions frequency and an increase in real money holding.

Finally, suppose that after some finite interval, the expansionary monetary policy is terminated. Specifically, both m^s/P and $P_b b^s/P$ return to their original levels. This reversal would imply an immediate decrease in P^* and an immediate increase in r^*. It would also return all the exogenous and predetermined variables to their original values, except for the accumulated increase in M and the accumulated decreases in B, i, and v. Because of the accumulated changes in M, B, and i, r^* would remain permanently below its original value and P^* would remain permanently above its original value. However, the permanent increase in P^* would be less than equiproportionate to the accumulated increase in M. Also, k^* would remain above its original value. Figure 3.5 depicts the time paths of m/P, M/P^*, and r^* in this example.

In the basic model of chapter 1, an increase in M was neutral. It caused equiproportionate increases in P and W, but no change in any of the real variables of the system. In contrast, as we have just seen,

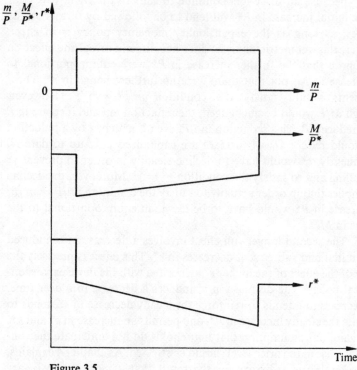

Figure 3.5

Time paths of $\dfrac{m}{P}$, $\dfrac{M^*}{P^*}$ and r^*

an increase in M in the present context is not neutral. The essential reason for this difference is the existence, in the present analysis, of interest-bearing government debt, the real value of which is, in part, a component of household nonwage wealth. The increase in M in the above example was not neutral, because the corresponding reduction in i and resulting increase in P reduced i/P. Moreover, this nonneutrality does not require that, as in the above example, the increase in M result from open-market operations. For example, if, alternatively, the increase in M corresponds to a period of reduced τ, with no net change in B and i, the resulting increase in P alone would serve to reduce i/P. In this case, M/P^* would again rise and r^* would again decline, although these changes would be smaller than in the case of open-market operaations. We could reestablish the property of neutrality of the stock of money by making either one of two modifications to the present analysis. One possibility would be to modify the structure of the model, as suggested above, to make Ω_0 independent of i/P. Another possibility would be to constrain monetary and fiscal policy to hold fixed the ratio of M to i by increasing i equiproportionately to any increase in M. In this case equiproportionate increases in P would keep both M/P and i/P constant.[40]

3.3.5 Growth of the capital stock

As a final example of comparative-statics analysis, consider an increase in the capital stock, K. Such an increase occurs over time whenever investment, k, is positive. Because we have assumed that changes in K have no effect on the marginal product of labor and, hence, on labor demand, and that labor supply is constant, changes in K do not affect $(W/P)^*$.

Consider first the $y^d = y^s$ locus, as described by equation (3.21). An increase in K directly induces a decrease in k^d and an increase in y^s. In addition, with W/P and l^d constant, profits, $\pi = y^s - (W/P)l^d$, increase by the same amount as y^s. The rise in π increases Ω_0 and induces an increase in c^d. We assume here that the induced increase in c^d is roughly equal to the increase in π and, hence, is roughly equal to the increase in y^s. Therefore, because k^d has declined, the net effect of the increase in K is to raise y^s by more than y^d and hence to shift the $y^d = y^s$ locus to the left.

Consider next the $f^d/P = f^s/P$ locus. The decrease in k^d implies a corresponding decrease in f^s/P. The increase in π induces, by assumption, a roughly equal increase in c^d, but does not affect m^d/P. Thus, f^d/P remains roughly constant. Therefore, the $f^d/P = f^s/P$ locus shifts to the right. Finally, because neither changes in K nor changes in π affect either m^s/P or m^d/P, as given by equation (3.17), the $m^d/P = m^s/P$ locus does not shift.

---

[40] Another possibility would be to vary i/B with changes in P such that i/PB remained constant. With such purchasing power adjustment, increases in M with no net change in B would be neutral, but increases in M resulting from open-market operations would not be neutral. For further discussion of the neutrality of money, see Metzler (1951), Patinkin (1965, esp. pp. 288–302), and Grossman (1967).

Figure 3.6 depicts the effects of an increase in K. The dashed lines represent the new market-clearing loci. The new market-clearing situation involves lower values for both the price level and the rate of return. Regarding the composition of output, the increase in π, as already noted, increases c^d by about as much as the increase in y^s. The induced

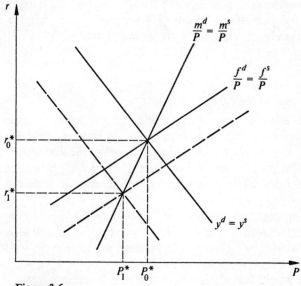

Figure 3.6
Effect of increase in capital stock under general-market-clearing conditions

decreases in P^* and r^* both imply further increases in c^d. Consequently, on net, k^d and k must decline. Thus, whenever k is positive, so that K increases over time, the effect of an increasing K is to reduce k over time. For given technology, household tastes and age structure, and government policy, the capital stock converges to a steady-state value – that is, a value of K which corresponds to zero investment.[41] The reader may wish to analyze, through comparative-statics techniques, the effect of a change in the underlying parameters of the model on the steady-state value of K.

[41] For a rigorous analysis of the determination of the level of and path of convergence to the steady-state capital stock, see, for example, Burmeister and Dobell (1970) and Stein (1971).

3.4   Investment and the rate of return under excess supply of labor services and commodities

This section revives the assumption of section 2.2 that the values of W and P are such that excess supply exists in the markets for both labor services and commodities. We begin by analyzing the behavior of firms and households under these conditions. Throughout the discussion we assume that the rate of return takes that value which is consistent with effective clearing of the financial asset market. We then analyze the determination of the levels of output and employment and the rate of return. Finally, we analyze how changes in government behavior affect output, employment, and the rate of return.

3.4.1   *The behavior of firms under excess supply of commodities*

The problem faced by the representative firm here is identical to the problem which it faced in section 3.2.1 above, *except* that the representative firm now acts as a quantity taker with respect to its sales, in addition to acting as a wage, price, and rate-of-return taker. The existence of current excess supply in the commodity market means that the representative firm will not be able to sell its current notional supply y^s. Its actual current sales y will equal the quantity demanded and thus will be less than y^s.

Since the adjustment of capital stock involves a penalty cost, the optimal pattern of capital accumulation will depend on the firm's expectations regarding future levels of demand-determined constraints on sales, in addition to the current value of this constraint. We assume here that the representative firm has the same pattern of expectations that the representative household had in chapter 2. Specifically, the representative firm expects to be effectively constrained to the current level of sales, y, until date $\hat{N}$, and expects to be unconstrained after date $\hat{N}$.

Under these conditions, maximization of real profit per share involves the following two calculations: First, the firm plans to produce now and until date $\hat{N}$ just output quantity y,[42] and to do so at each date with the minimum possible amount of labor, given the stock of capital existing at each date. Second, given this strategy for employing labor, the firm chooses an optimal pattern for the accumulation of capital.

---

[42] Given $y < y^s(0)$ and the expected constancy of y, W, P, and r, it follows that $y < y^s(t)$ for $t \leq \hat{N}$. This conclusion obtains unambiguously since we are neglecting depreciation and the possibility of a firm's planning to sell redundant capital, both of which would allow $y^s(t)$ to decrease over time.

Thus, the current effective demand for labor services is

$$l^{d'} = l^{d'}(y, g, K),$$ (3.28)
$$\phantom{l^{d'} = l^{d'}(}{(+)(-)(-)}$$

such that $\Phi(l^{d'}, g, K) = y$. As in the effective labor demand function of section 2.2, W/P no longer appears as an argument, but is replaced by y, which represents the level of the demand-determined constraint on sales. Note also that, whereas the notional demand function for labor involved $\delta\Phi/\delta l = W/P$, $\delta\Phi/\delta l$ again exceeds W/P along the effective demand function for labor because y is less than y^s ($W/P, g, K$).

In the long run, the firm again can also choose K. Profit is now given by

$$\pi = y - \frac{W}{P}\, l^{d'},$$

and profit per share is again π/E. The financing constraint is still

$$\frac{P_e}{P}\, dE = dK.$$

Denote by $\tilde{K}$ the value of K which, in the absence of adjustment costs, would maximize π/E for given values of y and g, subject to the financing constraint. The choice of $\tilde{K}$ and the associated value of $l^{d'}$, given by equation (3.28), amounts to the selection of the most efficient combination of K and l along the given isoquant associated with y and g. Specifically, at $\tilde{K}$ and the associated value of $l^{d'}$, the ratio of the marginal product of capital to the marginal product of labor is equal to the ratio of the rate of return to the real wage rate. Thus, $\tilde{K}$ satisfies the relation

$$\tilde{K} = \tilde{K}\left(y, g, \frac{r}{W/P}\right),$$
$$\phantom{\tilde{K} = \tilde{K}(}{(+)(-)\ (-)}$$

such that $\left.\dfrac{\delta\Phi/\delta K}{\delta\Phi/\delta l}\right|_{\Phi(l,g,K)=y} = \dfrac{r}{W/P}.$

Because, as we have already noted, the $l^{d'}$ function implies $\delta\Phi/\delta l > W/P$, it also follows that $\delta\Phi/\delta K$ exceeds r along the $\tilde{K}$ function. Because the notional target capital stock involved $\delta\Phi/\delta K = r$, $\tilde{K}$ must be smaller than K°, for given values of g, r, and W/P.[43] However, as y approaches y^s, $\tilde{K}$ approaches K° and $l^{d'}$ approaches l^d.

Because the representative firm expects y to be below y^s only until date $\hat{N}$, $\tilde{K}$ represents the 'target' capital stock only for this period.

---

[43] A formal proof of this result involves the condition that production is subject to diminishing returns to scale.

After date $\hat{N}$, the target capital stock is

$$K^\circ = K^\circ \underset{(-)}{(r)}.$$

Given that changes in K involve costs of adjustment, the weighing of these costs against the profits foregone by allowing K to be unequal to its target value is now complicated by the nonconstancy of the target over time. If $\hat{N}$ were large, the firm currently would be concerned principally with the gap between K and $\tilde{K}$, whereas, if $\hat{N}$ were small, the firm currently would be concerned principally with the gap between K and K°. We may suppose that, for the purpose of the representative firm's optimal adjustment policy, the effective, target capital stock denoted by K', is a weighted average of $\tilde{K}$ and K°, with a relatively larger weight for $\tilde{K}$ the larger is $\hat{N}$. Thus, we have

$$K' = K' \underset{(+)(+)\ (-)}{(\tilde{K}, K^\circ, \hat{N})},$$

with the property that

$$\tilde{K} \le K'(\tilde{K}, K^\circ, \hat{N}) \le K^\circ.$$

If we again assume that the firm's investment demand is related to its target capital stock by a simple linear adjustment mechanism, we obtain the effective investment demand function

$$k^{d'} = \lambda'_k (K' - K) \equiv k^{d'} \underset{(+)(-)(-)\ (+)\ (-)}{(y, g, r, W/P, K)}, \tag{3.29}$$

where λ'_k is positive and, for simplicity, is treated as a constant. Because K' is smaller than K°, if λ'_k is not larger than λ_k, $k^{d'}$ must be smaller than k^d.[44] This effective investment demand function implies that the effective flow supply of equity is

$$\frac{P_e}{P} e^{s'} = k^{d'} \underset{(+)(-)(-)\ (+)\ (-)}{(y, g, r, W/P, K)}. \tag{3.30}$$

We also assume for simplicity that for each individual firm, K' is at least as large as K, so that $k^{d'}$ and $e^{s'}$ are nonnegative.

In equations (3.3) and (3.4) derived above, notional investment demand and equity supply were functions of r and K, but were not functions of the level of output.[45] Output had been maximized out as a

---

[44] In general, the relation between λ'_k and λ_k is ambiguous. See Grossman (1972b).

[45] The k^d function also did not involve W/P and g. However, that simplification obtained only because of the assumption that $\Phi_{iK} = \Phi_{Kg} = 0$.

separate choice variable. The principal modification in the effective investment demand and equity supply functions, given by equations (3.29) and (3.30), is that these latter functions do have current output as an argument.[46] As with the effective demand for labor services, the level of demand for commodities here imposes output as a constraint on effective investment demand and effective equity supply.

3.4.2 *The behavior of households under excess supply of labor services*

The problem faced by the representative household here is identical to the problem which it faced in section 3.2.2 above, *except* that the representative working household now acts as a quantity taker with respect to its employment, in addition to acting as a wage, price, and rate-of-return taker. The existence of current excess supply in the labor market means that the representative working household will not be able to obtain the quantity of employment given by its current notional supply l^s. Its actual employment l will equal the quantity demanded and will be less than l^s.

Because utility maximization is an intertemporal problem, as in chapter 2, the household's optimal behavior will depend on its expectations regarding future employment possibilities, in addition to the employment currently obtainable. In section 2.2, we assumed that the representative household expects to be effectively constrained to the current level of employment, l, until date $\hat{N}$, where $0 < \hat{N} < N'$, and expects to be unconstrained during the remaining $N' - \hat{N}$ working years. We employ the same assumption here. In addition, we assume that the representative household expects π to be constant at its current level until date $\hat{N}$ and then to rise to π^*. This assumption also parallels the specification of profit expectations in section 2.2. Finally, we continue to assume that the representative household expects W, P, r, and τ to be constant over time.

---

[46] Effective investment demand, as specified by equation (3.29), depends on the level of output. However, over time the effect of investment is to change the stock of capital K. Noting that $k \equiv dK/dt$, if equation (3.29) were solved as a differential equation, we would find that, over the long run, effective investment demand depends on the rate of change of the level of the demand-imposed constraint on output. Thus, an income-investment accelerator-type relation is implicit in equation (3.29), although in the present chapter we are treating K as a constant. In addition, we have assumed that the representative firm expects the rate of change of output to be zero. An accelerator can also occur if the representative firm, in response to actual experience, anticipates a nonzero rate of change of output. See Grossman (1972b) for a derivation of these accelerator relations.

Recall that the anticipated rate or return, r, represents the discount rate at which the present value of the expected future stream of profits per share equals the current share price. Thus, the representative household's expectations regarding the future behaviour of π/E and P now imply that r satisfies the following relation:

$$P_e(0) \equiv \frac{P\pi(0)}{E} \int_0^N e^{-rt} dt + \frac{P\pi^*}{E} \int_N^\infty e^{-rt} dt,$$

which implies

$$r \equiv \frac{P\pi}{P_e E} + \frac{P}{P_e E} (\pi^* - \pi) e^{-r\hat{N}}.$$

In addition, the further expectation that r is constant over time combined with the expected increase in π at date $\hat{N}$ implies that the representative household expects $P_e E/P$ to increase steadily until date $\hat{N}$. For given values of E and P, the expected rate of capital gain until date $\hat{N}$, denoted by ρ_e, is determined by the derivative of $P_e(0)$ with respect to $\hat{N}$ – specifically,

$$\rho_e = -\frac{1}{P_e} \frac{dP_e}{d\hat{N}} = \frac{P}{P_e E} (\pi^* - \pi) e^{-r\hat{N}}.$$

Thus, the anticipated rate of return can now be expressed as the sum of the dividend return plus the expected rate of capital gain – namely,

$$r \equiv \frac{P\pi}{P_e E} + \rho_e.$$

Given the above assumptions, the representative household's formal problem, as in chapter 2, is to maximize

$$U = \int_0^{\hat{N}} u[c^{d'}(t), l] \, dt + \int_{\hat{N}}^{N'} u[c^{d'}(t), l^{s'}(t)] \, dt$$
$$+ \int_{N'}^N u[c^{d'}(t), 0] \, dt,$$

subject to the given constant values of W, P, r, τ, and l, the horizons $\hat{N}$, N', and N, and initial asset holdings $A(0)$. However, one essential effect of the expectation of changes over time in P_e is to create a divergence between the representative household's saving – which is defined as the nominal value of the flow of assets, $a \equiv m + P_e e + P_b b$ – and the anticipated rate of change in its nominal asset holdings, dA/dt. The real amount of planned saving for working households is now

$$\frac{a^{d'}}{P} = \frac{W}{P} l + \pi + \frac{i}{P} - \tau - c^{d'} - \gamma v. \tag{3.31}$$

The anticipated rate of change in asset holdings is equal to saving plus anticipated changes in the value of existing asset holdings due to the expected change in equity prices – that is

$$\frac{1}{P}\left(\frac{\mathrm{d}A}{\mathrm{d}t}\right)^{d'} = \frac{a^{d'}}{P} + \rho_e \frac{P_e E}{P} = \frac{W}{P} l$$

$$+ r\left(\frac{A}{P} - \frac{M}{P}\right) - \tau - c^{d'} - \gamma v.$$

The anticipated rate of change in asset holdings can be used to accumulate either equity shares, bonds, or money. However, in the case of equity, the anticipated change in nominal holdings now equals the value of equity flow plus the anticipated effect of equity price changes on the value of existing nominal holdings – that is,

$$\frac{1}{P}\left[\frac{\mathrm{d}(P_e E)}{\mathrm{d}t}\right]^{d'} = \frac{P_e}{P} e^{d'} + \rho_e \frac{P_e E}{P}.$$

Given the definition,

$$\frac{f^{d'}}{P} \equiv \frac{P_e}{P} e^{d'} + \frac{P_b}{P} b^{d'},$$

we have

$$\frac{1}{P}\left(\frac{\mathrm{d}A}{\mathrm{d}t}\right)^{d'} = \frac{1}{P}\left[\frac{\mathrm{d}(P_e E)}{\mathrm{d}t}\right]^{d'} + \frac{P_b}{P} b^{d'} + \frac{m^{d'}}{P}$$

$$\equiv \frac{f^{d'}}{P} + \rho_e \frac{P_e E}{P} + \frac{m^{d'}}{P}. \tag{3.32}$$

The pattern of accumulating savings first as money, with periodic purchases of earning assets, is still appropriate. The average money balance is $(a^{d'}/P)/2v$. Abstracting from adjustment costs associated with changes in v and M/P, the optimal transactions frequency would now be

$$\tilde{v} = \left(\frac{ra^{d'}/P}{2\gamma}\right)^{1/2},$$

which is obtained by replacing v° and a^d/P by $\tilde{v}$ and $a^{d'}/P$ in equation (3.7). The corresponding average real money balance would be

$$\left(\frac{\tilde{M}}{P}\right) = \frac{a^{d'}/P}{2\tilde{v}} = \left(\frac{\gamma a^{d'}/P}{2r}\right)^{1/2},$$

which is analogous to equation (3.8). In the aggregate, the functions for $\tilde{v}$ and $(\widetilde{M/P})$ would take the forms

$$\tilde{v} = \tilde{v}\,(|a^{d'}/P|, r, \gamma), \quad \text{and}$$
$$\underset{(+)\quad(+)(-)}{}$$

$$\left(\frac{\tilde{M}}{P}\right) = \left(\frac{\tilde{M}}{P}\right)(|a^{d'}/P|, r, \gamma),$$
$$\underset{(+)\quad(-)(+)}{}$$

which correspond to equations (3.9–3.10) above, where $|a^{d'}/P|$ is now the aggregate absolute saving flow at the employment level l and profit level π. As in the case of the firm's choice of capital stock, $\tilde{v}$ and $(\widetilde{M/P})$ represent the effective targets only until date $\hat{N}$. After date $\hat{N}$, the relevant targets are $v°$ and $(M/P)°$. We may suppose that, for the purpose of the representative household's optimal adjustment policy, the effective target transactions frequency, denoted by v', is a weighted average of $\tilde{v}$ and $v°$, and the effective target real money balance, denoted $(M/P)'$, is a weighted average of $(\widetilde{M/P})$ and $(M/P)°$. The relative weights for $\tilde{v}$ and $(\widetilde{M/P})$ are larger the larger is $\hat{N}$. Thus we have

$$v' = v'\,(\tilde{v}, v°, \hat{N}) \quad \text{and}$$
$$\underset{(+)(+)(-)}{}$$

$$\left(\frac{M}{P}\right)' = \left(\frac{M}{P}\right)'\left[\left(\frac{\tilde{M}}{P}\right), \left(\frac{M}{P}\right)°, \hat{N}\right].$$
$$\underset{(+)\qquad(+)\qquad(-)}{}$$

Assuming that $|a^{d'}/P|$ is no larger than $|a^d/P|$, for a given r and γ, these functions also have the property that

$$\tilde{v} \le v'(\tilde{v}, v°, \hat{N}) \le v° \quad \text{and}$$

$$\left(\frac{\tilde{M}}{P}\right) \le \left(\frac{M}{P}\right)'\left[\left(\frac{\tilde{M}}{P}\right), \left(\frac{M}{P}\right)°, \hat{N}\right] \le \left(\frac{M}{P}\right)°.$$

Again assuming linear adjustment, the effective desired rates of change of average transactions frequency and aggregate money holdings are

$$\frac{dv}{dt} = \lambda_v'(v' - v) \quad \text{and} \tag{3.33}$$

$$\frac{1}{P}\left(\frac{dM}{dt}\right)^{d'} \equiv \frac{m^{d'}}{P} = \lambda_m'\left[\left(\frac{M}{P}\right)' - \frac{M}{P}\right]$$

$$= \frac{m^{d'}}{P}\left(|a^{d'}/P|, |a^d/P|, r, \gamma, \frac{M}{P}\right), \tag{3.34}$$
$$\underset{(+)\qquad(+)\quad(-)(+)(-)}{}$$

where $|a^d/P|$ refers to the saving flow magnitude which is expected after date $\hat{N}$.

Optimal lifetime behavior for the household again entails the exhaustion of assets at date N. However, the new assumptions regarding profit expectations and the effective targets for trasactions frequency and money balances imply a revised specification of the present value of lifetime nonwage resources, Ω_0. Specifically, we now have

$$\Omega_0 \equiv \frac{A(0)}{P} - \left[r\left(\frac{M}{P}\right)' + \gamma v'\right] \int_0^{\hat{N}} e^{-rt}dt$$

$$- \left[r\left(\frac{M}{P}\right)^\circ + \gamma v^\circ\right] \int_{\bar{N}}^N e^{-rt}dt - \tau \int_0^N e^{-rt}dt,$$

where

$$\frac{A(0)}{P} \equiv \frac{M(0)}{P} + \frac{P_e}{P}E(0) + \frac{P_b}{P}B(0)$$

$$= \frac{M(0)}{P} + \pi(0)\int_0^{\hat{N}} e^{-rt}dt + \pi^* \int_{\hat{N}}^\infty e^{-rt}dt + \frac{i(0)/P}{r}.$$

The asset-exhaustion condition can then be written as

$$\Omega_0' \equiv \Omega_0 + \frac{W}{P}l\int_0^{\hat{N}} e^{-rt}dt = \int_0^N c^{d'}(t)e^{-rt}dt$$

$$- \frac{W}{P}\int_{\hat{N}}^{N'} l^{s'}(t)e^{-rt}dt. \quad (3.35)$$

Condition (3.35) says that the present value of lifetime nonwage income plus the present value of wage income until date $\hat{N}$, which are now exogenous, must equal the present value of lifetime consumption less the present value of wage income from date $\hat{N}$ until date N'.

The maximization of U, given the values of $\hat{N}$, N', and N and the asset-exhaustion condition of equation (3.35), implies that the current level of $c^{d'}$ is determined by a function of the following form:[47]

$$c^{d'} = c^{d'}(\Omega_0', W/P, r). \quad (3.36)$$
$$\phantom{c^{d'} = c^{d'}(}{\scriptstyle(+)}{\scriptstyle(+)}{\scriptstyle(?)}$$

The important difference between the effective demand function of equation (3.36) and the notional demand function of equation (3.14) is that $c^{d'}$ depends on the level of employment, l, which enters through Ω_0'. Substitution of the optimal value of current $c^{d'}$ from equation (3.36)

---

[47] We again assume the inequality constraints, $[c^{d'}(t), M(t), E(t), B(t)] \geq 0$, to be ineffective and deal only with the interior solution for $c^{d'}$.

into equation (3.31) yields for working households the following expression for current effective saving demand:

$$\frac{a^{d'}}{P} = \frac{a^{d'}}{P}\left(\underset{(-)}{\Omega_0'}, \underset{(-)(?)}{\frac{W}{P}, r, \frac{W}{P}l} + \pi + \underset{(+)}{\frac{i}{P}} - \tau - \gamma v\right).$$ (3.37)

For retired households the existence of excess supply of labor services is irrelevant. Their consumption and saving demands continue to depend only on Ω_0, r, and $\pi + i/P - \tau - \gamma v$, as in section 3.2.3 above. Consequently, retired households can again be included without altering the forms of the aggregate effective consumption and saving demand functions.

Equation (3.34) specifies the effective flow demand for money as a function of $|a^{d'}/P|$, $|a^d/P|$, r, γ, and M/P. Changes in Ω_0, r, and $\pi + i/P - \tau - \gamma v$ again involve offsetting effects on $|a^{d'}/P|$ and $|a^d/P|$ from households, typically working, for whom saving is positive, and from households, typically retired, for whom saving is negative. We again ignore these ambiguous net effects. However, an increase in $(W/P)l$, like an increase in W/P in section 2.2.3 above, raises the planned after-retirement consumption of working households and so raises their current saving.[48] Consequently, because current saving is typically positive for working households, an increase in $(W/P)l$ raises $|a^{d'}/P|$. Substituting into equation (3.33), we obtain

$$\frac{m^{d'}}{P} = \frac{m^{d'}}{P}\left(\underset{(+)}{\frac{W}{P}l}, \underset{(-)(+)(-)}{r, \gamma, \frac{M}{P}}\right).$$ (3.38)

Finally, as indicated by equation (3.32), the real effective flow demand for earning assets, $f^{d'}/P$, is the difference between $a^{d'}/P$ and $m^{d'}/P$. Therefore, by subtracting equation (3.38) from equation (3.37), we obtain

$$\frac{f^{d'}}{P} = \frac{f^{d'}}{P}\left(\underset{(-)}{\Omega_0'}, \underset{(?)}{\frac{W}{P}l}, \underset{(+)(+)}{r, \frac{M}{P}}, \pi + \underset{(+)}{\frac{i}{P}} - \tau - \underset{(-)}{\gamma v, \gamma}\right).$$ (3.39)

The net effect of a change in $(W/P)l$ is ambiguous. We assume, as before, that the effect of a change in r on $m^{d'}/P$ outweighs the ambiguous effect of a change in r on $a^{d'}/P$. The direction of effect of the other variables is readily apparent.

[48] Given $(W/P)l$, an increase in W/P would reduce $|a^{d'}/P|$, but would raise future $|a^d/P|$. The net effect on $m^{d'}/P$ would be ambiguous, and we have not included W/P as a separate argument in equation (3.38).

Mathematical note

The interior solution for optimal values of $c^{d'}(t)$ satisfies the following conditions:

$$\frac{\delta u}{\delta c^{d'}(t)} = \frac{\lambda(t)}{1 + [r/2v'(t)]} \quad \text{for } 0 \leq t \leq \hat{N},$$

$$\frac{\delta u}{\delta c^{d'}(t)} = \frac{\lambda(t)}{1 + [r/2v^\circ(t)]} \quad \text{for } \hat{N} < t \leq N',$$

$$\frac{\delta u}{\delta c^{d'}(t)} = \frac{\lambda(t)}{1 - [r/2v^\circ(t)]} \quad \text{for } N' < t \leq N,$$

$$\frac{\delta u}{\delta l^s(t)} = \frac{-\lambda(t)}{1 + [r/2v^\circ(t)]} \cdot \frac{W}{P} \quad \text{for } \hat{N} < t \leq N',$$

$$\frac{d\lambda}{dt} = \frac{-\lambda(t)}{1 + [r/2v'(t)]} \cdot r \quad \text{for } 0 \leq t \leq \hat{N},$$

$$\frac{d\lambda}{dt} = \frac{-\lambda(t)}{1 + [r/2v^\circ(t)]} \cdot r \quad \text{for } \hat{N} < t \leq N', \text{ and}$$

$$\frac{d\lambda}{dt} = \frac{-\lambda(t)}{1 - [r/2v^\circ(t)]} \cdot r \quad \text{for } N' < t \leq N,$$

assuming $\hat{N} < N'$, $a^{d'}(t) \geq 0$ for $0 \leq t \leq \hat{N}$, $a^d(t) \geq 0$ for $\hat{N} < t \leq \hat{N}'$, and $a^d(t) \leq 0$ for $N' < t \leq N$. The constant $\lambda(0)$ is determined so as to satisfy equation (3.35).

3.4.3 The determination of output, employment and the rate of return under general excess supply

This section considers the determination of the levels of output, employment, and the rate of return under the assumption that the existing wage-price vector implies excess supply for both labor services and commodities. As in chapter 2, a range of wage-price vectors can have this implication, including the vector $[(W/P)^*, P_1]$, where $P_1 > P^*$, which was the example used in chapter 2. This section does not focus on any particular wage-price vector, but in order to concentrate on quantity determination, we do take W and P to be fixed throughout the discussion.

With excess supply for both labor services and commodities, output and employment, as in chapter 2, are determined by the effective demands in the respective markets – that is,

$$l = l^{d'} \underset{(+)(-)(-)}{(y, g, K)} < l^s(\Omega_0, W/P, r), \text{ and} \tag{3.40}$$

$$y = k^{d'} \underset{(+)(-)(-)(+)(-)}{\left(y, g, r, \frac{W}{P}, K\right)} + c^{d'} \underset{(+)\ (+)\ (?)}{\left(\Omega'_0, \frac{W}{P}, r\right)}$$

$$+ \gamma v + g^d < y^s \left(\frac{W}{P}, g, K\right). \tag{3.41}$$

In accord with the above discussion of firm and household behavior, we assume that the financial asset market always clears. Given the effective demand for earning assets and the effective supply of equity, this market-clearing condition is

$$\frac{f^{d'}}{P} \underset{(-)\ \ (?)\ \ (+)(+)}{\left(\Omega'_0, \frac{W}{P} l, r, \frac{M}{P}, \underset{(+)}{\pi + \frac{i}{P}} - \underset{(-)}{\tau - \gamma v}, \gamma\right)}$$

$$= k^{d'} \underset{(+)(-)(-)(+)(-)}{\left(y, g, r, \frac{W}{P}, K\right)} + \frac{P_b}{P} b^s = \frac{f}{P}. \tag{3.42}$$

To simplify the notation, we denote aggregate effective commodity demand by $y^{d'}$ – that is, $y^{d'} \equiv k^{d'} + c^{d'} + \gamma v + g^d$ – and we denote aggregate effective earning asset supply by $f^{s'}/P$ – that is, $f^{s'}/P \equiv k^{d'} + P_b b^s/P$.

Given the exogenous and predetermined variables – $W, P, g^d, \tau, P_b b^s/P, K, E, M, B, i, \gamma,$ and v – and given the definitions of Ω'_0 and π, conditions (3.40–3.42) comprise a system of three equations involving the three endogenous variables – $l, y,$ and r. The analysis of the determination of $l, y,$ and r is facilitated by observing that, for a given K, condition (3.40) provides a simple relation between l and y. Substituting this relation into conditions (3.41) and (3.42) reduces the system to a set of two equations involving only y and r. Substituting for Ω'_0 from equation (3.35) and for π from the relation $\pi = y - (W/P)l$, and suppressing the exogenous variables, we obtain a simplified expression of these two equations:

$$y = y^{d'} \underset{(+)(-)}{(y, r)} \quad \text{and} \tag{3.43}$$

$$\frac{f^{d'}}{P} \underset{(?)\ (+)}{(y, r)} = \frac{f^{s'}}{P} \underset{(+)(-)}{(y, r)}. \tag{3.44}$$

The principal new consideration here involves the effect on $y^{d'}$ and $f^{d'}/P$ of a change in y. Consider the effect of an increase in y on Ω_0' as defined in equation (3.35). The expression for Ω_0' involves the sum of discounted wage income and profit income from date 0 to date $\hat{N}$. Given that $y = \pi + (W/P)l$, the marginal effect of y on Ω_0', on this account, is positive and is given by

$$\frac{\delta\Omega_0'}{\delta y} = \int_0^{\hat{N}} e^{-rt}dt.$$

An increase in y, to the extent that it involves an increase in $(W/P)l$, also raises $(M/P)'$ and v'. These changes represent an offset, which is presumably minor, to the positive effect of the increase in y on Ω_0'. Because an increase in y, given r, increases Ω_0', it also raises $c^{d'}$. Moreover, the full effect of an increase in y, given r, in raising $y^{d'}$ also includes the effect of an increase in y in raising $k^{d'}$.

An increase in y would also raise $a^{d'}/P$ as long as $c^{d'}$ rises less than one-to-one with y. However, to the extent that the increase in y involves an increase in $(W/P)l$, $m^{d'}/P$ also increases. Consequently, the full effect of a change in y on $f^{d'}/P$ is ambiguous.

Analogous to the notional demand functions, the effects of a change in r on $y^{d'}$ and $f^{d'}/P$ involve both the substitution and wealth effects for a given Ω_0' indicated in conditions (3.41–3.42) and the additional wealth effect involving the inverse relation between Ω_0' and r. Assuming, as before, that the substitution effect outweighs the ambiguous net wealth effect, an increase in r, given y, reduces $c^{d'}$ and raises $a^{d'}/P$. Hence, an increase in r reduces $y^{d'}$ and raises $f^{d'}/P$.

Again, the economy-wide budget constraint is of interest. By combining the momentary household budget constraint,

$$c^{d'} + \gamma v + \frac{f^{d'}}{P} + \frac{m^{d'}}{P} + \tau = \frac{W}{P}l + \pi + \frac{i}{P},$$

the firm financing constraint,

$$k^{d'} = \frac{P_e}{P}e^{s'},$$

the government budget constraint,

$$\tau = g^d + \frac{i}{P} - \frac{P_b}{P}b^s - \frac{m^s}{P},$$

and the definition of profits,

$$\pi = y - \frac{W}{P}l^{d'},$$

we obtain

$$(y^{d'} - y) + \frac{W}{P}(l^{d'} - l) + \frac{1}{P}(f^{d'} - f^{s'}) + \frac{1}{P}(m^{d'} - m^{s}) = 0.$$

$$(3.45)$$

Assuming that equation (3.40), $l^{d'} = l$, is satisfied, equation (3.45) implies that the combination of y and r which satisfies equations (3.43–3.44) also satisfies

$$\frac{m^{d'}}{P}\underset{(+)(-)}{(y, r)} = \frac{m^{s}}{P}.$$

$$(3.46)$$

From equation (3.38), we write $m^{d'}/P$ as an increasing function of y, given r, because an increase in $(W/P)l$ implies an increase in y.

Figure 3.7 provides a diagrammatic representation of equations (3.43), (3.44), and (3.46). The ($>$, $<$) signs on either side of the loci in

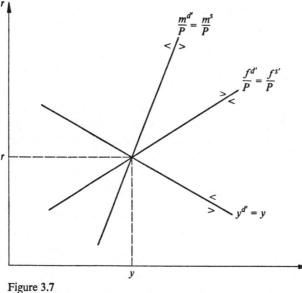

Figure 3.7
Output and the rate of return with excess supply of commodities and labor services

this diagram have the usual meaning in identifying the nature of the regions separated by the loci. The locus labeled $y^{d'} = y$ depicts combinations of values of y and r which are consistent with equation (3.43), given the values of W, P, and the other exogenous and predetermined variables.[49] To determine the slope of this locus consider the following thought experiment. Suppose that equation (3.43) was initially satisfied, but that r was then increased. The result would be a decrease in $y^{d'}$ which would cause output to exceed effective commodity demand. What change in y would reestablish the equality between $y^{d'}$ and y? A sufficient decrease in y would reduce y to $y^{d'}$ unless the effect of reducing y on $y^{d'}$ – through the effects of y on $k^{d'}$ and $c^{d'}$ – were greater than or equal to one-to-one. In the subsequent analysis we assume that $\delta y^{d'}/\delta y < 1$.[50] This assumption insures that the $y^{d'} = y$ locus is downward sloping.[51]

The locus labeled $f^{d'}/P = f^{s'}/P$ depicts combinations of values of y and r which are consistent with the financial asset market-clearing condition of equation (3.44). To determine the slope of this locus, consider another thought experiment. Suppose that equation (3.44) was initially satisfied, but that y was then increased. The result would be an increase in $f^{s'}/P$ and an ambiguous movement in $f^{d'}/P$. Assuming that the increase in $f^{s'}/P$ is dominant, an increase in r would be required to cause $f^{d'}/P$ to rise and $f^{s'}/P$ to decline. Thus, the earning-asset market-clearing locus is upward sloping.

To facilitate the analysis, figure 3.7 also includes the locus labeled $m^{d'}/P = m^s/P$, which depicts combinations of values of y and r which are consistent with equality between the effective flow demand and the flow supply of money balances. This locus is upward sloping because an increase in r would require an increase in y in order to keep $m^{d'}/P$ unchanged. The economy-wide budget constraint, equation (3.45), also implies that the locus $m^{d'}/P = m^s/P$ must pass through the intersection of the other two loci, and that it must be either in the region of $y^{d'} > y$ and $f^{d'}/P < f^{s'}/P$ or in the region of $y^{d'} < y$ and $f^{d'}/P > f^{s'}/P$.

[49] This locus corresponds to the conventional *I–S* curve. To establish this correspondence, note that the household's budget equation and the definition of profit imply, assuming $l = l^{d'}$,

$$y - c^{d'} - \gamma v = a^{d'}/P + \tau - i/P.$$

Therefore, equation (3.43) is equivalent to the condition

$$a^{d'}/P + \tau = k^{d'} + g^d + i/P.$$

[50] The marginal effects of y on both $c^{d'}$ and $k^{d'}$ are both increasing functions of $\hat{N}$. A sufficiently small value of $\hat{N}$ would insure $\delta y^{d'}/\delta y < 1$.

[51] An upward sloping $y^{d'} = y^s$ locus might create some problems for dynamic stability, depending on the specification of the $f^{d'}/P = f^{s'}/P$ locus and on the specific form of dynamic adjustment. For example, the dynamic system, $dy/dt = \lambda_y(y^{d'} - y)$ and $dr/dt = \lambda_r(f^{s'}/P - f^{d'}/P)$, would be dynamically stable if the slope of the $y^{d'} = y$ locus is less than the slope of the $f^{d'}/P = f^{s'}/P$ locus.

Consequently, the locus $m^{d'}/P = m^s/P$ must be more steeply sloped than the locus $f^{d'}/P = f^{s'}/P$.[52]

The intersection of the three loci identifies the single combination of y and r which is simultaneously consistent with equations (3.43), (3.44), and (3.46). At this combination of y and r, output will equal aggregate effective commodity demand and the financial asset market will be clearing. The effective flow demand for money balances will also be equal to the flow supply. As we noted above, the level of employment can be determined by substituting the value of y into the effective labor demand function, according to equation (3.40). Finally, we can determine the amount of investment by substituting the values of y and r into the $k^{d'}$ function of equations (3.29) and (3.41).

3.4.4 Comparative-statics analysis under general excess supply

In this context, comparative-statics analysis is concerned with the effects of exogenous disturbances on the values of the endogenous variables which satisfy conditions (3.43), (3.44), and (3.46). We shall focus here on the effects of shifts in fiscal and monetary policy on y and r. Note that figure 3.7, which provides a diagrammatic framework for the present analysis, corresponds to figure 3.1, which depicted the general-market-clearing situation, with the exception that the horizontal axis now measures y rather than P. Thus, the form of the present analysis corresponds closely to the form of the comparative-statics analysis under general-market-clearing conditions which was discussed above.

First, consider a shift toward a more expansionary fiscal policy, involving a reduction in τ and a corresponding increase in $P_b b^s/P$. The initial effects of this disturbance will be to raise Ω_0' and shift the $y^{d'} = y$ locus to the right, [53] to leave the $m^{d'}/P = m^s/P$ locus unchanged, and to shift the $f^{d'}/P = f^{s'}/P$ locus on net to the left. As a result of these shifts, these loci will now intersect at higher levels of both y and r. The higher r

---

[52] Although the $m^{d'}/P = m^s/P$ locus has the same slope as the conventional
L–M curve, which corresponds to the equation of $(M/P)'$ to M/P,
these loci differ in position as long as $m^s/P \neq 0$. However, the larger
the value of λ_m' in equation (3.33), the smaller this difference in position.
Also, as λ_m' becomes larger, the $f^{d'}/P = f^{s'}/P$ locus approaches
coincidence with the $m^{d'}/P = m^s/P$ locus.

[53] As in the general-market-clearing case, the present analysis of fiscal
policy assumes that the representative household does not take account
of the implications of an increase in $P_b b^s/P$ for future interest payments
and taxes. If the representative household did take these implications
fully into account and if its horizon for capitalization of future taxes
were infinite, 'expansionary' fiscal policy would have no effect on
Ω_0' and, hence, would also have no impact on y and r.

reflects the increase in bond supply which was required to balance the reduction in tax receipts. This higher r tends to offset the stimulus to $y^{d'}$ produced by the reduction in τ, and thereby moderates the net increase in y. The more steeply sloped is the $m^{d'}/P = m^s/P$ locus, the more will r increase and the less will y increase.

If r were fixed, the determination of y would result from a multiplier process similar to that analyzed in section 2.2. Specifically, in the present case, the gross demand multiplier would be equal to $1/(1 - \delta y^{d'}/\delta y)$. However, because r increases, the net change in y is smaller than the amount given by this gross demand multiplier. Specifically, the net increase in y may be larger or smaller than the decrease in τ – that is, the net demand multiplier may be greater or less than unity.

Because y increases, with g^d and γv unchanged, the sum of $c^{d'}$ plus $k^{d'}$ must also increase. However, because r also increases, the relative size of the increases in $c^{d'}$ and $k^{d'}$ is ambiguous. Possibly, either one of them might even decline. Finally, the increase in y, given g and K, implies an increase in $l^{d'}$ and l, according to equation (3.40).

The tendency for an increase in r to dampen the effects of expansionary fiscal policy on y is the basis for the so-called 'Treasury View' position. This position, which chronically arises in public discussions, holds that active fiscal policy alone cannot cause an increase in aggregate commodity demand and output (even with excess supply in the commodity market), because the financing of a reduction in taxes or an increase in government expenditure drives up the rate of return, with the effect of offsetting the apparent direct effects of fiscal policy on aggregate commodity demand. From figure 3.7, it is clear that for this position to be valid the $m^{d'}/P = m^s/P$ locus would have to be vertical. In other words, the partial derivative $\delta(m^{d'}/P)/\delta r$ would have to be zero, so that an increase in r would not stimulate the conversion of wealth from money balances into earning assets. Thus, in our model, r cannot rise sufficiently to offset completely the effects of an active fiscal policy on y. It is worth noting that analogous considerations also arise in the general-market-clearing context. If the $m^d/P = m^s/P$ locus in figure 3.1 were vertical, reflecting $\delta(m^d/P)/\delta r = 0$, then a more expansionary fiscal policy would not affect P^* either.

The above analysis again deals only with the initial effects associated with the initial change in flows. Over time, the induced increases in B, i, and v' would also become relevant. The analysis of the effects of these shifts again corresponds to the analysis in the general-market-clearing context. The reader can work out the details for himself, noting that figure 3.3, which depicts time paths of τ, P^*, and r^*, remains applicable, but with y and r replacing P^* and r^*.

Next consider a shift toward a more expansionary monetary policy, involving an increase in m^s/P and a corresponding decrease in $P_b b^s/P$. The initial effects of this disturbance will be to shift the $f^{d'}/P = f^{s'}/P$ locus to the right, to shift the $m^{d'}/P = m^s/P$ locus to the right and to leave the $y^{d'} = y$ locus in place.[54] As a result of these shifts, these loci now intersect at a higher level of y and a lower level of r. In this case, the reduction in $P_b b^s/P$ depresses r, which, in turn, raises $y^{d'}$ and leads to an increase in y. Again, because y has increased, the sum of $c^{d'}$ plus $k^{d'}$ must increase. Moreover, because r has declined, in contrast to the case of expansionary fiscal policy, we can now be sure that both $k^{d'}$ and $c^{d'}$ have increased. Over time, the induced increase in M and the induced decreases in B, i, and v' reinforce these initial effects, as in the general-market-clearing case. Section 6.1 below analyzes the exact form of the time paths of y and r implied by a specific time path of M and B.

Finally, the opposite of the extreme 'Treasury View' position, discussed above, is the 'liquidity trap' case.[55] In the liquidity trap, the partial derivative $\delta(m^{d'}/P)/\delta r$ is extremely large, so that the $m^{d'}/P = m^s/P$ locus is horizontal. In this hypothetical situation, a shift in monetary policy would not affect r, and changes in y would result solely from the effect on Ω_0' of the changes over time in M, B, and i.

[54] This result is again based on the assumption that the representative household does not take account of the implications of a change in $P_b b^s/P$ for future values of τ.

[55] Keynes (1936) mentioned the liquidity trap as a possible theoretical hypothesis, but the empirical evidence has led to its rejection. See Laidler (1969). See also the discussion of speculative demand for money in Section 6.3.3 below.

4 *Inflation and rates of return*

This chapter introduces into the analytical framework
expectations of nonzero rates of price and wage change and
focuses on one important implication of these expectations–
the divergence between the nominal and the real rate of return.
Section 4.1 explains these two rate-of-return concepts. Section
4.2 analyzes how inflationary or deflationary expectations
affect firm and household behavior. Section 4.3 analyzes the
comparative-statics implications of shifts in these expectations.
Section 4.4 develops a dynamic analysis of the interplay between
inflation, expected inflation, and rates of return.

4.1   Rates of return and expected rates of price and wage change

In chapter 3 we analyzed the determination of the values of the endogenous variables – including the levels of output, employment, the wage
rate, the price of commodities, and the rate of return – which would be
consistent with general-market-clearing conditions. The analysis focused
on exogenous disturbances which would alter the general-market-
clearing vector of wages and prices and, consequently, would result in
corresponding changes in actual wages and prices. However, despite the
existence of these disturbances, the analysis in chapter 3, like the analysis
in chapters 1 and 2, assumed that firms and households, in attempting to
maximize profits and utility, took P, W and r to be constant over time.

By taking P and W, in particular, to be constant, firms and
households made their plans as if nominal and real rates of return were
equivalent. Assuming i/B and P_b to be constant, the anticipated rate of
return on bonds was $r = r_b = i/P_bB$, and, assuming $P\pi/P_eE$ and P_e to
be constant, the anticipated rate of return on equity was $r = r_e = P\pi/P_eE$.
The variable r represented both the anticipated real and the anticipated
nominal rates of return on earning assets. The main purpose of the
present chapter is to relax the assumption that firms and households
take P and W to be constant over time and, thus, that they take nominal
and real rates of return to be equivalent. To facilitate the discussion, let
the lower case r now denote only real rates of return, and let the upper
case R denote nominal rates of return.

Consider first the specification of the anticipated nominal
rates of return on earning assets, R_b and R_e. The variable R_b [R_e] represents the implied discount rate at which the present value of the expected
future stream of nominal interest payments per bond [nominal dividend

payments per share] equals the current nominal asset price, $P_b(0)[P_e(0)]$. Given that the representative household regards equity and bonds as perfect substitutes, we must have $R_b = R_e = R$. Continue to assume that the representative household expects π/E and R to be constant over time, but assume that it expects P to change over time at the constant proportionate rate ρ. Consequently, the representative household anticipates that the time path of prices will be

$$P(t) = P(0)e^{\rho t}.$$

Under these conditions, the anticipated nominal rate of return on earning assets satisfies the following two relations:

$$P_b(0) \equiv \frac{i}{B} \int_0^\infty e^{-Rt}dt \quad \text{and}$$

$$P_e(0) \equiv \frac{\pi}{E} \int_0^\infty P(t)e^{-Rt}dt.$$

Solving these two relations yields

$$R \equiv \frac{i}{P_b(0)B} \equiv \frac{P(0)\pi}{P_e(0)E} + \rho.$$

The specification of R implies, given anticipated constancy of π/E and R, that the representative household expects P_b to be constant over time, and that it expects the proportionate rate of change of equity prices to be equal to ρ. Thus, i/P_bB still measures the nominal rate of return on bonds, but $P\pi/P_eE$ no longer measures the nominal rate of return on equity. Because real dividends per share, π/E, are constant, nominal dividends per share increase with commodity prices. The nominal rate of return on equity equals $P\pi/P_eE$ plus the anticipated rate of capital gain, which is equal to the anticipated rate of increase of commodity prices.

Consider now the specification of the anticipated real rates of return on earning assets, r_b and r_e. The variable r_b [r_e] represents the implied discount rate at which the present value of the expected future stream of real interest payments per bond [real dividend payments per share] equals the current real asset price, $P_b(0)/P(0)$ [$P_e(0)/P(0)$]. Perfect substitutability between equity and bonds implies $r_b = r_e = r$. Given anticipated constancy of π/E, r, and ρ, r satisfies the following two relations:

$$\frac{P_b(0)}{P(0)} \equiv \frac{i}{B} \int_0^\infty \frac{1}{P(t)} e^{-rt}\, dt \quad \text{and}$$

$$\frac{P_e(0)}{P(0)} \equiv \frac{\pi}{E} \int_0^\infty e^{-rt}dt.$$

Solving these two relations yields

$$r \equiv \frac{i}{P_b(0)B} - \rho \equiv \frac{P(0)\pi}{P_e(0)E} \equiv R - \rho.$$

The anticipated real rate of return equals the anticipated nominal rate of return minus the anticipated rate of inflation. $P\pi/P_eE$ now measures the real rate of return on equity. However, because nominal interest payments per bond, i/B, are constant, real interest payments decrease with an increase in commodity prices. Thus, the anticipated real rate of return on bonds equals i/P_bB minus the anticipated rate of inflation.[1]

Finally, consider the rate of return on money. In chapters 1, 2, and 3, both the anticipated real and nominal rates of return on money were zero. In this chapter, we still assume that the nominal rate of return on money equals zero. However, this assumption now implies that the anticipated real rate of return on money is $-\rho$.

4.2   Expected price changes and firm and household behavior

This section analyzes how inflationary and deflationary expectations affect the behavior of firms and households. The analysis shows that, given the specification that firms do not incur transactions costs and, hence, do not hold money, the behavior of firms is independent of price change expectations. In other words, equations (3.1–3.4) and (3.28–3.30) of chapter 3 continue to describe labor demand, output supply, invest-ment demand, and equity supply, under market-clearing and general-excess-supply conditions, respectively, with the variable r representing the real rate of return. In contrast, the analysis shows that inflationary and deflationary expectations do have significant effects on household behavior. The most important aspect of these effects involves household evaluation of real wealth and household evaluation of the differential between the rates of return on financial assets and money. Finally, government behavior remains subject to the government budget con-straint, equation (3.19), specified in chapter 3.

In the interest of brevity, we limit consideration to the frame-work in which exchange takes place only under general-market-clearing

---

[1] Note that, although ρ is not a directly observable variable, we can infer its value by subtracting the real rate of return, $r \equiv P\pi/P_eE$, from the nominal rate of return, $R \equiv i/P_bB$. In practice, differences between the rates of return on equity and bonds involve other considerations in addition to expectations of price change, such as expectations about future real profits per share and risk factors.

conditions. Under conditions of excess supply or excess demand, the implied modifications of household behavior are basically similar. The analysis of the general-market-clearing case should enable the reader to work out the implications under non-market-clearing conditions.

4.2.1 The behavior of firms

In chapter 3, the objective of the representative firm was to maximize the market price of its equity shares. Now, although individual firms and households continue to regard P as exogenous, they do not necessarily anticipate P to be constant over time. Consequently, it is useful now to specify the firm's objective in real terms – that is, to maximize the ratio P_e/P. Given the definition of the real rate of return r, maximizing P_e/P is equivalent to maximizing π/Er. Because the representative firm regards r as exogenous, maximizing P_e/P then amounts to maximizing, as in chapter 3, real profits per share, π/E.

Given the definition of real profits as $\pi = y - (W/P)l$, and the assumed production function, $y = \Phi(l, g, K)$ of chapter 3, the maximization of short-run real profit per share – with K and E fixed – implies the same labor demand and output supply behavior as derived in chapter 3. Specifically, under general-market-clearing conditions, we have

$$l^d = l^d \underset{(-)}{\left(\frac{W}{P}\right)} \quad \text{and} \tag{3.1}$$

$$y^s = y^s \underset{(-)\,(+)(+)}{\left(\frac{W}{P}, g, K\right)}. \tag{3.2}$$

Turning to the long run, maximization of π/E involves choosing optimal time paths for K and E. Assuming that the representative firm regards r as constant over time, and given the assumed adjustment costs of chapter 3, optimal investment demand and equity supply behavior is also the same as that derived in chapter 3. Specifically, under general-market-clearing conditions, we have

$$k^d = \frac{P_e}{P} e^s = \underset{(-)(-)}{k^d(r, K)}. \tag{3.3, 3.4}$$

In sum, firm behavior continues to depend only on the predetermined real stock K, on the real exchange ratio W/P, and on the real rate of return r. In this model, the expected rate of price change does not affect the behavior of firms.[2]

The key to this independence is the assumption that firms do not incur transaction costs either in paying wages or dividends, in selling commodities or equity shares, or in buying new capital goods, and, hence, have no motivation to hold money. Because firms do not hold money, anticipated changes in the real value of money, as determined by the value of ρ, have no effect on firm behavior. Alternatively, if firms did hold money, the expected rate of price change would affect their behavior. The nature of this effect, however, would be very similar to the effect of ρ on household behavior, as analyzed below. Thus, for simplicity, we continue to assume that firms do not hold money.

4.2.2 *The behavior of households: optimal transactions frequency and money holding*

The objective of households continues to be to maximize utility as given by

$$U = \int_0^N u[\underset{(+)}{c^d(t)}, \underset{(-)}{l^s(t)}] \, dt.$$

An essential effect of the expectation of changes over time in P and P_e is to create a divergence between the representative household's saving and the anticipated rate of change in its real asset holdings. Again, saving is defined as the nominal value of the flow of assets, $a \equiv m + P_e e + P_b b$, so that, as in chapter 3, the real amount of planned saving for working households is

$$\frac{a^d}{P} = \frac{W}{P} l^s + \pi + \frac{i}{P} - \tau - c^d - \gamma v. \tag{3.5}$$

The anticipated rate of change in real asset holdings, which we denote by

$$\left[\frac{d(A/P)}{dt} \right]^d \equiv \left(\frac{a}{P} \right)^d,$$

now includes the real amount of saving plus anticipated changes in the real value of existing asset holdings due to expected changes in P and P_e.

---

[2] If we had not assumed $\Phi_{lK} = 0$, the target capital stock, K°, would depend on W/P. In that case, the optimal adjustment of K, which determines k^d, would involve both current and expected future values of W/P. However, if the representative firm anticipated that the relative rate of change of W and P were independent of the rate of change of commodity prices, ρ, the firm's behavior would still not depend on ρ.

Given the nominal stock of money balances M, the expected rate of change in its real value, $d(M/P)/dt$, is given by $-\rho M/P$. Thus, when ρ is positive, the expected depreciation of the real value of money holdings adds a negative term to the anticipated change in real asset holdings. Similarly, given the nominal stock of bonds $P_b B = i/(r + \rho)$, the expected rate of change in its real value, $d(P_b B/P)/dt$, is given by $-\rho(P_b B/P)$. Finally, given the real stock of equity, $P_e E/P = \pi/r$, the expected change in its real value is zero, because P and P_e are expected to change at the same rate, ρ. Thus, the anticipated rate of change in real asset holdings is[3]

$$\left[\frac{d(A/P)}{dt}\right]^d \equiv \left(\frac{a}{P}\right)^d = \frac{a^d}{P} - \rho\left(\frac{M}{P} + \frac{P_b B}{P}\right)$$

$$= \frac{W}{P} l^s + r\left(\frac{A}{P} - \frac{M}{P}\right) - \rho\frac{M}{P} - \tau - c^d - \gamma v. \quad (4.1)$$

The anticipated rate of change in real asset holdings can be used to accumulate either shares, bonds, or money. However, in the case of each of these assets, the anticipated change in real holdings now equals the sum of the real value of the nominal flow plus the anticipated effect of price changes on the real value of existing nominal holdings. Given the definitions,

$$\left(\frac{P_b}{P} b\right)^d \equiv \frac{P_b}{P} b^d - \rho\frac{P_b B}{P},$$

$$\left(\frac{m}{P}\right)^d \equiv \frac{m^d}{P} - \rho\frac{M}{P}, \quad \text{and}$$

$$\frac{f^d}{P} \equiv \frac{P_e}{P} e^d + \frac{P_b}{P} b^d,$$

we have

$$\left(\frac{a}{P}\right)^d = \frac{P_e}{P} e^d + \left(\frac{P_b}{P} b\right)^d + \left(\frac{m}{P}\right)^d = \frac{f^d}{P} + \frac{m^d}{P} - \rho\left(\frac{M}{P} + \frac{P_b B}{P}\right).$$

$$(4.2)$$

[3] An alternative procedure would be to redefine saving as net changes in the real value of existing asset holdings. Specifically, given that the representative household expects π/E, r, and ρ to be constant over time, this procedure would specify anticipated disposable income as $\frac{W}{P} l^s + \pi + \frac{i}{P} - \tau - \rho\left(\frac{M}{P} + \frac{P_b}{P} B\right)$, and would specify the real amount of planned saving as $(a/P)^d$, rather than as a^d/P. These alternative definitions would not alter any of the substantive conclusions reached in the analysis which follows.

Equations (4.1) and (4.2) represent a generalization of equations (3.5) and (3.6), the two formulations being equivalent when $\rho = 0$.

As in chapter 3, the household accumulates savings first as money, and then makes periodic purchases of earning assets. Given this pattern, the representative working household's average real money balance still equals $(a^d/P)/2v$, where v measures the frequency of transactions.[4] However, given that prices are expected to change at the proportionate rate ρ, the amount of real income foregone by holding money is now

$$(r + \rho)\frac{a^d/P}{2v} = R\frac{a^d/P}{2v}.$$

The opportunity cost involved in holding money equals the difference between the anticipated real rate of return on earning assets, r, and the anticipated real rate of return on money, $-\rho$. This cost may be measured equivalently as the difference between the anticipated nominal rate of return on earnings assets, R, and the zero nominal rate of return on money. Consequently, given a^d/P, the target value $v°$ will now be chosen to minimize the sum

$$(r + \rho)\frac{a^d/P}{2v} + \gamma v,$$

which requires setting

$$v° = \left[\frac{(r + \rho)a^d/P}{2\gamma}\right]^{1/2}. \tag{4.3}$$

The target average real money balance is then

$$\left(\frac{M}{P}\right)° = \left[\frac{\gamma a^d/P}{2(r + \rho)}\right]^{1/2}. \tag{4.4}$$

Equations (4.3) and (4.4) correspond to equations (3.7) and (3.8), with the exception that $r + \rho$ now replaces r.[5]

---

[4] The calculation of the average real money balance as $(a^d/P)/2v$ neglects the effect of inflation on the real value of money which is accumulated over the period $1/v$. In terms of the calculations of income foregone from holding money, this approximation is analogous to neglecting the compounding of interest over the interval $1/v$. The overall approximation is satisfactory as long as $(r + \rho)/v$ is much less unity.

[5] The specification in equation (4.4) that $(M/P)°$ depends only on the nominal rate of return, $r + \rho = R$, requires the assumption that transactions costs are incurred only in buying and selling earning assets. Alternatively, if transaction costs were incurred in buying

The choice of $v°$ and $(M/P)°$ by retired households again corresponds to the choice by working households, but with a^d/P, when it is negative, replaced by its absolute value. Thus, taking working and retired households together, the aggregate target transactions frequency and aggregate target money holding functions have the form

$$v° = v° \, (\underset{(+)}{|a^d/P|}, \underset{(+)}{r + \rho}, \underset{(-)}{\gamma}), \quad \text{and} \tag{4.5}$$

$$\left(\frac{M}{P}\right)° = \left(\frac{M}{P}\right)° (\underset{(+)}{|a^d/P|}, \underset{(-)}{r + \rho}, \underset{(+)}{\gamma}), \tag{4.6}$$

where $|a^d/P|$ again represents the aggregate of absolute saving flows. Equations (4.5) and (4.6) correspond to equations (3.9) and (3.10), but with $r + \rho$ again replacing r.

We assume that desired adjustment of average v toward the average value of $v°$ again corresponds to the simple gradual-adjustment relation given by equation (3.11). For the flow demand for money balances, we again assume that, in aggregate, the desired adjustment of actual real money holdings toward $(M/P)°$ also conforms to a linear gradual adjustment relation. However, as was indicated above, the anticipated change in real money holdings now includes the anticipated effect of price changes on the real value of existing nominal money holdings as well as the real value of the nominal money flow. In other words, we have

$$\left[\frac{d(M/P)}{dt}\right]^d \equiv \left(\frac{m}{P}\right)^d = \frac{m^d}{P} - \rho\frac{M}{P}.$$

Consequently, the assumption

$$\left(\frac{m}{P}\right)^d = \lambda_m\left[\left(\frac{M}{P}\right)° - \frac{M}{P}\right] = \left(\frac{m}{P}\right)^d \left(\underset{(+)}{|a^d/P|}, \underset{(-)}{r + \rho}, \underset{(+)}{\gamma}, \underset{(-)}{\frac{M}{P}}\right)$$

also implies

$$\tag{4.7}$$

$$\frac{m^d}{P} = \lambda_m\left[\left(\frac{M}{P}\right)° - \frac{M}{P}\right] + \rho\frac{M}{P}.$$

Equation (3.12) now appears as a special case of equation (4.7), applicable when $\rho = 0$.

---

commodities, and commodities were storable, then $(M/P)°$ would also depend separately on ρ, which, neglecting storage costs, would represent the difference between the rates of return on money and commodities. For an explicit consideration of commodity inventories in this context, see Feige and Parkin (1971) and Santomero (1974).

4.2.3 The behavior of households: labor supply, consumption demand, and saving

Having considered the effect of expected changes over time in P on the optimal disposition of the household's given saving flow, we now consider the effect of such expectations on the primary choice of optimal flows of labor services, consumption, and saving. Optimal behavior again implies the exhaustion of asset holdings at date N. The specification of the anticipated rate of change of real asset holdings in equation (4.1) now represents the relevant first-order differential equation in A/P. The solution to this equation determines the planned amount of real asset holding at any point in time. Specifically, assuming that the representative household takes r, ρ, W/P, and τ to be constant over time,[6] that it also treats $(M/P)^\circ$ and v° as constant over time, and that it treats M/P and v as equal to $(M/P)^\circ$ and v° at all future times, the solution for real asset holdings at date N is

$$\frac{A}{P}(N) = \frac{A}{P}(0)\, e^{rN} + \frac{W}{P} \int_0^{N'} l^s(t) e^{r(N-t)}\, dt$$

$$- \int_0^N [\tau + c^d(t) + (r+\rho)\left(\frac{M}{P}\right)^\circ + \gamma v^\circ]\, e^{r(N-t)}\, dt.$$

The assumption that the representative household takes W/P to be constant over time implies that it expects the proportionate rate of change of wages, $(1/W)(dW/dt)$, to be equal to the proportionate rate of change of prices, ρ.

The asset-exhaustion condition, $(A/P)(N) = 0$, can, as in chapter 3, be expressed in present value terms by multiplying through the above expression for $(A/P)(N)$ by e^{-rN}. After rearranging terms, we obtain

$$\Omega_0 \equiv \frac{A}{P}(0) - [\tau + (r+\rho)\left(\frac{M}{P}\right)^\circ + \gamma v^\circ] \int_0^N e^{-rt}dt$$

$$= \int_0^N c^d(t) e^{-rt} dt - \frac{W}{P} \int_0^{N'} l^s(t) e^{-rt}\, dt, \tag{4.8}$$

---

[6] In assuming that the representative household expects τ to be constant over time, we are assuming that the representative household does not take account of the effect of the anticipated change in the price level on the government's budget constraint. Specifically, the representative household ignores the fact that, given B and i, an increase in P would reduce i/P, and that, given g^d, m^s/P, and $P_b b^s/P$, a reduction in i/P would imply a reduction in τ. This treatment of household behavior accords with the treatment in section 3.3.3, where we assumed that the representative household ignored the possible effect of current government borrowing on future taxes.

where $\dfrac{A}{P}(0) \equiv \dfrac{M}{P}(0) + \dfrac{P_e}{P} E(0) + \dfrac{P_b B}{P}(0)$

$$\equiv \dfrac{M}{P}(0) + \pi(0)/r + \dfrac{i}{P}(0)/R.$$

Equation (4.8) represents a generalization of the asset-exhaustion condition of chapter 3, equation (3.13). Equation (3.13) now appears as a special case, applicable when $\rho = 0$.

The phenomenon of central interest here is the effect of the level of ρ on the present value of lifetime nonwage resources, Ω_0. It will be useful to consider two separate cases: in one, the real rate of return, r, is held constant, so that the nominal rate of return R increases with an increase in ρ; in the other case, R is held constant, so that r decreases with an increase in ρ. With r held constant, an increase in ρ, and hence in R, has two effects on Ω_0. First, an increase in ρ and R depresses the value of the outstanding stock of bonds, and thereby tends to reduce Ω_0.[7] Second, an increase in ρ and R raises the opportunity cost of the average real money balance, lowers the optimal real money balance, and raises the optimal transactions frequency. This second effect also involves a net inverse relation between ρ and Ω_0, because, from equations (4.3) and (4.4), the elasticity of the sum, $(r + \rho) (M/P)^\circ + \gamma v^\circ$, with respect to $r + \rho$ is positive and equal to one-half. Thus, through both effects, given r, an increase in ρ implies a decrease in Ω_0. An exact relation between Ω_0 and ρ can be obtained by differentiating Ω_0, as given in equation (4.8), with respect to ρ, holding r constant, yielding

$$\left.\dfrac{\delta\Omega_0}{\delta\rho}\right|_{dr=0} = -\dfrac{i/P}{(r + \rho)^2} - \left(\dfrac{M}{P}\right)^\circ \int_0^N e^{-rt}\,dt < 0. \qquad (4.8.1)$$

In the alternative case where R is held constant, an increase in ρ, and the consequent decrease in r, again have two effects on Ω_0. First, the increase in ρ and decrease in r raise the value of the outstanding stock of equity. Second, the increase in ρ and decrease in r raise the present value of the liability term which includes taxes, income foregone by holding money, and transactions cost. (With R constant, the streams to be discounted – $R(M/P)^\circ$ and γv° – are unchanged.) Thus, the first effect tends to raise Ω_0 and the second effect tends to reduce Ω_0. The net result depends on the size of π relative to the sum, $\tau + R(M/P)^\circ + \gamma v^\circ$, and on the size of N. The larger is π, the larger is the first effect. The larger is either $\tau + R(M/P)^\circ + \gamma v^\circ$ or N, the larger is the second effect.

[7] This effect on Ω_0 would be offset if the representative household took account of the effect of a higher ρ in reducing the real value of taxes needed to finance the lower value of future real interest payments.

Because π is capitalized over an infinite horizon whereas N is finite, the first effect will be larger if π is either larger than or not much smaller than $\tau + R(M/P)^\circ + \gamma v^\circ$. An exact relation between Ω_0 and ρ can be obtained by differentiating Ω_0, as given in equation (4.8), with respect to ρ, holding $R = r + \rho$ constant, yielding

$$\left.\frac{\delta\Omega_0}{\delta\rho}\right|_{dR=0} = \frac{\pi}{r^2} - [\tau + R(M/P)^\circ + \gamma v^\circ] \int_0^N te^{-rt}dt \gtreqless 0.$$

$$(4.8.2)$$

Given the asset-exhaustion condition and Ω_0, as now specified by equation (4.8), and the values of N' and N, the maximization of U implies, as a close approximation, that functions of the form of equations (3.14) and (3.15) again determine the current levels of c^d and l^s. For convenience, we rewrite these forms as

$$c^d = c^d(\Omega_0, W/P, r) \quad \text{and} \tag{4.9}$$
$${(+)} \quad {(+)} \quad {(?)}$$

$$l^s = l^s(\Omega_0, W/P, r). \tag{4.10}$$
$${(-)} \quad {(+)} \quad {(?)}$$

The nature of the approximation in equations (4.9) and (4.10) is that they neglect the direct substitution effect of ρ on the choice between current and future expenditures.[8]

Substitution of the optimal values of c^d and l^s from equations (4.9) and (4.10) into equations (3.5) and (4.1) yields for working households the following expression for asset accumulation and saving:

$$\left(\frac{a}{P}\right)^d = \frac{a^d}{P}\left(\Omega_0, \frac{W}{P}, r, \pi + \frac{i}{P} - \tau - \gamma v\right) - \rho\left(\frac{M}{P} + \frac{P_b B}{P}\right).$$
$$\phantom{\left(\frac{a}{P}\right)^d = \frac{a^d}{P}\Big(}{(-)} \;{(+)}\,{(?)} \quad\;\; {(+)}$$

$$(4.11)$$

Equation (4.11) represents a generalization of equation (3.16). As in the previous chapters, neglecting the effect of W/P, equations (4.9) and

---

[8] The substitution effect of ρ, given r, on the time paths of c^d and l^s arises because each dollar saved or dissaved is held for some amount of time in the form of a money balance. Consequently, given Ω_0 and W/P, a change in ρ, like a change in r, would involve a substitution effect on the margin between current and future expenditure. Formally, in the mathematical note to section 3.2.3, the term $r/2v^\circ(t)$, which derived from the interest foregone on the average money balance, must be replaced by $(r + \rho)/2v^\circ(t)$. However, since this term enters as $1 \pm (r + \rho)/2v^\circ(t)$, its effect is negligible if $(r + \rho)/2v^\circ(t)$ is much less than unity, which is essentially the condition which we assumed to hold in neglecting the compounding of interest over the period between trips to the financial asset market.

(4.11) also apply to retired households. Thus, the aggregate c^d, l^s, and $(a/P)^d$ functions have the same form as the functions given in equations (4.9–4.11), where Ω_0, $\pi + i/P - \tau - \gamma v$, and $\rho(M/P + P_b B/P)$ are interpreted as aggregate quantities.

What does equation (4.11) imply about the aggregate absolute saving flow, $|a^d/P|$? Again, the effect of all variables except W/P is ambiguous. As in chapter 3, we take $|a^d/P|$ to be simply an increasing function of W/P. Substituting this relation into equation (4.7), we obtain for the aggregate notional flow demand for money balances

$$\frac{m^d}{P} = \left(\frac{m}{P}\right)^d \underset{(+) \quad (-) \quad (+) \quad (-)}{(W/P, r + \rho, \gamma, M/P)} + \rho \frac{M}{P}. \tag{4.12}$$

Finally, as indicated in equation (4.2), the real notional flow demand for earning assets is given by

$$\frac{f^d}{P} \equiv \frac{P_e}{P} e^d + \frac{P_b}{P} b^d \equiv \frac{a^d}{P} - \frac{m^d}{P}.$$

Thus, by subtracting m^d/P in equation (4.12) from the a^d/P function in equation (4.11), we obtain

$$\frac{f^d}{P} = \frac{f^d}{P} \underset{(-) \quad (?) \quad (?) \quad (+) \quad (+) \quad\qquad (+) \qquad (-)}{\left(\Omega_0, \frac{W}{P}, r, r + \rho, \frac{M}{P}, \pi + \frac{i}{P} - \tau - \gamma v - \rho \frac{M}{P}, \gamma\right)} \tag{4.13}$$

Equations (4.12) and (4.13) represent generalizations of equations (3.17) and (3.18).

The preceding discussion has explicitly introduced the phenomenon of anticipated inflation into the analysis of household behavior. In this context, the question naturally arises of the implications of divergences between anticipated and actual rates of price change. Of course, this question could also have been raised in the context of chapter 3, where, because we assumed the anticipated rate of price change to be zero, we would have been concerned simply with the implications of a nonzero actual rate of price change. The demand and supply functions of equations (4.9–4.13), like those of equations (3.14–3.18) and (3.36–3.39), do not involve the actual rate of price change. Consequently, a divergence between ρ and the actual rate of price change has no immediate effect on the quantities demanded and supplied. However, given the real amount of planned saving, a^d/P, such a divergence implies that the anticipated rate of change of real asset holdings differs from the actual rate of change of real asset holdings. Moreover, if equity and commodity prices rise as expected at the same rate, so that P_e/P is constant, un-anticipated inflation causes unanticipated changes only in the real value of existing holdings of money and bonds. Although unanticipated inflation does not affect current demands and supplies, it affects Ω_0 over time and probably also influences the formulation of ρ, and these effects would, in turn, influence the quantities demanded and supplied.

4.3 Comparative-statics effect of expected price changes

This section analyzes how a change in inflationary or deflationary expectations, treated as an exogenous disturbance, affects the values of the endogenous variables which would be consistent with general-market-clearing conditions. There are various possible sources of exo-genous shifts in ρ. Some examples might include government pronounce-ments regarding its economic objectives, changes in government policies which are believed to affect inflation, such as price and wage controls, changes in prospects for war or peace, changes in exchange rates, etc. However, in general, ρ is not a completely exogenous variable, but is presumably related to some extent to actual past and present price movements. Section 4.4 below considers the role of endogenous changes in ρ. In the present section, we first specify and discuss the market-clearing conditions implied by the generalized formulation of household and firm behavior developed in the preceding section. We then consider, as a specific exogenous disturbance, an increase in ρ.

4.3.1 *Market-clearing conditions*

According to the analysis of the preceding section, allowing for ex-pected price and wage changes implies that the clearing conditions for the labor, commodity, and financial asset markets must now be specified as follows:

$$l^d \underset{(-)}{\left(\frac{W}{P}\right)} = l^s \left(\underset{(-)}{\Omega_0}, \underset{(+)}{\frac{W}{P}}, \underset{(?)}{r}\right) = l, \tag{4.14}$$

$$\underset{(-)(-)}{k^d(r, K)} + c^d \left(\underset{(+)}{\Omega_0}, \underset{(+)}{\frac{W}{P}}, \underset{(?)}{r}\right) + \gamma v + g^d = y^s \left(\underset{(-)}{\frac{W}{P}}, \underset{(+)}{g}, \underset{(+)}{K}\right) = y, \tag{4.15}$$

$$\text{and } \frac{f^d}{P} \left(\underset{(-)}{\Omega_0}, \underset{(?)}{\frac{W}{P}}, \underset{(?)}{r}, \underset{(+)}{r + \rho}, \underset{(+)}{\frac{M}{P}}, \underset{(+)}{\pi + \frac{i}{P} - \tau - \gamma v - \rho \frac{M}{P}}, \underset{(-)}{\gamma}\right)$$

$$= \underset{(-)(-)}{k^d(r, K)} + \frac{P_b}{P} b^s = \frac{f}{P}. \tag{4.16}$$

To simplify the notation, we again denote aggregate notional commodity demand by y^d – that is, $y^d \equiv k^d + c^d + \gamma v + g^d$ – and we denote aggregate notional earning asset supply by f^s/P – that is, $f^s/P \equiv k^d + P_b b^s/P$.

In form, the market-clearing conditions (4.14) and (4.15) are identical to the market-clearing conditions (3.20) and (3.21) of chapter 3. However, r now represents the real rate of return. Further, the specification of Ω_0 in equation (4.8) includes an effect of ρ, and therefore differs from the specification of Ω_0 in equation (3.13). In addition, market-clearing condition (4.16) includes a direct effect of ρ, and therefore differs in form from the corresponding market-clearing condition (3.22).

In order to facilitate the analysis of the implications of these market-clearing conditions, it will again be helpful to rewrite these conditions, now in terms of ρ and the three exchange ratios – W/P, P, and r. Substituting for Ω_0 from equation (4.8) and for π from the relation $\pi = y^s - (W/P)l^d$, and suppressing the other exogenous and predetermined variables, we obtain

$$l^d \underset{(-)}{\left(\frac{W}{P}\right)} = l^s \underset{(+)\,(+)(+)(+)}{\left(\frac{W}{P}, P, r, \rho\right)} = l, \tag{4.17}$$

$$y^d \underset{(+)\,(-)(-)(-)}{\left(\frac{W}{P}, P, r, \rho\right)} = y^s \underset{(-)}{\left(\frac{W}{P}\right)} = y, \text{ and} \tag{4.18}$$

$$\frac{f^d}{P} \underset{(?)\;(-)(+)(+)}{\left(\frac{W}{P}, P, r, \rho\right)} = \frac{f^s}{P} \underset{(-)}{(r)} = \frac{f}{P}. \tag{4.19}$$

Equations (4.17–4.19) correspond to equations (3.23–3.25) of chapter 3. Moreover with one minor exception, the qualitative effects of changes in W/P, P, and r are the same in equations (4.17–4.19) as in equations (3.23–3.25). The one exception involves the effect of P, for a given ρ, on the rate of depreciation of the real value of existing money balances. Recall the discussion of the effect of P on f^d/P in equation (3.25). An increase in P reduces Ω_0, thereby raising a^d/P, and tending to raise f^d/P. At the same time, an increase in P also reduces M/P, thereby raising m^d/P, and tending to reduce f^d/P. Now, in addition, an increase in P reduces the term $\rho(M/P)$, thereby reducing m^d/P, and tending to raise f^d/P. In regard to equation (3.25), we assumed that the coefficient λ_m was large enough for the second effect to dominate the first. Now, if λ_m is also much larger than ρ, the second effect will still dominate over the combination of the first and third effects.[9] Thus, equation (4.19) continues to specify the relation between P and f^d/P as inverse.

The completely new consideration which enters into equations (4.17–4.19) is the expected rate of price change, ρ. Given W/P, P, and r, the direction of the effects of changes in ρ on l^s and y^d involves simply the inverse relation between ρ and Ω_0 for a given value of r, as specified by equation (4.8.1).[10] However, the effect of changes in ρ on f^d/P involves three components: the inverse relation between ρ and Ω_0, the inverse relation between ρ and $(M/P)^{\circ}$, and the relation between ρ and the rate of depreciation of the real value of existing money balances, $\rho M/P$. The first two of these components imply that an increase in ρ would tend to raise f^d/P, whereas the third component implies the opposite effect. However, if the coefficient λ_m is again much larger than ρ, the effects of the second component will dominate the effects of the third component.[11]

As in chapters 1 and 3, the specification of general-market-clearing conditions does not require a separate statement of the equality between the notional flow demand and flow supply of money balances. Walras' Law of Markets, in the form of equation (3.26), again applies. Thus, the combination $(W/P)^*$, P^*, and r^* which satisfies equations (4.17–4.19) also satisfies the equality $m^d/P = m^s/P = m/P$. Taking account of the relation $m^d/P \equiv (m/P)^d + \rho\, M/P$, this money flow equality can be expressed as

$$\frac{m^d}{P} \equiv \left(\frac{m}{P}\right)^d \underset{(+)(+)\ \ (-)}{\left(\frac{W}{P}, P, r + \rho\right)} + \rho\,\frac{M}{P} = \frac{m^s}{P} = \frac{m}{P}. \qquad (4.20)$$

Again, let us consider the possibility of divergences between ρ and the actual rate of price change. The actual rate of change of real money balances is given by

$$\frac{d(M/P)}{dt} = \frac{m}{P} - \left(\frac{1}{P}\frac{dP}{dt}\right)\frac{M}{P}.$$

[9] From equation (4.7), the net of the second and third effects alone is given by $(\lambda_m - \rho)M/P$.

[10] If commodities were storable, changes in ρ would also affect commodity demand through the effect on the return from holding commodity inventories.

[11] From equations (4.4) and (4.7), the net effect of these two components is given by

$$\frac{1}{2}\frac{\lambda_m}{r+\rho}\left(\frac{M}{P}\right)^{\circ} - \frac{M}{P}.$$

Substituting for m/P from equation (4.20) yields

$$\frac{d(M/P)}{dt} = \left(\frac{m}{P}\right)^d + \left(\rho - \frac{1}{P}\frac{dP}{dt}\right)\frac{M}{P}.$$

Thus, although the actual rate of change of nominal money balances equals the desired rate of change based on the anticipated rate of inflation, the actual rate of change of real money balances differs from the anticipated rate of change in accordance with the difference between ρ and $\dot{P}/P$. Similarly, for the rate of change of real bond holdings we have

$$\frac{d(P_bB/P)}{dt} = \left(\frac{P_b}{P}b\right)^d + \left(\rho - \frac{1}{P}\frac{dP}{dt}\right)\frac{P_bB}{P}.$$

Equations (4.17–4.20) specify the market-clearing conditions in terms of ρ, W/P, P, and the real rate of return, r. However, it will also be instructive, for the comparative-statics analysis which follows, to specify the market-clearing conditions in terms of the nominal rate of return, R. Proceeding as in deriving equations (4.17–4.20), but substituting in addition for r from the relation $r = R - \rho$, we obtain

$$l^d\left(\frac{W}{P}\right) = l^s\left(\frac{W}{P}, P, R, \rho\right) = l, \qquad (4.21)$$

$$\underset{(-)}{} \qquad \underset{(+)(+)(+)(?)}{}$$

$$y^d\left(\frac{W}{P}, P, R, \rho\right) = y^s\left(\frac{W}{P}\right) = y, \qquad (4.22)$$

$$\underset{(+)(-)(-)(+)}{} \qquad \underset{(-)}{}$$

$$\frac{f^d}{P}\left(\frac{W}{P}, P, R, \rho\right) = \frac{f^s}{P}(R, \rho) = \frac{f}{P} \quad \text{and} \qquad (4.23)$$

$$\underset{(?)\,(-)(+)(-)}{} \qquad \underset{(-)(+)}{}$$

$$\left(\frac{m}{P}\right)^d\left(\frac{W}{P}, P, R\right) + \rho\frac{M}{P} = \frac{m^s}{P} = \frac{m}{P}. \qquad (4.24)$$

$$\underset{(+)(+)(-)}{}$$

The effects of changes in W/P and P in equations (4.21–4.24) are the same as in equations (4.17–4.20). In addition, given ρ, the effects of changes in R in equations (4.21–4.24) are the same as the effects of changes in r in equations (4.17–4.20). However, the effects of changes in ρ in equations (4.21–4.24) differ from the effects of changes in ρ in equations (4.17–4.20).

The effect of changes in ρ on l^s, for a given value of R, involves two components: the relation between ρ and Ω_0 and the inverse relation between ρ and r. As was indicated in equation (4.8.2), with R rather than r held fixed, the relation between ρ and Ω_0 is ambiguous. The relation between r and l^s, given Ω_0, is also ambiguous. Hence, we have left the full effect of ρ on l^s in equation (4.21) as ambiguous.

The effect of changes in ρ, given R, on y^d now involves three components: the inverse relation between ρ and r with regard to k^d, the relationship between ρ and Ω_0, and the inverse relation between ρ and r with regard to c^d. The first component implies that an increase in ρ would raise y^d. Assuming that this effect dominates over the ambiguous effect of the second and third components, an increase in ρ on net raises y^d.[12]

Turning to the financial asset market, the effect of changes in ρ, given R, on f^d/P now involves three components: the relation between ρ and Ω_0; the inverse relation between ρ and r, operating through the effect of r on a^d/P; and the relation between ρ and the rate of depreciation of the real value of existing money balances. Note that, because R is held fixed, $(M/P)^o$ does not change with ρ. The third component implies an inverse relation between ρ and f^d/P. If this effect dominates over the ambiguous effect of the first and second components, an increase in ρ on net lowers f^d/P.[13] The effect of changes in ρ on f^s/P involves the inverse relation between ρ and r working through k^d. Finally, because ρ enters the $(m/P)^d$ function only through the sum $r + \rho = R$, $(m/P)^d$ is independent of ρ, given the value of R.

4.3.2 *Comparative-statics analysis*

Comparative-statics analysis here is concerned with the effects of changes in the anticipated rate of price change, treated as an exogenous variable, on the values of the endogenous variables which satisfy the market-clearing conditions.[14] The general form of the analysis corresponds

---

[12] The second component reinforces the first component if an increase in ρ, given R, raises Ω_0. This result follows if π is not much smaller than the sum, $\tau + R(M/P)^o + \gamma v^o$. The third component also reinforces the first component if, for a given value of Ω_0, the substitution effect of r on c^d dominates over the wealth effect.

[13] The first component reinforces the third component if an increase in ρ, given R, raises Ω_0. The second component also reinforces the third component if, for a given value of Ω_0, the substitution effect of r on a^d/P dominates over the wealth effect.

[14] An alternative disturbance, which would be more interesting in a long-run context, would be a change in ρ accompanied by an equal change in the growth rate of the money stock, m/M. Assuming that the government distributes the new money via transfer payments to the households, a change in m/M would imply a change in τ in accordance with the term, m/P, and a corresponding change in Ω_0. However, this additional effect on Ω_0 would not alter any of the qualitative conclusions regarding the effects of a change in ρ discussed below. We leave the verification of this result as an exercise for the reader.

closely to the comparative-statics analysis of chapter 3. Specifically, in order to accommodate the analysis to a two-dimensional diagram, we again employ an approximation which neglects the dependence of l^s on W/P, Ω_0, and r. Consequently, the value of $(W/P)^*$ follows immediately from the labor-market clearing condition. Within this context, we focus on the effects of changes in ρ on P^*, r^*, and R^*.

The solid lines in figure 4.1 depict, for given values of W/P and ρ, the combinations of values of r and P which are consistent with

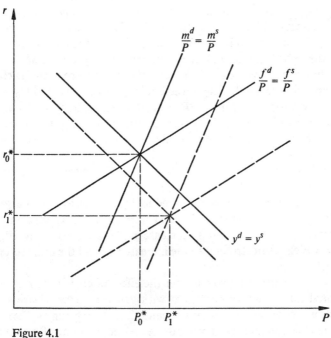

Figure 4.1
Effect of exogenous increase in expected rate of price change on r^* and P^*

clearing of the commodity and financial asset markets and with equality between the notional flow demand and supply of money balances. The loci depicted in figure 4.1 have the same slopes as the corresponding loci in figure 3.1, and the discussion of these slopes will not be repeated. The dashed lines in figure 4.1 depict the effects of an exogenous increase in ρ.

To analyze these effects, consider first the $y^d = y^s$ locus, as described by equations (4.15) and (4.18). The increase in ρ depresses

c^d, thereby reducing y^d and shifting this locus downward. This shift reflects the inverse relation between ρ and Ω_0. Next, consider the $f^d/P = f^s/P$ locus, as described by equations (4.16) and (4.19). The increase in ρ raises f^d/P, thereby also shifting this locus downward. This shift reflects primarily the substitution away from money holding and toward earning asset holding as ρ increases. The new general-market-clearing situation involves unambiguously a lower real rate of return.

The construction in figure 4.1 also assumes that the new general-market-clearing situation involves a higher price level. This result corresponds to the assumption that the downward displacement of the $f^d/P = f^s/P$ locus is greater than the downward displacement of the $y^d = y^s$ locus. In other words, the conclusion that an increase in ρ raises P^*, and thereby lowers M/P^* and i/P^*, depends on the assumption that the substitution away from money holding and toward earning asset holding as ρ increases is a more important force than the effect on consumption demand of the inverse relation between ρ and Ω_0.

Consider now the $m^d/P = m^s/P$ locus, as described by equation (4.20). The increase in ρ depresses $(m/P)^d$, but raises $\rho M/P$. However, if the coefficient λ_m is much greater than ρ, the first effect must dominate, so that m^d/P decreases. As a result, this locus shifts rightward, which is consistent with the rightward shifting of the intersection of the $y^d = y^s$ and $f^d/P = f^s/P$ loci.

Because an increase in ρ reduces r^*, an increase in ρ also raises k^*. The assumption that l^s is fixed implies that a change in ρ must depress c^*. The corresponding decrease in c^d reflects primarily a decrease in Ω_0, which results from both the increase in ρ and the induced increase in P^*.[15]

We also want to consider the effect of changes in ρ on R^*, the nominal rate of return consistent with general market clearing. These effects are especially important because in the long run the level of R^* will determine the level of γv and, hence, the amount of resources devoted to providing transactions services. The solid lines in figure 4.2 depict, for given values of W/P and ρ, the combinations of R and P which are consistent with clearing of the commodity and financial asset markets and with equality between the notional flow demand and supply of money balances. With ρ equal to zero, the solid lines depicted in figure 4.2 are identical to the solid lines depicted in figure 4.1. The dashed lines in figure 4.2 again depict the effects of an exogenous increase in ρ.

[15] Because c^d declines on net, given the initial value of W/P, it is reasonable to suppose that desired leisure would also decline so that l^s would increase. Accordingly, in a fuller analysis, the increase in ρ would tend to raise l and y and to reduce W/P.

To analyze these effects, consider first the $y^d = y^s$ locus, as described by equations (4.15) and (4.22). The increase in ρ, given R, raises y^d and shifts this locus upward. Next, consider the $f^d/P = f^s/P$ locus, as described by equations (4.16) and (4.23). The increase in ρ, given R, lowers f^d/P and raises f^s/P, thereby also shifting this locus

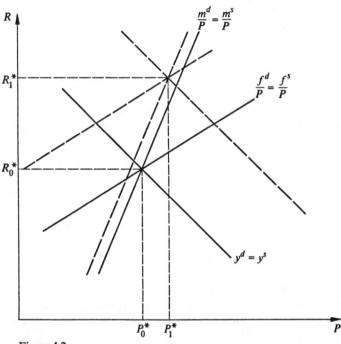

Figure 4.2
Effect of exogenous increase in expected rate of price change on R^* and P^*

upward. The new general-market-clearing situation involves unambiguously a higher nominal rate of return. In addition, to be consistent with the assumption used in the construction of figure 4.1, figure 4.2 also depicts the new general-market-clearing situation as involving a higher price level. This assumption now implies that, in (P, R) space, the upward displacement of the $y^d = y^s$ locus is greater than the upward displacement of the $f^d/P = f^s/P$ locus. Finally, the increase in ρ raises $\rho M/P$, thereby shifting the $m^d/P = m^s/P$ locus, as described by equation (4.24), to the left

Although figure 4.2 shows that an increase in ρ raises R^*, figure 4.1 showed that an increase in ρ also lowers r^*. Thus, the induced increase in R^* is smaller than the increase in ρ. Because $\rho \equiv R - r$, an increase in inflationary expectations must widen the gap between the anticipated real and nominal rates of return which is consistent with general-market-clearing conditions. This widened gap involves to some extent a higher nominal rate and to some extent a lower real rate. On the one hand, the increase in R^* is necessary to reclear the commodity and financial asset markets because, at the initial value of R^*, an increase in ρ creates excess demand for commodities, by raising y^d, and excess supply of financial assets, by lowering f^d/P and raising f^s/P. On the other hand, the decrease in r^* is necessary because, at the initial value of r^*, an increase in ρ creates excess supply of commodities, by lowering c^d, and excess demand for financial assets, by raising f^d/P.[16,17]

Because the increase in ρ causes an increase in R^*, it also causes an increase in the target transactions frequency, $v°$, as given by equation (4.3). Initially, the actual transactions frequency was predetermined. However, over time, as households adjust v toward the higher $v°$, they also increase their demand for transaction services, γv. As was discussed in section 3.3.3, this increase in γv over time would raise r^* and P^* and would reduce k^* and c^*. With a given total output, y^*, the increases in r^* and P^* were necessary to reduce k^* and c^* in order to accommodate the greater demand for financial services. Thus, the longer-run effect of the increase in ρ on γv tends to intensify both the initial increase in P^* and R^* and the initial decrease in c^*. However, the increase in γv over time tends to offset both the initial decrease in r^* and the initial increase in k^*.[18] In other words, if the longer-run effect of ρ on γv were neglected,

[16] The analysis by Mundell (1965) leads to similar conclusions, although the direct effect of ρ on the $y^d = y^s$ locus, as shown in figure 4.1, is not considered in his analysis.

[17] The present analysis holds K fixed and thus deals only with the short run. Karni (1972) discusses some long-run implications of changes in ρ associated with induced changes in K.

[18] In a full long-run analysis it is possible that r returns to its original value. When $v = v°$ the increase in γv would approximately offset the reduction in c^d associated with the increase in $\gamma v°$ and corresponding decline in Ω_0. If, as in n. 14 above, the increase in ρ is associated with an equal change in the growth rate of money, m/M, with the money issue distributed as transfers to households, then the implied reduction in τ would balance the increase in $\rho(M/P)°$ and leave Ω_0 unchanged on this count. The effect of ρ in reducing the real value of government bonds would not affect Ω_0 if households took account (over an infinite horizon) of the negative effect of higher future prices on the taxes needed to finance future real interest payments. Finally, the real interest foregone by holding money, $r(M/P)°$, declines with the increase in ρ which implies an increase in Ω_0. In the infinite horizon case this last effect implies that Ω_0 depends on $M/P - (M/P)°$ – that is, on real balances relative to desired real balances – rather than on M/P itself. In this case the long-run effect of

we would conclude that an increase in ρ would bring about a one-to-one substitution away from current consumption and toward the accumulation of physical capital. However, the induced increase over time in γv implies that an increase in ρ causes a reduction in the total output available for consumption and investment. Accordingly, any net increase in investment must correspond to a greater than one-to-one reduction in current consumption.[19]

Mathematical note

Given W/P, we can determine the effect of a change in ρ on P^* and r^* by solving the following system of equations obtained by differentiating equations (4.18) and (4.19):

$$
\begin{bmatrix}
\dfrac{\delta y^d}{\delta P} & \dfrac{\delta y^d}{\delta r} \\[2ex]
\dfrac{\delta(f^d/P)}{\delta P} & \dfrac{\delta(f^d/P)}{\delta r} - \dfrac{\delta(f^s/P)}{\delta r}
\end{bmatrix}
\begin{bmatrix}
\dfrac{dP^*}{d\rho} \\[2ex]
\dfrac{dr^*}{d\rho}
\end{bmatrix}
=
\begin{bmatrix}
-\dfrac{\delta y^d}{\delta \rho} \\[2ex]
-\dfrac{\delta(f^d/P)}{\delta \rho}
\end{bmatrix}.
$$

The solutions are

$$
\frac{dP^*}{d\rho} =
\begin{vmatrix}
-\dfrac{\delta y^d}{\delta \rho} & \dfrac{\delta y^d}{\delta r} \\[2ex]
-\dfrac{\delta(f^d/P)}{\delta \rho} & \dfrac{\delta(f^d/P)}{\delta r} - \dfrac{\delta(f^s/P)}{\delta r}
\end{vmatrix}
$$

$$
\div
\begin{vmatrix}
\dfrac{\delta y^d}{\delta P} & \dfrac{\delta y^d}{\delta r} \\[2ex]
\dfrac{\delta(f^d/P)}{\delta P} & \dfrac{\delta(f^d/P)}{\delta r} - \dfrac{\delta(f^s/P)}{\delta r}
\end{vmatrix},
$$

an increase in ρ can be shown graphically in figure 4.1 by a rightward shift in the $y^d = y^s$ locus to intersect the other two loci at the initial real interest rate, r_0^*, and a higher price level, P_1^*. (This analysis neglects any induced changes in labor supply.) In this long-run analysis of an increase in ρ, capital accumulation would be unaffected, the nominal interest rate would rise one-to-one with ρ, and the only real effect would be a diversion of a part of output from consumption to financial services.

[19] The same result would obtain if firms incurred transaction costs and, hence, held money in order to reduce the amount of labor services which they employ in providing transaction services. In that case, a reduction in real money holdings would imply the drawing of labor services away from the production of consumption and investment goods. See Stein (1971, chapter 1) and Barro and Santomero (1974) for a discussion of this case.

which is positive if the numerator is negative, and

$$\frac{dr^*}{d\rho} = \begin{vmatrix} \dfrac{\delta y^a}{\delta P} & -\dfrac{\delta y^a}{\delta \rho} \\[3mm] \dfrac{\delta(f^a/P)}{\delta P} & -\dfrac{\delta(f^a/P)}{\delta \rho} \end{vmatrix} \div \begin{vmatrix} \dfrac{\delta y^a}{\delta P} & \dfrac{\delta y^a}{\delta r} \\[3mm] \dfrac{\delta(f^a/P)}{\delta P} & \dfrac{\delta(f^a/P)}{\delta r} - \dfrac{\delta(f^s/P)}{\delta r} \end{vmatrix},$$

which is unambiguously negative.

Similarly, we can determine the effect of a change in ρ on P^* and R^* by solving the following system of equations obtained by differentiating equations (4.22) and (4.23):

$$\begin{bmatrix} \dfrac{\delta y^a}{\delta P} & \dfrac{\delta y^a}{\delta R} \\[3mm] \dfrac{\delta(f^a/P)}{\delta P} & \dfrac{\delta(f^a/P)}{\delta R} - \dfrac{\delta(f^s/P)}{\delta R} \end{bmatrix} \begin{bmatrix} \dfrac{dP^*}{d\rho} \\[3mm] \dfrac{dR^*}{d\rho} \end{bmatrix} = \begin{bmatrix} -\dfrac{\delta y^a}{\delta \rho} \\[3mm] \dfrac{\delta(f^s/P)}{\delta \rho} - \dfrac{\delta(f^a/P)}{\delta \rho} \end{bmatrix}.$$

The solutions are

$$\frac{dP^*}{d\rho} = \begin{vmatrix} -\dfrac{\delta y^a}{\delta \rho} & \dfrac{\delta y^a}{\delta R} \\[3mm] \dfrac{\delta(f^s/P)}{\delta \rho} - \dfrac{\delta(f^a/P)}{\delta \rho} & \dfrac{\delta(f^a/P)}{\delta R} - \dfrac{\delta(f^s/P)}{\delta R} \end{vmatrix}$$

$$\div \begin{vmatrix} \dfrac{\delta y^a}{\delta P} & \dfrac{\delta y^a}{\delta R} \\[3mm] \dfrac{\delta(f^a/P)}{\delta P} & \dfrac{\delta(f^a/P)}{\delta R} - \dfrac{\delta(f^s/P)}{\delta R} \end{vmatrix},$$

which is positive if the numerator is negative, and

$$\frac{dR^*}{d\rho} = \begin{vmatrix} \dfrac{\delta y^a}{\delta P} & -\dfrac{\delta y^a}{\delta \rho} \\[3mm] \dfrac{\delta(f^a/P)}{\delta P} & \dfrac{\delta(f^s/P)}{\delta \rho} - \dfrac{\delta(f^a/P)}{\delta \rho} \end{vmatrix}$$

$$\div \begin{vmatrix} \dfrac{\delta y^a}{\delta P} & \dfrac{\delta y^a}{\delta R} \\[3mm] \dfrac{\delta(f^a/P)}{\delta P} & \dfrac{\delta(f^a/P)}{\delta R} - \dfrac{\delta(f^s/P)}{\delta R} \end{vmatrix},$$

which is unambiguously positive.

4.4 Dynamic analysis of inflation, expected inflation, and rates of return

The preceding section discussed the comparative-statics effects of a change in inflationary expectations, treated as an exogenous variable. This discussion suffers from two major and related shortcomings. First, the treatment of ρ as a completely exogenous variable seems unduly restrictive. In general, viewed as a prediction of future inflation, ρ should have important endogenous components. Specifically, ρ should be related to some extent to actual past and present inflationary experiences. Second, in the preceding analysis, the satisfaction of the general-market-clearing conditions over time may be inconsistent, even in the long run, with the fulfillment of expectations. In other words, nothing in the preceding analysis insures that, either in the short run or in the long run, the movement of P over time in accord with changes in P^* corresponds to expectations regarding changes in P, as specified by the value of ρ.

This section endeavors to rectify both of these shortcomings. First, we specify a simple adaptive mechanism for generating ρ endogenously, by relating it to actual past and present price movements. Second, we devise a more general specification of the price-adjustment relation which incorporates a direct role for inflationary expectations. This generalized formulation serves to reconcile the fulfillment of expectations with the satisfaction of general-market-clearing conditions over time. Finally, in order to see the implications of these new considerations, we present a dynamic analysis of the effects of a shift toward a more expansionary monetary policy.

4.4.1 Adaptive expectations

In order to generate the variable ρ endogenously, we view ρ as a prediction formulated by the representative firm and the representative household for the actual rate of price change to obtain in the future. We assume that the representative firm or household bases its prediction on the actual record of price change – specifically, that it continually adjusts (or adapts) its expectations to bring them into line with experience. For simplicity, we assume that this adaptation mechanism operates at a finite speed and is linear in form – that is,[20]

$$\frac{d\rho}{dt} = \theta \left(\frac{1}{P} \frac{dP}{dt} - \rho \right), \tag{4.25}$$

---

[20] Cagan (1956) presents an early formulation and application of the linear-adaptive expectations hypothesis. Cagan shows that the solution of equation (4.25) as a differential equation yields ρ as a weighted average of all current and past values of $\dot{P}/P$. In this context, see also Allais (1966).

where the coefficient θ is positive and is treated, for simplicity, as a constant.

Although equation (4.25) is convenient in its simplicity, this particular model of expectations formation lacks generality. First, it neglects all the sources of exogenous shifts in ρ mentioned in the preceding section. Second, even if the representative firm and household views the process generating inflation to be independent of other economic phenomena, equation (4.25) would represent an optimal predictor of the rate of inflation only under very special conditions.[21,22] However, the linear form of equation (4.25) is not essential for any of the discussion which follows.

4.4.2 *The price-adjustment relation with expected price changes*

The analysis in chapters 1 and 2 employed the concept of a price-setting agent whose job it was to find the price level P^*, which would be consistent with the general-market-clearing conditions. We assumed that the price-setting agent knew the signs of the partial derivatives of the commodity demand and supply functions, and that he consequently would increase or decrease P according to whether he observed excess demand or supply for commodities. Thus, equations (1.17) and (2.27) specified the rate of price change to be solely an increasing function of the difference between aggregate commodity demand and supply.

However, such adjustment strategy seems appropriate only if the market-clearing price is not expected to change over time. Suppose instead that the price-setting agent expects P^* to change over time. Denote this anticipated rate of change by ρ^*. It would seem plausible that optimal adjustment policy would take account of this anticipated trend without waiting for it to add to the finite discrepancy between P and P^*. Given this consideration, and assuming the notional demand and supply of commodities to be relevant, it would seem appropriate to express the price adjustment relation as

$$\frac{1}{P}\frac{dP}{dt} = \lambda_P(y^d - y^s) + \rho^*. \tag{4.26}$$

---

[21] Sargent and Wallace (1973) discuss this issue in the context of a 'rational expectations' model, in which expectations depend on the full information available to market participants. For further development of the rational expectations approach, see Muth (1961), Lucas (1972), and Sargent (1973).

[22] One plausible possibility, not allowed by equation (4.25), would be for the expected rate of price change to depend on the period to which it applies.

According to equation (4.26), price adjustment results from the summation of two component forces: first, an attempt to correct any existing discrepancy between the current values of P and P^* and, second, an attempt to anticipate and prevent any potential future discrepancies between P and P^*.[23]

Finally, in order to analyze the significance of the variable ρ^*, we must specify the process by which it is generated. A simple and plausible formulation is to assume that the price-setting agent bases his prediction of ρ^* on the actual record of price change. In particular, assume, for simplicity, that the linear adaptation mechanism specified in equation (4.25) generates ρ^* as well as ρ. This assumption has the convenient implication that ρ^* is equal to ρ.

Two important implications of equation (4.26), together with the equality between ρ^* and ρ, are especially worth noting. First, equation (4.26) reconciles the clearing of the commodity market with the fulfillment of expectations regarding the rate of change of commodity prices. In equation (4.26), y^d is equal to y^s if and only if $(1/P)(dP/dt)$ is equal to ρ. Thus, equation (4.26) implies that the values of the endogenous variables which satisfy the general-market-clearing conditions also are consistent with the fulfillment of currently held price expectations. Second, equation (4.26) suggests that expectations of price change affect the actual rate of price change through two distinct channels. The first channel involves the effects of a change in ρ on y^d – effects which were analyzed in sections 4.2 and 4.3 above. The second channel is the direct one-to-one effect of ρ on $(1/P)(dP/dt)$, for given values of y^d and y^s, operating through the adjustment strategy of the price-setting agent.

4.4.3 Dynamic effects of monetary policy

Chapter 3 above contained an analysis of the comparative-statics effects of a shift toward a more expansionary monetary policy. For a given value of ρ, specifically ρ equal to zero, this analysis showed that an increase in m^s/P and a corresponding decrease in $P_b b^s/P$ would initially shift the $f^d/P = f^s/P$ locus to the right, thereby raising P^* and lowering r^*. In addition, over time, as M increased and B decreased, the $y^d = y^s$ locus would continually shift to the right and the $f^d/P = f^s/P$ locus would

---

[23] The analogue of equation (4.26) for the labor market would be

$$\frac{1}{W}\frac{dW}{dt} = \lambda_w(l^d - l^s) + \rho_w^*,$$

where ρ_w^* is the anticipated rate of change of W^*, which may or may not equal ρ^*.

continually shift further to the right. Consequently, over time, P^* would continue to increase, and to the extent that the representative household views the present value of the interest on government bonds as a net addition to wealth, r^* would continue to decrease. The present section expands this analysis in two ways. First, it focuses on the actual movement of prices and rates of return over time, bringing in explicitly dynamic analysis to supplement the comparative-statics analysis of changes in P^* and r^*. Second, it considers the nature and effect of endogenous changes in ρ, which are produced by the movement of P, and analyzes the feedback mechanism among ρ, P, r, and R.[24] However, the analysis continues to abstract from the dynamics of changes in the stock of capital – that is, the analysis assumes throughout a fixed value of K.

We can usefully analyze the dynamic effects of a shift toward a more expansionary monetary policy as occurring in three stages. The analysis assumes that, prior to the disturbance, the general market-clearing conditions are satisfied and ρ equals zero, so that R equals r.

Stage one: Assume, as in chapter 3, that the adjustment of the rate of return is instantaneous in the sense that it always takes that value which is consistent with effective clearing of the financial-asset market. In contrast, assume that the adjustment of prices conforms to equation (4.26). Thus, the first stage of a more expansionary monetary policy involves the decline in R and r which is necessary to clear the financial-asset market, given the initial levels of P and ρ. Because the decline in R and r, with P and ρ fixed, creates excess demand in the commodity market, clearing of the financial asset market involves equating of effective, rather than notional, demand and supply of financial assets. For simplicity, figure 4.3 does not explicitly depict the distinction between the $f^d/P = f^s/P$ and the $f^{d\prime}/P = f^{s\prime}/P$ loci. Given, as can be readily shown, that both these loci are positively sloped, this distinction has no apparent significance for the present discussion. The vertical arrow in figure 4.3 illustrates the fall in R and r from R_0^* to R_1 in stage one.

Stage two: Although the initial level of P is given, the movement in the first stage into the region in which y^d is greater than y^s causes $(1/P)(dP/dt)$ to become positive. In the second stage, the positive level of $(1/P)(dP/dt)$ causes P to increase over time. If the market-clearing loci did not shift further, and if ρ remained equal to zero, the increases in P would mean that R and r would also have to increase to maintain clearing of the financial asset market. Under these conditions, the second

[24] Friedman (1968) contains an earlier, less formalized, discussion along these same lines. For some interesting evaluations of the empirical relevance of these considerations, see Fand (1972) and Carr and Smith (1972).

stage would involve a gradual movement up the given financial-asset market-clearing locus towards the $y^d = y^s$ locus. The values of P and R, which remains equal to r, would steadily increase as they asymptotically approached their new market-clearing values. Figure 4.3 denotes these new market-clearing values as P_1^* and $R_1^* = r_1^*$. In this case, stage one would unambiguously involve an undershooting of the new value for R^* and r^*. The rapid adjustment of rates of return in response to

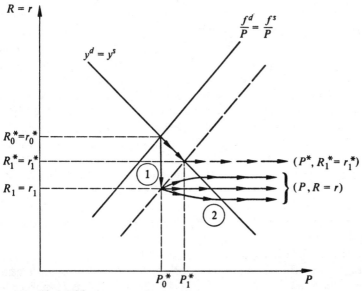

Figure 4.3
Dynamic effects of expansionary monetary policy: stage one and stage two

excess demand in the financial asset market, relative to the adjustment of P in response to excess demand in the commodity market, implies that R and r would first fall sharply and then rise gradually in response to the increase in P.

Recall, however, that as m^s remains positive and b^s remains negative, M increases and B decreases, and the $f^d/P = f^s/P$ and $y^d = y^s$ loci both shift steadily rightward. Thus, given ρ, P^* steadily increases. However, in order to simplify the analysis, we neglect here the effect of the increase in M and decrease in B on r^* and R^*. We assume in stage two that R^* and r^* remain equal to R_1^* and r_1^*. This simplification involves the approximation that Ω_0 is independent of i/P – that is, that the present value of i/P approximately equals the present value of the tax liability which it implies and, hence, that the representative household does not view the present value of the interest on government bonds as a net addition to wealth. In other words, the present analysis for simplicity ignores the result from chapter 3 that the existence of government bonds may violate the neutrality of changes in the stock of money.

Given the steady rightward shifting of the $f^d/P = f^s/P$ locus, the initial movement in R and r in the second stage involves the net effect of two opposing forces: first, the tendency for R and r to increase as P rises, which involves a movement along a given financial-asset market-clearing locus; and, second, the tendency for R and r to decrease as M increases, which involves a rightward movement of the financial-asset market-clearing locus. Assuming that government bonds have no effect on wealth, the net effect of these two forces depends only on the initial size of $(1/P)(dP/dt)$ relative to the rate of monetary expansion, m/M. The initial size of $(1/P)(dP/dt)$ depends in turn on the price adjustment coefficient, λ_P, and on the distance of the starting point for the second stage from the $y^d = y^s$ locus. If this combination is sufficiently large, $(1/P)(dP/dt)$ is larger than m/M initially. In that case, M/P is declining initially, and in order to maintain clearing of the financial asset market, R and r must be increasing initially. However, the decreases in M/P and increases in r and R imply decreases in y^d, which imply, in turn, decreases in $(1/P)(dP/dt)$. This decline in the rate of price inflation continues until $(1/P)(dP/dt)$ is equal to m/M, at which point M/P, R, and r are no longer changing. Alternatively, if $(1/P)(dP/dt)$ is smaller than m/M initially, so that M/P is rising, R and r must be decreasing initially, in order to maintain clearing of the financial asset market. In this case, y^d and $(1/P)(dP/dt)$ increase until $(1/P)(dP/dt)$ is equal to m/M, at which point M/P, R, and r are again constant.

Regardless of the starting point for the second stage, the values of P, R, and r would eventually approach a time path along which P is rising while R and r are constant. Because P continues to rise, and, by assumption, ρ is still equal to zero, y^d must remain greater than y^s along any of these second-stage paths. This persistence of excess demand for commodities implies that R and r remain below R^* and r^*. Moreover, given $\rho = 0$, these time paths also exhibit perpetual nonfulfillment of expectations, reflecting an excess of $(1/P)(dP/dt)$ over ρ.

Figure 4.3 illustrates the various possibilities for stages one and two. The dashed arrow depicts the time path of P^* and $R^* = r^*$. The value of P^* increases continually and the value of $R^* = r^*$ declines to $R_1^* = r_1^*$ and then remains constant. As indicated above, the vertical solid arrow depicts the decline in R and r from R_0^* to R_1 in stage one. The three subsequent solid arrows depict possible time paths for P and $R = r$ in stage two. Along the upper path, the initial value of $(1/P)(dP/dt)$ is sufficiently large to more than offset the effect of the continual rightward shifting of the $f^d/P = f^s/P$ locus. Hence, $R = r$ rises and then approaches a constant value below R_1^* but above R_1. Along the lower path, the initial value of $(1/P)(dP/dt)$ is sufficiently small to be more than offset by the effect of the continual rightward shifting of the $f^d/P = f^s/P$ locus. Hence, $R = r$ falls and then approaches a constant value below both R_1^* and R_1. Along the middle path, the initial value of $(1/P)(dP/dt)$ exactly offsets the effect of the continual rightward shifting of the $f^d/P = f^s/P$ locus. Hence, $R = r$ remains constant at R_1.

Stage three: The preceding discussion of the second stage assumed that the anticipated rate of price change remained equal to zero, despite the positive actual rate of price change. The third stage involves the effects of induced changes in the anticipated rate of price change. According to equation (4.25), ρ adapts gradually in response to changes in $(1/P)(dP/dt)$. Consequently, P, R, and r do not actually follow out the time paths initiated in the second stage. The level of $(1/P)(dP/dt)$ over time causes ρ to become positive, and this increase in ρ disturbs the time paths of P, r, and R in two ways: First, according to equation (4.26), an increase in ρ feeds back one-for-one into $(1/P)(dP/dt)$. Second, according to the comparative-statics analysis of section 4.3, an increase in ρ shifts the market-clearing loci and drives a wedge between r and R. We analyze these two considerations in turn.

Taken by itself, the effect of the first consideration would be to cause the time path of P, r, and R to converge to the general-market-clearing path, depicted by the dashed arrow in figure 4.3, rather than to any lower parallel path. This new convergence property is independent of the starting point of the actual time path and of its initial direction in the second stage. The mechanism of this effect is straightforward. According to equation (4.25), the tendency of ρ is to converge to equality with $(1/P)(dP/dt)$. Moreover, according to equation (4.26), as ρ moves to equality with $(1/P)(dP/dt)$, $y^d - y^s$ tends to zero. Thus, with ρ both adapting to $(1/P)(dP/dt)$ and feeding back one-for-one into $(1/P)(dP/dt)$, P, r, and R would tend toward a time path along which $(1/P)(dP/dt)$ is positive and perpetually consistent with clearing of the commodity market. In addition, $(1/P)(dP/dt)$ would be equal to ρ along this path, so that expectations would be fulfilled. In other words, P, r, and R would converge to a dynamic equilibrium.

The effect of the second consideration is to displace the time paths of P^*, r^*, and R^*. According to the comparative-statics analysis of section 4.3, an increase in ρ raises P^* and R^* and lowers r^*.[25] Consider

---

[25] See, however, n. 18 above.

first the implications for dynamic behavior in (P, r) space. The increase in ρ, in response to the positive level of $(1/P)(\mathrm{d}P/\mathrm{d}t)$, reinforces the existing tendency for P^* to increase and also causes r^* to decrease. In figure 4.4, the dashed arrow depicts the time path of P^* and r^*, taking into account the increase in ρ. In the third stage, assuming the dynamics to be stable,

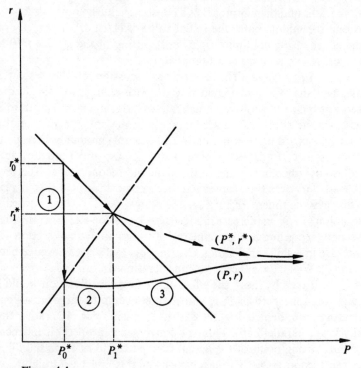

Figure 4.4
Dynamic effects of expansionary monetary policy on P and r: stages one, two, and three

the actual time path of P and r will converge to this time path of P^* and r^*. The solid arrow in figure 4.4 depicts one possibility for the time path of P and r through stages one, two, and three.[26]

Consider finally the implications of the third stage for dynamic behavior in (P, R) space. The increase in ρ in response to the positive

[26] Depending on the parameter values, the time path of P, R, and r can now be stable or unstable, direct or oscillatory. The mathematical note at the end of this section analyzes the relevant stability conditions.

level of $(1/P)/(dP/dt)$, again reinforces the existing tendency for P^* to increase, and also tends to make R^* increase. In figure 4.5, the dashed arrow depicts the time path of P^* and R^*, taking into account the increase in ρ. In the third stage, assuming the dynamics to be stable, the actual time path of P and R will converge to this time path of P^* and R^*.

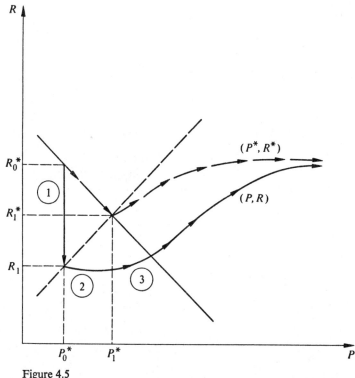

Figure 4.5
Dynamic effects of expansionary monetary policy on P and R: stages one, two, and three

The solid arrow in figure 4.5 depicts one possibility for the time path of P and R through stages one, two, and three. An important observation is that, although a shift to a more expansionary monetary policy initially, in stage one, depresses the nominal rate of return and may cause, in stage two, a further decline in the nominal rate of return for a period thereafter, the eventual increase in inflationary expectations implies a further period, stage three, during which the nominal rate of return will be rising. Thus, the overall long-run effect of a shift to a more expansionary monetary policy on R is ambiguous. In figure 4.5, the long-run level of R^* must be above R_1^* and, depending on the parameters of the model, may be either above or below R_0^*.[27,28]

Mathematical note

Given W/P, the dynamic motion of P, r, and ρ conforms to the following relations:

$$\frac{1}{P}\frac{dP}{dt} = \lambda_P \underset{(-)(-)(-)}{[y^d(P, r, \rho)} - y^s] + \rho, \tag{A.1}$$

$$\frac{d\rho}{dt} = \theta \left(\frac{1}{P}\frac{dP}{dt} - \rho \right), \quad \text{and} \tag{A.2}$$

$$\underset{(-)(+)(+)}{\frac{f^d}{P}(P, r, \rho)} = \underset{(-)}{\frac{f^s}{P}(r)}. \tag{A.3}$$

We can solve equation (A.3) for r as a function of P and ρ. Substitution of this solution into the y^d function eliminates r from equations (A.1) and (A.2) and enables us to rewrite equations (A.1) and (A.2) in the following form:

$$\frac{1}{P}\frac{dP}{dt} = \lambda_P F(P, \rho) + \rho, \tag{A.5}$$

$$\frac{d\rho}{dt} = \theta \lambda_P F(P, \rho) \tag{A.6}$$

where

$$\frac{\delta F}{\delta P} = \frac{\delta y^d}{\delta P} + \frac{\delta y^d}{\delta r}\frac{\delta(f^d/P)}{\delta P} \bigg/ \left(\frac{\delta(f^s/P)}{\delta r} - \frac{\delta(f^d/P)}{\delta r} \right),$$

which is unambiguously negative, and

$$\frac{\delta F}{\delta \rho} = \frac{\delta y^d}{\delta \rho} + \frac{\delta y^d}{\delta r}\frac{\delta(f^d/P)}{\delta \rho} \bigg/ \left(\frac{\delta(f^s/P)}{\delta r} - \frac{\delta(f^d/P)}{\delta r} \right),$$

---

[27] The long-run levels of $v°$ and γv depend on the long-run level of R^*. As explained in section 4.3.2 above, if, for example, the long-run level of R^* is above R_0^*, $v°$ and γv in the long run will be above their initial levels, and the increase in γv over time will tend to raise R^* further.

[28] The long-run relation of R^* to R_0^* is ambiguous because in the present example the expansion of the money stock occurs through open-market operations. If, alternatively, the monetary expansion occurred through transfer payments, the long-run level of R^* would be unambiguously above R_0^*.

which, from the mathematical note to section 4.3.2, is positive if $dP^*/d\rho$ is positive. The stability of the time path of P and ρ depends on the characteristic roots, ψ, which are determined by solving the equation

$$\begin{vmatrix} \lambda_P \dfrac{\delta F}{\delta P} - \psi & \lambda_P \dfrac{\delta F}{\delta \rho} + 1 \\[2mm] \theta \lambda_P \dfrac{\delta F}{\delta P} & \theta \lambda_P \dfrac{\delta F}{\delta \rho} - \psi \end{vmatrix} = 0.$$

If the real parts of these roots are negative, the motion of P, r, and ρ will be locally stable. The condition for stable roots is

$$\frac{\delta F}{\delta \rho} < -\frac{\delta F/\delta P}{\theta}.$$

If $\delta F/\delta \rho$ is positive, because $\delta F/\delta P$ is negative, a sufficiently large value of θ would produce instability. Note that the stability condition does not involve λ_P. If these roots are complex, the motion of P, r, and ρ will be oscillatory. The condition for complex roots is

$$-\frac{\delta F/\delta P}{\theta} - 2\left(\frac{-\delta F/\delta P}{\theta \lambda_P}\right)^{\frac{1}{2}} < \frac{\delta F}{\delta \rho} < -\frac{\delta F/\delta P}{\theta} + 2\left(\frac{-\delta F/\delta P}{\theta \lambda_P}\right)^{\frac{1}{2}}.$$

In summary, the motion of P, r, and ρ can take four possible forms:

(1) direct convergence to P^*, r^*, and ρ^* if

$$\frac{\delta F}{\delta \rho} < -\frac{\delta F/\delta P}{\theta} - 2\left(\frac{-\delta F/\delta P}{\theta \lambda_P}\right)^{\frac{1}{2}},$$

(2) oscillatory convergence to P^*, r^*, and ρ^* if

$$-\frac{\delta F/\delta P}{\theta} - 2\left(\frac{-\delta F/\delta P}{\theta \lambda_P}\right)^{\frac{1}{2}} < \frac{\delta F}{\delta \rho} < -\frac{\delta F/\delta P}{\theta},$$

(3) oscillatory divergence from P^*, r^*, and ρ^* if

$$-\frac{\delta F/\delta P}{\theta} < \frac{\delta F}{\delta \rho} < -\frac{\delta F/\delta P}{\theta} + 2\left(\frac{-\delta F/\delta P}{\theta \lambda_P}\right)^{\frac{1}{2}}, \quad \text{and}$$

(4) direct divergence from P^*, r^* and ρ^* if

$$-\frac{\delta F/\delta P}{\theta} + 2\left(\frac{-\delta F/\delta P}{\theta \lambda_P}\right)^{\frac{1}{2}} < \frac{\delta F}{\delta \rho}.$$

5 Inflation and unemployment

This chapter shifts the analytical focus to the market for
labor services and considers in detail the coincident behavior
of the rate of change of wages and the level of employment.
Section 5.1 discusses the concepts of wage inflation,
underemployment, and unemployment within the context
of a single labor market as developed in the preceding chapters.
Section 5.2 generalizes this analytical framework by
introducing heterogeneous labor services and deriving a
richer model of the coincident behavior of unemployment and
wage inflation. Sections 5.3, 5.4, and 5.5 expand this model to
consider the implications of asymmetrical wage response, gradual
adjustment of measured unemployment, and inflationary
expectations.

5.1 Wage inflation, underemployment, and unemployment in a single labor market

The analysis developed in chapter 2 above considered the relations
between the quantities of labor services demanded and supplied, the
rate of change of nominal wages, and the level of employment. Let us
briefly review the results of this analysis. Figures 2.8–2.11 illustrate
effective market-clearing loci for labor services, labeled $l^{d'} = l^s$ and
$l^d = l^{s'}$. These loci divide $(M/P, W/P)$ space into a region of excess
labor demand to the right and a region of excess labor supply to the
left. In the excess demand region employment equals the quantity
supplied, whereas in the excess supply region employment equals the
quantity demanded.

Figures 2.9 and 2.11 illustrate iso-employment loci. The
maximum employment level l^* coincides with the unique combination
of M/P and W/P which is consistent with general market clearing.
Movement away from l^* in any direction, including movement along
the effective market-clearing loci, implies lower levels of employment.
At each point, actual employment is equal to the smaller of the quantities
effectively supplied and demanded – that is, $l = \min(l^{d'}, l^{s'})$. Recall
that $l^{d'}$ is less than l^d if there is excess supply in the commodity market.
Otherwise, $l^{d'}$ coincides with l^d. Similarly, $l^{s'}$ is less than l^s if there is
excess demand in the commodity market. Otherwise, $l^{s'}$ coincides with
l^s.

Figure 2.10 associates $(M/P, W/P)$ space with the dynamics of wages and prices. The wage adjustment relation was assumed to be

$$\frac{1}{W}\frac{dW}{dt} = \lambda_w(l^{d'} - l^{s'}).$$

This relation implied that nominal wages are constant at points on the effective market-clearing loci, that nominal wages are rising in the region of excess demand, and that nominal wages are falling in the region of excess supply.

5.1.1   *Wage inflation and underemployment*

The difference between l^* and l represents the amount by which actual employment falls short of the maximum level of employment. We refer to this shortfall as the amount of underemployment. Through the production function, the current amount of underemployment corresponds to the shortfall of output below the maximum level of output. The results just summarized imply that the coincident behavior of the rate of change of wages and the amount of underemployment does not involve a unique relation. Because $(1/W)(dW/dt)$ equals zero at all points on the effective market-clearing loci, a constant wage does not imply zero underemployment, and positive underemployment does not imply that wages are changing. However, because the effective market-clearing loci include the general market-clearing point, zero underemployment does imply a constant wage, and any non-zero value for $(1/W)(dW/dt)$ implies positive underemployment.

Figure 5.1 illustrates the coincident behavior of the rate of change of wages and the amount of underemployment. Any combination in the shaded area is possible, depending on the existing values of M/P and W/P. We depict the boundaries of the shaded area as linear for convenience only.

5.1.2   *Unemployment*

Most popular discussions of labor market conditions focus not on the level of employment or underemployment, but rather on the amount of 'unemployment'. Unfortunately, the concept of unemployment is not unambiguous, and we must exercise caution in associating particular theoretical constructs with particular empirical definitions which are employed in the collection of unemployment data. The theoretical concept of unemployment which emerges naturally in the present context is the difference between the quantity of labor effectively supplied and the level of employment, that is

$$U \equiv l^{s'} - l$$

where U represents the flow of unemployment, measured in man-hours per year.[1]

In general, this theoretical concept of unemployment does not correspond to the concept of underemployment. Specifically, although

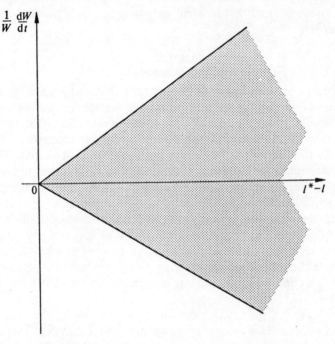

Figure 5.1
Wage inflation and underemployment

the existence of general market clearing and zero underemployment implies zero unemployment, the clearing of the labor market and zero unemployment does not imply zero underemployment. Thus, to the extent that $l^{s'}$ differs from l^*, U differs from the amount of underemployment and, hence, does not measure the actual potential for increasing employment. However, a main reason for focusing on unemployment is that it is apparently more readily measurable than is underemployment.

In this regard, we can also note that our theoretical concept

---

[1] The use of the symbol U to represent unemployment has obvious notational advantages, despite the fact that we have already used this symbol to represent utility.

represented by U does not correspond precisely to the measured unemployment statistic reported by the US Bureau of Labor Statistics. There are at least three possible sources of discrepancy. First, the measured unemployment statistic involves a stock of men rather than a flow of man-hours. Section 5.4 below discusses the possibility that these two measures diverge and the implications of such a divergence. Second, offers to sell labor services as reported in the BLS survey may differ from the effective supply of labor services. For example, under excess supply conditions, if households think that actual employment is directly related to the amount which they offer to work, they may offer to work in excess of their desired employment. Alternatively, if looking for work is costly, households may not bother to make offers which they do not expect to be successful.[2] Third, the measured unemployment statistic involves a broader concept than is encompassed by our theoretical construct. In the BLS survey, an individual might report himself as unemployed in either of two situations. As one possibility, he might be offering to accept employment, for which he is qualified, at the wage generally being paid to people currently employed in that labor market, but be currently unable to find such a job. This situation would reflect the existence of excess supply in the labor market. As a second possibility, he might have job offers in hand, but be unwilling to accept any of them, because they do not measure up to his subjective beliefs regarding the wages being offered elsewhere to people with his qualifications. This situation would result from incomplete information on the part of labor suppliers regarding the relevant alternatives which they face. The present analysis deals only with the first of these two situations – that is, it concentrates on the failure of labor markets to clear, but abstracts from the informational problem involved in the employment-acceptance decision. Chapter 7 below discusses this latter problem.

Figure 5.2 illustrates the coincident behavior of the rate of change of wages and the amount of unemployment. Along the effective labor market-clearing loci, both $(1/W)(dW/dt)$ and U are zero. To the right of the effective market-clearing loci, $(1/W)(dW/dt)$ is positive but U remains zero. To the left of the effective market-clearing loci, $(1/W)(dW/dt)$ is negative but U is positive. Moreover, in this region each combination of M/P and W/P implies an amount of excess supply of labor services and, hence, a specific combination of $(1/W)(dW/dt)$ and U.

5.2 Wage inflation and unemployment with heterogeneous labor

The discussion in the preceding sections has been limited to the context of a single labor market for homogeneous labor services. As is illustrated

---

[2] These considerations involve the behavior of secondary workers and the phenomenon of discouraged workers. See, also, Grossman (1974*a*).

by figure 5.2, this framework yields a limited model of the coincident behavior of unemployment and wage inflation. Specifically, figure 5.2 associates all nonnegative rates of wage change with zero unemployment, and permits an inverse relation between $(1/W)(dW/dt)$ and U only for negative rates of wage change. Both of these implications are counter to empirical evidence.

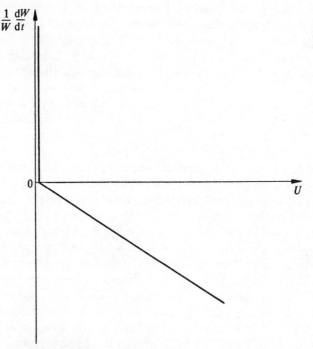

Figure 5.2
Wage inflation and unemployment in a single labor market

In order to generate a richer model of the coincident behavior of unemployment and wage inflation, this section generalizes the analytical framework by introducing heterogeneous labor services. Consider a framework of n different labor markets for n different types of labor, which are distinguished either by quality or by location. Each type of labor is homogenous and in each labor market the wage currently being paid is uniform. We want to analyze the coincident behavior of the rate of change of average wages and the aggregate unemployment rate. This analysis requires that we derive relations between each of these observed variables and an aggregate measure of excess demand. We derive these relations by aggregating the structural relations between the rate of wage change and excess demand and between unemployment and excess demand in each of the n labor markets.

5.2.1 The rate of average wage inflation

Consider first the relation between wage change and excess demand. Assume that the rate of change of the wage for each type of labor depends on the amount of excess demand for that type of labor – that is,

$$\frac{1}{W_i}\frac{dW_i}{dt} = \lambda_w \frac{l_i^{d'} - l_i^{s'}}{l_i^{s'}}, \, i \, \varepsilon \, N \tag{5.1}$$

where the variables are defined as follows:

N is the set of all labor markets, i.e., $N \equiv \{1,2, \ldots, n\}$,
W_i is the wage rate for the ith type of labor,
$l_i^{d'}$ is the quantity demanded of the ith type of labor,
$l_i^{s'}$ is the quantity supplied of the ith type of labor.

Note that equation (5.1), in order to simplify the computations which follow, measures excess demand as a fraction of the quantity supplied.

The determination of the rate of average wage inflation requires aggregation of equation (5.1) over the n labor markets. Define the average level of wages as

$$W \equiv \frac{1}{l} \sum_{i \varepsilon N} l_i W_i, \text{ where } l \equiv \sum_{i \varepsilon N} l_i,$$

and l_i represents employment of the ith type of labor. Taking the derivative of W with respect to time, holding the l_i fixed, gives for the rate of change of the average level of wages

$$\frac{dW}{dt} \equiv \frac{1}{l} \sum_{i \varepsilon N} l_i \frac{dW_i}{dt}.$$

This definition of dW/dt amounts to a Laspeyres Index. Using these definitions to aggregate equation (5.1) yields

$$\frac{1}{W}\frac{dW}{dt} = \lambda_w \sum_{i \varepsilon N} \frac{l_i W_i}{lW} \cdot \frac{l_i^{d'} - l_i^{s'}}{l_i^{s'}} \equiv \lambda_w H. \tag{5.2}$$

Equation (5.2) says that the proportionate rate of change of average money wages varies directly with a weighted average measure of excess demand for labor, denoted by H, where the weights are the share of each type of labor in the total wage bill.

The analysis in this chapter assumes that H is exogenously determined, either by the parameters of the system or as a policy instrument. Specifically, we ignore any feedback on H associated with changes in W. In this framework it is the exogenously generated cycle in H which is responsible for any observed cycles in wage inflation.

5.2.2   The aggregate level of unemployment

Consider next the relation between unemployment and excess demand. In the present context, the determination of the aggregate unemployment rate involves both the relation between excess demand and unemployment in each market and the form of the intermarket distribution of excess demands. The assumptions of homogenous labor and a uniform wage in each labor market imply a simple and unambiguous measure of unemployment – namely,

$$U_i = l_i^{s'} - l_i \text{ and } u_i = U_i/l_i^{s'}, i \ \varepsilon \ N, \tag{5.3}$$

where U_i represents unemployment of the ith type of labor, and u_i is the unemployment rate for the ith type of labor.

The relation between unemployment and excess demand involves the nature of the restrictions on actual transactions in each market. We have assumed previously that in each market exchange is voluntary, which implies $l_i \leq \min \ (l_i^{d'}, l_i^{s'})$, and that in each market exchange exhausts all possibilities which are mutually advantageous at the current wage, which implies $l_i \geq \min \ (l_i^{d'}, l_i^{s'})$. Taken together, these two assumptions imply

$$l_i = \min \ (l_i^{d'}, l_i^{s'}), i \ \varepsilon \ N. \tag{5.4}$$

Combining equations (5.3) and (5.4) yields

$$U_i = \max \ (l_i^{s'} - l_i^{d'}, 0), i \ \varepsilon \ N. \tag{5.5}$$

According to equation (5.5), in each market, unemployment equals the absolute amount of excess demand, whenever excess demand is negative. Otherwise, unemployment is zero.

The determination of aggregate unemployment requires the aggregation of equation (5.5) over the n labor markets. The aggregate unemployment rate, represented by u, is defined as

$$u \equiv \frac{1}{l^{s'}} \sum_{i \varepsilon N} U_i \equiv \sum_{i \varepsilon N} \frac{l_i^{s'}}{l^{s'}} u_i, \text{ where } l^{s'} = \sum_{i \varepsilon N} l_i^{s'}.$$

According to this (standard) definition, u is a weighted average of the unemployment rate in each market, where the weights are the share of each market in the total labor force.

The immediate problem is to relate u to H, the aggregate measure of excess demand introduced in the preceding section.[3] To obtain the desired properties, assume that the rate of excess demand, weighted by the labor-force share, in each market is a linear increasing function of H – that is,

$$\frac{l_i^{s'}}{l^{s'}} \cdot \frac{l_i^{d'} - l_i^{s'}}{l_i^{s'}} = F_i(H), \; F_i' > 0, \; F_i'' = 0, \; i \; \varepsilon \; N. \tag{5.6}$$

Equation (5.6) says that an increase in H has the effect of increasing excess demand in each market and that the magnitude of these effects is independent of the level of H.[4]

It is convenient to index the markets in order of decreasing rates of excess demand, weighted by labor-force share. Specifically, the first market has the largest rate of excess demand, weighted by labor-force share, and the nth market has the smallest rate of excess demand, weighted by labor-force share. The rate of excess demand in the nth market will typically be negative. According to this indexing scheme, $F_i(H)$ is algebraically larger the smaller the value of the index i. Moreover, the index of a particular market changes whenever its relative excess demand position changes.

Equation (5.6) implicitly assumes that the functions $F_i(H)$ are independent of time. This assumption implies that the distribution of excess demand magnitudes, weighted by labor-force share, is constant over time. This constancy, in turn, implies a balancing of two forces. First, the adjustment of wages over time, as specified by equation (5.1), is continually tending to reduce the absolute magnitudes of excess demands and thereby to reduce the dispersion of excess demand magnitudes. Any mobility across markets of workers and firms in response to perceived differentials in wages and unemployment rates would

---

[3] Hansen (1970) also develops a model along the lines of what follows.
[4] One troublesome aspect of equation (5.6) is that it relates labor-force-weighted rates of excess demand to the wage-bill-weighted average rate of excess demand. It might be more plausible to assume a linear relation between H and

$$\frac{l_i W_i}{lW} \cdot \frac{l_i^{d'} - l_i^{s'}}{l_i^{s'}}$$

However, this alternative assumption would lead to a relation between H and a wage-bill-weighted, rather than a labor-force-weighted, measure of aggregate unemployment. Whether such an alternative measure of unemployment would be more useful is an open empirical question. See Perry (1970) for some related evidence.

reinforce this effect. Second, unforeseen exogenous structural disturbances are by implication continually tending to increase the dispersion
of excess demand magnitudes. Note, however, that the constancy of
the functions $F_i(H)$ does not imply that the relative magnitude of excess
demand in each specific market is constant. Excess demand can be
declining in some markets, in response to wage adjustments, while
excess demand is increasing in other markets, because of exogenous
disturbances. In other words, the relative excess demand positions of
the markets can be changing, and, hence, the indexes applied to particular
markets can be changing, without altering the dispersion of excess
demands, as expressed by the $F_i(H)$ functions.

Combining equation (5.5) and (5.6) and the definition of u
yields

$$u = \sum_{i \epsilon N} \max \left[- F_i(H), 0 \right]. \tag{5.7}$$

To facilitate analysis of equation (5.7), divide the n markets into two
non-intersecting subsets, one comprising all markets which are experiencing nonnegative excess demand and the other comprising all
other markets. Specifically, define

$$N_1 \equiv \{i \; \epsilon \; N | l_i^{d'} - l_{i}^{s'} \geq 0\} \text{ and } N_2 \equiv \{i \; \epsilon \; N | l_i^{d'} - l_i^{s'} < 0\}.$$

Denote the number of markets in set N_1 by n_1 and the number of markets
in set N_2 by n_2. Using these definitions and equation (5.6), equation
(5.7) can be rewritten as

$$u = - \sum_{i \epsilon N_2} F_i(H). \tag{5.8}$$

Notice also that n_2 is a function of H – specifically, $n_2 = n_2(H)$, where
$n_2'(H) < 0$. Thus, equation (5.8) is a piece-wise linear function. Along
each segment, the derivative of u with respect to H is negative. At each
switching point, the left-hand derivative is less than the right-hand
derivative. Thus equation (5.8) is also a convex function. In other
words, as H increases, unemployment decreases in all markets in which
unemployment is positive – that is, in all markets in which excess demand
is negative. Moreover, as H increases, the number of such markets
decreases.

Two further characteristics of equation (5.8) are especially
worth noting. First, u is bounded from below by zero. However, this
boundary is not reached until H is so large that n_2 equals zero – that is,
until no market has positive excess supply. Second, the value of u
associated with H equal to zero, which we denote by u^*, is given by

$$u^* = - \sum_{i \epsilon N_2} F_i(0), \text{ where } n_2 = n_2 (0).$$

The important phenomenon is that $n_2(0) > 0$ implies $u^* > 0$. In other words, if structural imbalance is such that $H = 0$, i.e., if zero aggregate excess demand would be associated with positive excess demand in some markets and negative excess demand in other markets, then $H = 0$ would also be associated with positive aggregate unemployment. The counterpart of this positive unemployment would be a positive number of unfilled vacancies. The general point is that, even though in each market exchange exhausts all mutually advantageous possibilities, the existence of structural imbalance means that aggregate employment falls short of both the aggregate quantity supplied and the aggregate quantity demanded. Finally, if n is very large, we can approximate equation (5.8) as a smooth, decreasing and convex function – specifically,

$$u = G(H), \ G'(H) < 0, \ G''(H) > 0,$$

$$u^* \equiv G(0) > 0, \text{ and } \lim_{H \to \infty} G(H) = 0. \tag{5.9}$$

The above discussion has derived a structural relation between the rate of change of average wages and aggregate excess demand, given by equation (5.2), and a structural relation between the aggregate unemployment rate and aggregate excess demand, given by equation (5.9). Given an exogenous cycle in aggregate excess demand, these structural relations together generate coincident behavior of wage inflation and unemployment, which conforms to movements up and down the solid locus, depicted in figure 5.3. This locus, given by

$$u = G \left(\frac{1}{W} \frac{dW}{dt} \Big/ \lambda_W \right),$$

is downward sloping and convex, has a positive intercept on the u axis, and is asymptotic to the $\dot{W}/W$ axis. This solid locus corresponds to the empirical construct known as the Phillips curve. The dashed arrows in figure 5.3 are discussed in section 5.4 below.

5.3 Asymmetrical wage response

The discussion in the preceding section assumed the response of wage change to excess demand to be a symmetric relation. Some authors have suggested that the alternative assumption of asymmetrical wage response would help to explain the coincident behavior of unemployment and wage inflation. The essential idea involves replacing equations (5.1) and (5.2) with a formulation such as the following: Assume, in place of equation (5.1), that

$$\frac{1}{W_i}\frac{dW_i}{dt} = \lambda_1 \frac{l_i^{d'} - l_i^{s'}}{l_i^{s'}} \text{ for } i \, \varepsilon \, N_1 \text{ where } l_i^{d'} \geq l_i^{s'},$$

and

$$\frac{1}{W_i}\frac{dW_i}{dt} = \lambda_2 \frac{l_i^{d'} - l_i^{s'}}{l_i^{s'}} \text{ for } i \, \varepsilon \, N_2 \text{ where } l_i^{d'} < l_i^{s'}. \tag{5.10}$$

where $\lambda_1 > \lambda_2$.

Equations (5.10) say that wages adjust more rapidly in response to positive excess demand than in response to negative excess demand.

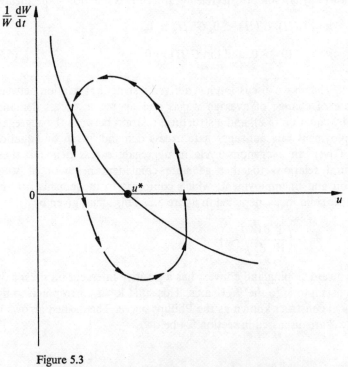

Figure 5.3
Wage inflation and unemployment with heterogeneous labor

What does this asymmetry imply for the relation between unemployment and the inflation of average wages? Aggregating equations (5.10) yields

$$\frac{1}{W}\frac{dW}{dt} = \lambda_1 \sum_{i \varepsilon N_1} \frac{l_i W_i}{l W} \cdot \frac{l_i^{d'} - l_i^{s'}}{l_i^{s'}} + \lambda_2 \sum_{i \varepsilon N_2} \frac{l_i W_i}{l W} \cdot \frac{l_i^{d'} - l_i^{s'}}{l_i^{s'}}. \tag{5.11}$$

Given that λ_1 exceeds λ_2, equation (5.11) implies that, unless $l_i^{d'} = l_i^{s'}$ for all i, a zero value for $(1/W)(dW/dt)$ requires a negative value for H. In other words, with this particular asymmetry in wage response, a zero rate of increase of average money wages implies a negative level of aggregate excess demand. Moreover, given an inverse relation between u and H, this asymmetry increases the level of unemployment associated with zero average wage increase.

However, if, as indicated by equation (5.9), the relation between u and H is inverse and convex, the introduction of asymmetrical wage response does not alter the qualitative nature of the coincident behavior of $(1/W)(dW/dt)$ and u. The relation remains downward sloping and convex. The increase in the positive intercept on the u axis represents a purely quantitative modification.

Alternatively, if we return to the framework involving a single labor market, whether or not wage response is symmetrical, the relation between $(1/W)(dW/dt)$ and H would pass through the origin. Thus, the relation between $(1/W)(dW/dt)$ and u would pass through the origin and zero wage increase would imply zero unemployment. In summary, the assumption of asymmetrical wage response seems to be neither necessary nor sufficient to generate the coincident behavior of unemployment and wage inflation illustrated in figure 5.3.[5]

5.4 Gradual adjustment of measured unemployment

The theoretical concept of unemployment discussed in the preceding sections represents a flow of man hours, the difference between the man hours of labor services supplied and the man hours of labor services actually worked. However, as noted above, the measured unemployment

[5] Asymmetrical wage response might be more important if the principal exogenous disturbance were not a cycle in H. For example, consider a cycle in the degree of structural imbalance. Specifically, assume that, although H is fixed, exogenous shifts in tastes and technology produce a cycle in $\sum_{i \varepsilon N_2} F_i(H)$. With symmetrical wage response, as specified by equation (5.2), the fixity of H means fixity of $(1/W)(dW/dt)$. Consequently, the cycle in $\sum_{i \varepsilon N_2} F_i(H)$ produces only a cycle in u, as determined by equation (5.8). However, with asymmetrical wage response, as specified by equation (5.11), the cycle in $\sum_{i \varepsilon N_2} F_i(H)$ also produces a cycle in $(1/W)(dW/dt)$. For a given H, when $- \sum_{i \varepsilon N_2} F_i(H)$ is relatively large, both u and $(1/W)(dW/dt)$ would be relatively large. Thus, with asymmetrical wage response, a cycle in $\sum_{i \varepsilon N_2} F_i(H)$ would produce an upward sloping relation between u and $(1/W)(dW/dt)$.

statistic involves a stock of men, the difference between the number of people who are supplying a positive amount of labor services and the number of people who are actually selling a positive amount of labor services. In particular, a person who is selling a positive amount of labor services, but less than his quantity supplied, makes no contribution to the measured unemployment statistic.

Suppose that changes in the quantity of employment in man hours first take the form of changes in number of hours worked per week by persons already employed. However, if the quantity of employment remains at its new level, the persons employed begin returning to working the normal number of hours per week, and the number of persons employed is gradually changed. This gradual adjustment in the number of persons employed may reflect higher short-run costs of adjusting the number of persons employed than of adjusting the number of hours worked by persons already employed.

This assumption suggests that, if we want to analyze the measured unemployment statistic, we should replace equation (5.4) with a relation of the form

$$\frac{dl_i}{dt} = \lambda_l[\min{(l_i^{d'}, l_i^{s'})} - l_i],\ i\ \varepsilon\ N, \tag{5.12}$$

where l_i now represents the number of employed people of the ith type of labor. Equation (5.12) says that employment in each market, measured as a stock of men, adjusts gradually towards the minimum of the quantities demanded and supplied. These quantities now represent total numbers of man hours per week divided by the number of man hours per week normally worked by one person.

Using the measure of unemployment given by equation (5.3), $U_i = l_i^{s'} - l_i$, but where U_i now represents the number of unemployed people of the ith type of labor, and assuming $l_i^{s'}$ to be constant, equation (5.12) can be rewritten as

$$\frac{dU_i}{dt} = \lambda_l[\max{(l_i^{s'} - l_i^{d'}, 0)} - U_i],\ i\ \varepsilon\ N. \tag{5.13}$$

Aggregating equation (5.13) over all the labor markets, using the definition $u \equiv \sum_{i\varepsilon N} U_i/l^{s'}$ with $l^{s'}$ constant, and substituting in the relation of equation (5.6) between excess demand in the ith market and aggregate excess demand, yields

$$\frac{du}{dt} = \lambda_l\left[\sum_{i\varepsilon N}\max{[-F_i(H), 0]} - u\right]. \tag{5.14}$$

Equation (5.14) can be rewritten as

$$\frac{du}{dt} = \lambda_l \left[- \sum_{i \varepsilon N_2} F_i(h) - u \right], \text{ where } n_2 = n_2\,(H). \tag{5.15}$$

Finally, utilizing the continuous approximation introduced in equation (5.9), equation (5.15) can be expressed as

$$\frac{du}{dt} = \lambda_l[G(H) - u], \tag{5.16}$$

where $G(H)$ is as specified in equation (5.9).

Equation (5.16) says that the aggregate unemployment rate, u, is always tending towards $G(H)$. Consequently, given an exogenous cycle in H, the average relation between u and H corresponds to $G(H)$. Moreover, u is below $G(H)$ whenever u is rising, and u is above $G(H)$ whenever u is falling.

The structural relation given by equation (5.16), together with the structural relation between $(1/W)(dW/dt)$ and H, given by equation (5.2), and an exogenous cycle in H, generates a counterclockwise cycle of four phases in the relation between u and $(1/W)(dW/dt)$.[6] The dashed arrow in figure 5.3 illustrates such a counterclockwise cycle. Such cycles correspond to the empirical observations of Phillips.

Consider, in turn, the four cyclical phases, starting with H at its trough. According to equation (5.2), a trough in H also implies a trough in $(1/W)(dW/dt)$. Also, assume that initially u is less than $G(H)$, which, according to equation (5.16), implies that du/dt is positive.

(1) In the first phase, H begins to increase. Consequently, $(1/W)(dW/dt)$ also begins to increase. However, with u less than $G(H)$, du/dt initially remains positive. Thus, at the trough in H, a rise in wage inflation is associated with a continued rise in unemployment.

(2) However, as H and u increase, u and $G(H)$ steadily converge. Eventually, the peak in u is reached when the actual path of wage inflation and unemployment crosses the Phillips curve. As H continues to increase, u exceeds $G(H)$, and du/dt becomes negative. Thus, a continued increase in wage inflation is eventually associated, in the second

---

[6] An alternative rationalization for a counterclockwise cycle, along the lines suggested by Lipsey (1960), would be that the degree of structural imbalance between labor markets varies inversely with the value of dH/dt. Specifically, one might assume that, for a given H, the value of $- \sum_{i \varepsilon N_2} F_i(H)$ is greater when dH/dt is positive than when dH/dt is negative. This explanation, in contrast to the explanation developed above, generates a cycle with only two phases, both negatively sloped, in the shape of a crescent.

phase, with declining unemployment. This second phase represents classic expansion.

(3) Eventually H reaches its peak and begins, in the third phase, to decline. At that point, $(1/W)(dW/dt)$ also peaks and begins to decline. However, because u exceeds $G(H)$, du/dt initially remains negative. Thus, at the peak, a decline in wage inflation is associated with a continued decline in unemployment.

(4) Eventually, the actual path of wage inflation and unemployment again crosses the Phillips curve as the trough in u is reached. Then, as H continues to decrease $G(H)$ exceeds u, and du/dt becomes positive. Thus, in the fourth phase, as H and $(1/W)(dW/dt)$ move toward the trough, declining wage inflation becomes associated with rising unemployment. This fourth phase represents classic contraction. When the trough is reached, the revival of H leads back into the first phase described above.

The temporal duration of the first and third phases of this cycle, relative to the more classic second and fourth phases, varies inversely with the rate of the exogenous change in H and with the speed of adjustment, λ_l. For example, if H and $(1/W)(dW/dt)$ rise rapidly from their trough, and if λ_l is large, so that u and $G(H)$ converge rapidly, then phase one, the period of transition from rising unemployment to declining unemployment, will be short. Similarly, if H declines rapidly from its peak and λ_l is large, phase three will be short.

5.5 Unemployment, wage inflation, and inflationary expectations

The discussion in this chapter thus far has ignored the role of expectations regarding the rate of change of the market-clearing wage. Equation (5.1) assumed that the rate of change of the wage for each type of labor depends only on the amount of excess demand for that type of labor. However, in chapter 4 we argued that a plausible adjustment policy for prices would take account of any anticipated change in P^* without waiting for it to add to the finite discrepancy between P and P^*. The adjustment of wages, with which we are concerned in the present chapter, should involve an analogous consideration. Consequently, it would seem appropriate to replace equation (5.1) with

$$\frac{1}{W_i}\frac{dW_i}{dt} = \lambda_w \frac{l_i^{d'} - l_i^{s'}}{l_i^{s'}} + \rho_i^*, i \, \varepsilon \, N, \qquad (5.17)$$

where ρ_i^* is the proportionate anticipated rate of change of the market-clearing wage for the ith type of labor. This expectation can be viewed as the sum of two components: first, the expected rate of change of output price, which indicates the rate of change of nominal wages which is consistent with stability of the real wage; second, the expected rate of change of the market-clearing real wage, which may reflect the expected trend of productivity. According to equation (5.17), wage adjustment results from the summing of two component forces: first, an attempt to correct any existing discrepancy between the current and market-clearing wage and, second, an attempt to anticipate and prevent any potential future discrepancies between actual and market-clearing wages.

Using the definitions of the average level of wages, $W \equiv \sum_{i\epsilon N} l_i W_i / l$, and of the rate of change of the average level of wages, $\dfrac{dW}{dt} = \sum_{i\epsilon N} l_i \dfrac{dW_i}{dt} \Big/ l$, to aggregate equation (5.17) yields

$$\frac{1}{W}\frac{dW}{dt} = \lambda_W \sum_{i\epsilon N} \frac{l_i W}{lW} \cdot \frac{l_i^{d'} - l_i^{s'}}{l_i^{s'}} + \sum_{i\epsilon N} \frac{l_i W_i}{lW} \rho_i^*$$

$$= \lambda_W H + \rho_W^*. \tag{5.18}$$

Equation (5.18) says that the proportionate rate of change of average money wages equals $\lambda_W H$ plus the weighted average expected rate of change of market-clearing money wages, denoted by ρ_W^*, where the weights are, as in H, the share of each market in the total wage bill. In other words, the level of H alone determines, not the actual rate of wage inflation, but rather the difference between the actual rate of wage inflation and the average expected rate of change of market-clearing wages. Consequently, a zero rate of change of average money wages requires a value of H which varies inversely with ρ_W^*, rather than simply H equal to zero. Equation (5.18) represents a generalization of equation (5.2).

Taken together, the structural relation between $(1/W)(dW/dt)$, ρ_W^*, and H, given by equation (5.18), and the structural relation $u = G(H)$, given by equation (5.9), imply that the coincident behavior of wage inflation and unemployment conforms to the relation

$$u = G\left(\frac{\dfrac{1}{W}\dfrac{dW}{dt} - \rho_W^*}{\lambda_W}\right).$$

Thus, given the value of ρ_W^*, the relation between $(1/W)(dW/dt)$ and u is downward sloping and convex, like the Phillips curve depicted in figure 5.3. However, the position of the Phillips curve relation between $(1/W)(dW/dt)$ and u now depends on the value of ρ_W^*. The solid loci in figure 5.4 depict a few of the possibilities. With ρ_W^* equal to zero, the Phillips curve passes through the point at which u equals u^* and $(1/W)$ (dW/dt) equals zero. However, each increase in ρ_W^* shifts the Phillips

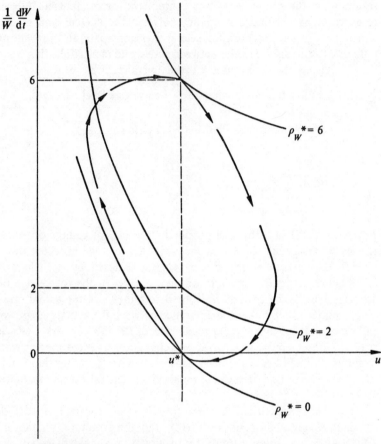

Figure 5.4
Wage inflation and unemployment with inflationary expectations

curve upward, so that, in general, u equal to u^* is associated with $(1/W)(dW/dt)$ equal to ρ_W^*.

5.5.1 *Clockwise cycles and accelerating inflation*

In order to analyze the cyclical significance of the variable ρ_W^*, we must specify the process by which it is generated. Following the formulation of chapter 4, we assume that the expectations ρ_W^* are based on the past experience of $(1/W_i)(dW_i/dt)$ in the form of a linear adaptation mechanism – that is,

$$\frac{d\rho_i^*}{dt} = \theta_\rho \left(\frac{1}{W_i} \frac{dW_i}{dt} - \rho_i^* \right), i \varepsilon N, \tag{5.19}$$

where the coefficient θ_ρ is a positive constant. Neglecting changes over time in the weights $l_i W_i / lW$, the definition of ρ_W^* implies

$$\frac{d\rho_W^*}{dt} = \sum_{i \varepsilon N} \frac{l_i W_i}{lW} \frac{d\rho_i^*}{dt}.$$

Aggregating equation (5.19) then gives

$$\frac{d\rho_W^*}{dt} = \theta_\rho \left(\frac{1}{W} \frac{dW}{dt} - \rho_W^* \right). \tag{5.20}$$

Equation (5.20) says that the average expected rate of change of market-clearing wages adjusts at a finite rate towards the actual rate of change of average wages. Combining equations (5.18) and (5.20) to eliminate the unobservable expectations variable yields

$$\frac{d \left(\frac{1}{W} \frac{dW}{dt} \right)}{dt} = \lambda_W \left(\theta_\rho H + \frac{dH}{dt} \right). \tag{5.21}$$

Abstract for the moment from gradual adjustment of employment, and consider the structural relation described by equation (5.21), together with the structural relation $u = G(H)$, given by equation (5.9). Given an exogenous cycle in H, this model also generates a cycle of four phases in the relation between u and $(1/W)(dW/dt)$. However, this cycle corresponds to the clockwise looping pattern which has been observed in recent years. The dashed arrow in figure 5.4 illustrates such a clockwise cycle.

Consider, in turn, the four phases of this cycle, again starting with H at its trough. According to equation (5.9), a trough in H implies a peak in u. Also, assume that initially $(1/W)(dW/dt)$ is less than ρ_W^*, which, according to equation (5.18), implies that H is negative, and, according to equation (5.20), implies that ρ_W^* is decreasing. With dH/dt equal to zero and H negative, according to equation (5.21), $(1/W)(dW/dt)$ is also initially decreasing.

(1) In the first phase, H begins to increase. Consequently, u begins to decrease. However, unless H rises very rapidly, the continued decline in ρ_W^* keeps $(1/W)(dW/dt)$ falling. According to equation (5.21), when H is negative, $(1/W)(dW/dt)$ is decreasing as long as $-(1/H)$

$(\mathrm{d}H/\mathrm{d}t)$ is less than θ_ρ. Thus, at the trough in H, a decrease in unemployment is associated with a continued decline in wage inflation.

(2) According to equation (5.20), as ρ_W^* approaches $(1/W)$ $(\mathrm{d}W/\mathrm{d}t)$, the rate of decrease of ρ_W^* declines. Equivalently, when H is negative, as H increases, $-(1/H)(\mathrm{d}H/\mathrm{d}t)$ also increases. According to equation (5.21), the trough in $(1/W)(\mathrm{d}W/\mathrm{d}t)$ is reached when $-(1/H)(\mathrm{d}H/\mathrm{d}t)$ equals θ_ρ. Notice that this point occurs before H reaches zero. As H continues to increase, $-(1/H)(\mathrm{d}H/\mathrm{d}t)$ exceeds θ_ρ, and $(1/W)(\mathrm{d}W/\mathrm{d}t)$ begins to increase. Thus, the continued decrease in unemployment is eventually associated, in the second phase, with a steady increase in wage inflation. The second phase again represents classic expansion.

In this phase, when H reaches zero, $(1/W)(\mathrm{d}W/\mathrm{d}t)$ momentarily equals ρ_W^*, and ρ_W^* is momentarily constant. As this point, the actual path of wage inflation and unemployment is tangent to a Phillips curve. However, as H continues to increase and becomes positive, $(1/W)$ $(\mathrm{d}W/\mathrm{d}t)$ exceeds ρ_W^*, which causes ρ_W^* to begin increasing. Through equation (5.18), this increase in ρ_W^* feeds back into $(1/W)(\mathrm{d}W/\mathrm{d}t)$, and the actual path of wage inflation and unemployment rises more steeply. If H remains positive, even if its value stabilizes, $(1/W)(\mathrm{d}W/\mathrm{d}t)$ increases indefinitely.[7]

(3) Eventually H reaches its peak and, in the third phase, begins to decline. Consequently, u reaches a trough and begins to rise. However, with H positive, $(1/W)(\mathrm{d}W/\mathrm{d}t)$ now exceeds ρ_W^*, and ρ_W^* is increasing. Unless H declines very rapidly, this continued increase in ρ_W^* keeps $(1/W)(\mathrm{d}W/\mathrm{d}t)$ rising. According to equation (5.21), when H is positive, $(1/W)(\mathrm{d}W/\mathrm{d}t)$ is increasing as long as $-(1/H)(\mathrm{d}H/\mathrm{d}t)$ remains less than θ_ρ. Thus, at the peak in H, an increase in unemployment is associated, not only with a continuation of wage inflation, but with a continued increase in wage inflation. This unfortunate coincidence represents what has been called stagflation.

(4) As ρ_W^* approaches $(1/W)(\mathrm{d}W/\mathrm{d}t)$, the rate of increase of ρ_W^* declines. Equivalently, as H decreases, $-(1/H)(\mathrm{d}H/\mathrm{d}t)$ increases, and the peak in $(1/W)(\mathrm{d}W/\mathrm{d}t)$ is reached when $-(1/H)(\mathrm{d}H/\mathrm{d}t)$ equals θ_ρ. Thus, given the reversal of the signs of $\mathrm{d}H/\mathrm{d}t$ and H, the condition for transition from phase three to phase four is the same as the condition for transition from phase one to phase two. Notice also that, analogously to the trough in $(1/W)(\mathrm{d}W/\mathrm{d}t)$, the peak in wage inflation occurs before H reaches zero. As H continues to decrease, $(1/W)(\mathrm{d}W/\mathrm{d}t)$ begins to decrease. In the fourth phase, the continued increase in unemployment

---

[7] Seminal discussions of this possibility of expectations-induced acceleration of wages include Phelps (1967) and Friedman (1968).

is associated with a steady decrease in wage inflation. The fourth phase again represents classic contraction.

In this phase, when H reaches zero, the actual path of wage inflation and unemployment is again momentarily tangent to a Phillips curve, although at a higher level of ρ_W^* than in phase two. As H continues to increase, ρ_W^* begins to decline, and the actual path of wage inflation and unemployment falls more steeply. If H stabilizes at a negative value, $(1/W)(dW/dt)$ declines indefinitely. More relevantly, when H becomes negative, and consequently, ρ_W^* exceeds $(1/W)(dW/dt)$, the revival of H leads back into the first phase described above.

The temporal duration of the first and third phases of this cycle, relative to the more classic second and fourth phases, is larger the smaller is the magnitude of the proportionate rate of change of aggregate excess demand, $(1/H)(dH/dt)$, and the larger is the speed of adjustment of expectations, θ_ρ.[8] For example, if H rises rapidly from its trough, so that u declines rapidly from its peak, and if θ_ρ is small, so that ρ_W^* declines only slowly towards $(1/W)(dW/dt)$, phase one, the period of transition from declining to increasing wage inflation, will be short. Moreover, the same conditions – that is, rapid adjustment of expectations relative to the absolute rate of change of excess demand – which would prolong this favorable phase would also produce a lengthy stagflation phase at the opposite side of the cycle.

Another important implication of the model developed in this section is that an inverse relation between unemployment and wage inflation would be apparent only because the expected rate of inflation lags behind the actual rate as H fluctuates. As we have seen, if H should stabilize at either a positive or negative value, $(1/W)(dW/dt)$ would either increase or decrease indefinitely. More generally, if the average value of H were either positive or negative over successive cycles, the average value of $(1/W)(dW/dt)$ would either increase or decrease from cycle to cycle. Figure 5.5 illustrates a situation in which the average value of H is positive. In the long run, wage inflation would either increase or decrease unless H averaged zero. An average value of H equal to zero in turn implies an average value of unemployment given by $u^* \equiv G(0)$. Thus, in the long run, the level of unemployment becomes independent of the rate of wage inflation.

From an empirical standpoint, an interesting question is whether, if we were to accept the model developed in this section, we would still expect to find the best-fitted relation between $(1/W)(dW/dt)$ and u over each cycle in H to be inverse. A pair of conditions which

---

[8] Recall that the present analysis treats H as exogenous. Specifically, H is independent of θ_ρ.

together would be sufficient to insure such an inverse relation are the following. First, the level of u at the trough of $(1/W)(dW/dt)$ should exceed the level of u at the peak of $(1/W)(dW/dt)$. If H is negative at the trough of $(1/W)(dW/dt)$ and positive at the peak of $(1/W)(dW/dt)$, this condition obtains. Second, the level of $(1/W)(dW/dt)$ at the trough

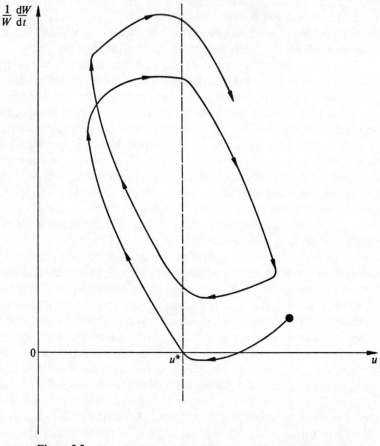

Figure 5.5
Wage inflation and unemployment with rising inflationary expectations

of u (peak of H) should exceed the level of $(1/W)(dW/dt)$ at the peak of u (trough of H). This second condition holds if θ_ρ is small enough relative to the absolute average value of H over the cycle. As a special case, if the average value of H over the cycle equals zero, this condition holds for all finite values of θ_ρ. In summary, even if u and $(1/W)(dW/dt)$ are independent in the long run, an average inverse relation between u and $(1/W)(dW/dt)$ over each cycle in H remains highly probable.

5.5.2 The dominant cyclical pattern

Section 5.2 developed a basic model of the average inverse relation between u and $(1/W)(dW/dt)$. Equation (5.2), $(1/W)(dW/dt) = \lambda_w H$, and equation (5.9), $u = G(H)$, summarized this model. Section 5.4 introduced partial adjustment into the relation between u and H. This modification generated equation (5.16), $du/dt = \lambda_l[G(H) - u]$, as a generalization of equation (5.9). With λ_l less than infinite, the model, summarized by equations (5.2) and (5.16), predicted a counterclockwise cyclical pattern. Section 5.5 introduced adaptive expectations into the relation between $(1/W)(dW/dt)$ and H. This modification generated equation (5.21),

$$\frac{d\left(\dfrac{1}{W}\dfrac{dW}{dt}\right)}{dt} = \lambda_w\left(\theta_\rho H + \frac{dH}{dt}\right),$$

as a generalization of equation (5.2). With θ_ρ greater than zero, the model summarized by equations (5.9) and (5.21), predicted a clockwise cyclical pattern.

We can specify the conditions which determine the dominant cyclical tendency by analyzing equations (5.16) and (5.21) as a general model of the cyclical pattern of unemployment and wage inflation. Adopting the linear approximation $G(H) \approx u^* - gH$, $g > 0$, and then combining equations (5.16) and (5.21) to eliminate H yields

$$\frac{d\left(\dfrac{1}{W}\dfrac{dW}{dt}\right)}{dt} = \frac{\lambda_w}{g}\left[\theta_\rho\left(u^* - u - \frac{1}{\lambda_l}\frac{du}{dt}\right) - \left(\frac{du}{dt} + \frac{1}{\lambda_l}\frac{d^2u}{dt^2}\right)\right].$$

$$(5.22)$$

Consider the point in the cycle at which $\dfrac{du}{dt} = 0$ and $\dfrac{d\left(\dfrac{1}{W}\dfrac{dW}{dt}\right)}{dt} > 0$.
This point represents either the peak or the trough in unemployment coincident with accelerating wage inflation. On a counterclockwise cycle this point will be the peak in u. Consequently, this point will also involve $d^2u/dt^2 < 0$ and $u^* - u < 0$. In contrast, on a clockwise cycle, this point will be the trough in u. In this case, this point will involve

$d^2u/dt^2 > 0$ and $u^* - u > 0$. Applying these conditions to equation (5.22) yields the following results: counterclockwise cycling requires

$$\lambda_l \theta_\rho < \frac{d^2u/dt^2}{u^* - u} > 0,$$

whereas clockwise cycling requires

$$\lambda_l \theta_\rho > \frac{d^2u/dt^2}{u^* - u} > 0.$$

Thus, the tendency for clockwise cycling will be the stronger (1) the larger is the product $\lambda_l \theta_\rho$, (2) the larger is $|u^* - u|$ at the peak and trough of u, and (3) the smaller is $|d^2u/dt^2|$ at the peak and trough of u. The larger is $|u^* - u|$ at the peak and trough the greater is the amplitude of the cycle in u. The smaller is $|d^2u/dt^2|$ at the peak and trough, the slower is the deceleration of u from its peak and the acceleration of u from its trough, and, given the amplitude of the cycle, the larger is the period of the cycle. In sum, the faster the adjustment of employment and expectations and the larger the amplitude and period of the cycle, the more likely that the cycle will be clockwise.[9]

[9] Grossman (1974b) contains some further discussion of the empirical implications of this analysis.

6 The dynamics of aggregate demand

This chapter explores the implications of various structural lags for the time paths of output, employment, and the rate of return. The various lags considered involve the responses of effective demands to their proximate determinants, the adjustment of expectations regarding future levels of income and the rate of return, and the response of the rate of return to divergences between the demand and supply of financial assets. The analysis focuses on the effects of a change in monetary policy. Section 6.1 considers the model, developed in chapter 3, dealing with the determination of output, employment, and the rate of return under general excess supply. Section 6.2 generalizes the implications of the gradual adjustment phenomenon. Section 6.3 deals with the implications of adaptive expectations. Section 6.4 considers gradual clearing of the financial asset market.

6.1 Gradual adjustment of money balances

As a point of departure for the present discussion, consider the analysis, developed in section 3.4 above, dealing with the determination of output, employment, and the rate of return under general excess supply. This analysis assumes that the given values of the wage rate and price level are such that excess supply exists in the markets for both labor services and commodities. Thus, the effective demands in the respective markets determine output and employment. The analysis also assumes that the rate of return takes that value which is consistent with effective clearing of the financial asset market. Given these assumptions, we determined in section 3.4 that the levels of output and the rate of return would conform to the following relations:[1]

$$y = y^{d'}(y, r), \tag{3.43}$$
$$\underset{(+)(-)}{}$$

[1] The specification of these relations involves the suppression of all exogenous and predetermined variables, including the stock of money, M/P, and the stock of bonds, $P_b B/P$. In the analysis below, open-market operations change the stock of money and bonds by equal but opposite amounts. According to the analysis in section 3.2.3 above, these equal changes alter the present value of lifetime nonwage resources, Ω_0, and thereby affect $y^{d'}$ and $f^{d'}/P$. By employing equations (3.43) and (3.44) in the analysis which follows, we are abstracting from the cumulative effects of open-market operations on Ω_0. According

$$\frac{f^{a'}}{P}(y, r) = \frac{f^{s'}}{P}(y, r), \text{ and} \tag{3.44}$$
$$\quad\;\;{\scriptstyle(?)\,(+)}\qquad\;\;{\scriptstyle(+)(-)}$$

$$\frac{m^{a'}}{P}(y, r) = \frac{m^s}{P} = \frac{1}{P}\frac{dM}{dt}. \tag{3.46}$$
$$\quad\;\;{\scriptstyle(+)(-)}$$

Three specific aspects of these relations warrant special mention. First, given the various exogenous and predetermined variables and the production function, the value of y implied by the above equations uniquely determines the level of employment.[2] Thus, we can suppress explicit analysis of the determination of l. Second, according to the economy-wide budget constraint, equation (3.45) above, only two of the above three equations are independent. Thus, we can determine y and r by solving any two of the three equations. In the discussion which follows, we focus for convenience on the equalities between y and $y^{a'}$ and between $m^{a'}/P$ and m/P. Third, the effective flow demand for money balances, $m^{a'}/P$, represents a gradual-adjustment relation. Specifically, the more basic formulation of the $m^{a'}/P$ function is

$$\frac{m^{a'}}{P} = \lambda'_m \left[\left(\frac{M}{P}\right)' - \frac{M}{P} \right], \text{ where}$$

$$\left(\frac{M}{P}\right)' = \left(\frac{M}{P}\right)'(y, r),$$
$$\qquad\qquad\qquad\;\;{\scriptstyle(+)(-)}$$

and λ'_m is positive and is treated, for simplicity, as a constant. The reader may recall from the analysis of chapter 3 that the effective target real money balance, $(M/P)'$, corresponds to an effective target transaction frequency, v'.

In order to facilitate explicit dynamic analysis, it will be helpful to ultilize linear approximations to the $y^{a'}$ and $(M/P)'$ functions – namely,

$$y^{a'}(y, r) = y_y y - y_r r \text{ and}$$
$$\quad\;{\scriptstyle(+)(-)}$$

$$\left(\frac{M}{P}\right)'(y, r) = M_y y - M_r r,$$
$$\qquad\;\;{\scriptstyle(+)(-)}$$

---

to the analysis in section 3.2.3, this case would arise only when the households did not capitalize their future tax liabilities. However, removing this simplifying assumption would not alter the main qualitative features of the structural lags which we examine in this chapter.

[2] This analysis does not introduce any structural relations which would generate a lagged relation between employment and output. In this respect an extended treatment could consider variations in capital stock (capacity), variations in hours worked, and training costs for new workers.

where y_y, y_r, M_y, and M_r are all positive coefficients and y_y is less than unity.[3] In addition, because, in the present context, the price level is given and held constant, we may simplify the notation by adopting the normalization, $P = 1$. Thus, the model, which was developed in chapter 3, dealing with the determination of y and r under general excess supply can now be expressed as

$$y = y_y y - y_r r \text{ and} \tag{6.1}$$

$$\frac{dM}{dt} = \lambda'_m (M_y y - M_r r - M). \tag{6.2}$$

The specific objective of the present analysis is to ascertain the timing of the effects of exogenous disturbances on output, employment, and the rate of return. As a specific example of an exogenous disturbance, we consider a shift in monetary policy. We assume that fiscal policy does not change, so that neither government demand for commodities nor taxes change, and the altered growth of the money stock is accomplished solely through open-market operations. However, the reader should appreciate that the same general form of analysis would apply in the case of any exogenous disturbance. In order to facilitate this analysis, we assume specifically that M behaves in the following simple way:

$$M(t) = \begin{cases} M_0 & \text{for } t \leq 0, \\ M_0 e^{\mu t} & \text{for } 0 < t \leq T \\ M_0 e^{\mu T} & \text{for } t > T. \end{cases} \tag{6.3}$$

In other words, M is constant at level M_0 until date zero, grows at the constant proportionate rate, μ, from date zero until date T, and then remains constant after date T. The important aspect of this behavior is the temporary acceleration of the growth of M. The constancy of the proportionate rate of growth as well as the normal zero growth are simplifying assumptions which are not essential for the analysis. Figure 6.1 illustrates the time path of M specified by equation (6.3).

The final section of chapter 3 considered the effect of a shift toward a more expansionary monetary policy within the context of the model developed in section 3.4. We noted that initially y would increase and r would decrease and that over time these initial effects would be reinforced. Within the context of this same model, we now want to

---

[3] For convenience, the constant terms in these linear approximations are omitted. The inclusion of these constant terms would not alter any of the results obtained below.

make this analysis more precise by analyzing the exact form of the time paths of y and r implied by the behavior of M as specified by equation (6.3). Figure 6.1 illustrates the time paths of M, y, and r implied by

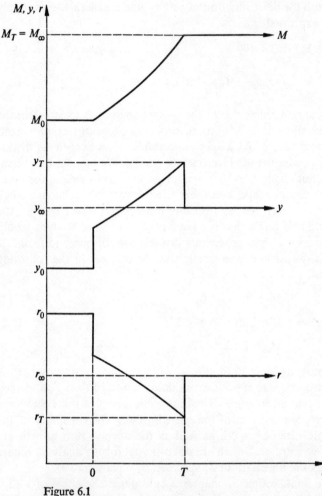

Figure 6.1
The paths of M, y and r with gradual adjustment of money balances: equations (6.1, 6.2, 6.3)

equations (6.1, 6.2, 6.3). The mathematical note at the end of this section explains the derivation of figures 6.1 and 6.2. The similarity between figure 6.1 and figure 3.5 above should be noted. The only new considerations present in figure 6.1 are that M grows at a constant proportionate rate, rather than simply at a constant rate, and that the endogenous variables are y and r, rather than $P*$ and $r*$.

The most striking feature of figure 6.1 is that the form of the time paths of y and r does not correspond to the form of the time path of M. Although the growth of M is continuous and monotonic from its initial value at date zero to its final value at date T, the time paths of y and r exhibit discrete changes as well as overshooting of their final values. Specifically, both y and r exhibit a discrete change at date zero, followed by continued smooth movement in the same direction until date T, and finally a discrete reversal at date T. In the present context, the essential element responsible for the lack of correspondence between the forms of these time paths and the time path of M is the gradual adjustment of money balances. This gradual adjustment implies that the change in $m^{d'}$ necessary to keep $m^{d'}$ equal to dM/dt requires a change in the target level of money balances, M', relative to M. Consequently, the discrete changes in dM/dt at dates zero and T necessitate discrete changes in M', which in turn imply discrete changes in r. These discrete changes in r imply discrete changes in y in order to keep $y^{d'}$ equal to y.

If the coefficient λ'_m were larger, the forms of the time paths of M and y and r would correspond more closely. In the limit as λ'_m becomes infinitely large, implying that the desired adjustment of money balances was instantaneous rather than gradual, equation (6.2) would be replaced by

$$M = M_y y - M_r r. \tag{6.4}$$

Given equations (6.1, 6.3, 6.4) the forms of the time paths of M, y, and r would correspond exactly. Figure 6.2 illustrates this case.

Mathematical note

The behavior of y and r described in figures 6.1 and 6.2 can be derived as follows. Equations (6.1) and (6.2) can be written as

$$\begin{bmatrix} 1 - y_y & y_r \\ \lambda'_m M_y & -\lambda'_m M_r \end{bmatrix} \begin{bmatrix} y \\ r \end{bmatrix} = \begin{bmatrix} 0 \\ (D + \lambda'_m)M \end{bmatrix},$$

where $D \equiv \dfrac{d}{dt}.$

Solving this pair of equations for y and r as functions of M yields

$$y = \frac{B}{A}\left(1 + \frac{D}{\lambda'_m}\right) M \text{ and}$$

$$r = -\frac{1-y_y}{y_r}\frac{B}{A}\left(1+\frac{D}{\lambda'_m}\right)M,$$

where $A \equiv 1 - y_y + M_y y_r/M_r$ and $B \equiv y_r/M_r$.

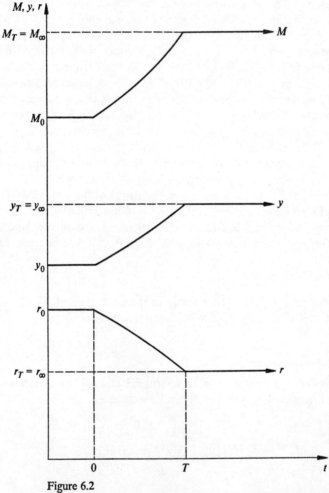

Figure 6.2
Time paths of M, y and r with no structural lags: equations (6.1, 6.3, 6.4)

Note that the negative value for r occurs only because we have omitted the constant terms in approximating the effective demand functions.

Given the time path for M specified by equation (6.3), the time paths of y and r are as follows:

$$y(t) = \begin{cases} \dfrac{B}{A} M_0 & \text{for } t \leq 0, \\[2ex] \dfrac{B}{A} \left(1 + \dfrac{\mu}{\lambda'_m}\right) M_0 e^{\mu t} & \text{for } 0 < t \leq T, \\[2ex] \dfrac{B}{A} M_0 e^{\mu T} & \text{for } t > T. \end{cases}$$

$$r(t) = \begin{cases} -\dfrac{1 - y_y}{y_r} \dfrac{B}{A} M_0 & \text{for } t \leq 0, \\[2ex] -\dfrac{1 - y_y}{y_r} \dfrac{B}{A} \left(1 + \dfrac{\mu}{\lambda'_m}\right) M_0 e^{\mu t} & \text{for } 0 < t \leq T, \\[2ex] -\dfrac{1 - y_y}{y_r} \dfrac{B}{A} M_0 e^{\mu T} & \text{for } t > T. \end{cases}$$

As long as the term μ/λ'_m is nonzero, both of these time paths exhibit discrete changes at dates zero and T. However, as λ'_m becomes infinitely large, both time paths become continuous.

6.2   Gradual adjustment of effective commodity demand

The preceding section considered gradual adjustment only as relating to the average money balance. However, other structural relations may be subject to gradual adjustment as well. This section considers the implications of gradual adjustment of effective commodity demand. Specifically, the analysis distinguishes between the effective commodity demand, $y^{d'}$, which is actually expressed in the market, and an ultimate target level of effective commodity demand, represented by y'. Assume that the household choice calculus analyzed in Section 3.4.2 above determines y', rather than $y^{d'}$, so that we have as an approximation

$$y' = y_y y - y_r r.$$

Assume in addition that the representative household gradually adjusts $y^{d'}$ to y' according to the mechanism

$$\frac{dy^{d'}}{dt} = \lambda'_y(y' - y^{d'}),$$

where λ'_y is positive and is treated, for simplicity, as a constant. This gradual adjustment relation is analogous to the gradual adjustment of

M to M', which was involved in the determination of $m^{a'}/P$. The corresponding rationalization for the gradual adjustment of $y^{a'}$ to y' involves a trade-off between the costs implied by $y^{a'}$ not being equal to y' and the costs involved in changing $y^{a'}$.[4]

Given the gradual adjustment of $y^{a'}$ to y', the equality between actual output y and effective demand $y^{a'}$, which is implied by the context of general excess supply, now requires

$$\frac{dy}{dt} = \lambda'_y(y_v y - y_r r - y). \tag{6.5}$$

Equation (6.5) represents an alternative to equation (6.1). Equation (6.1) may be thought of as a limiting case which arises as λ'_y becomes infinitely large.

Figure 6.3 illustrates the time paths of M, y, and r which are implied by equations (6.3, 6.4, 6.5). This model contains a lag in the adjustment of effective commodity demand, but no lag in the adjustment of money balances. The mathematical note at the end of this section explains the derivation of figures 6.3 and 6.4. The first important feature of figure 6.3 is that the adjustment of y lags behind the growth of M. This lag is the direct consequence of the gradual adjustment of effective commodity demand. With instantaneous adjustment of money balances, as implied by equation (6.4), the growth of M from date zero to date T causes a corresponding decline in r. However, the gradual adjustment of $y^{a'}$ to y' means that the growth of $y^{a'}$ and y is incomplete at date T and must continue on an asymptotic path beyond date T. In addition, the continued increase in y beyond date T implies that, with M constant, r must increase after date T in order to keep the target level of money

---

[4] An alternate type of gradual adjustment could involve a gap between actual output, y, and $y^{a'}$. However, within the context of general excess supply, the assumptions that output is not storable, that labor input can be changed instantaneously without incurring adjustment costs, and that exchange is voluntary and exhausts all mutually-advantageous trades imply that y must always equal $y^{a'}$. In order to allow y to adjust gradually to $y^{a'}$, we would have to relax at least one of these assumptions. For example, if the coordination of buyers and sellers involved in the exhaustion of all mutually-advantageous trades were a costly, and therefore, gradual, process, we could have

$$\frac{dy}{dt} = \lambda'_y(y^{a'} - y),$$

subject to $y \leq y^{a'}$. However, this sort of gradual adjustment of y to $y^{a'}$ would have implications which were identical to those of the gradual adjustment of $y^{a'}$ to y' which are being considered in the text.

balances constant. Thus, the time path of r undershoots its asymptotic value.

Comparison of figures 6.1 and 6.3 produces an interesting contrast. In figure 6.1, where gradual adjustment of money balances is

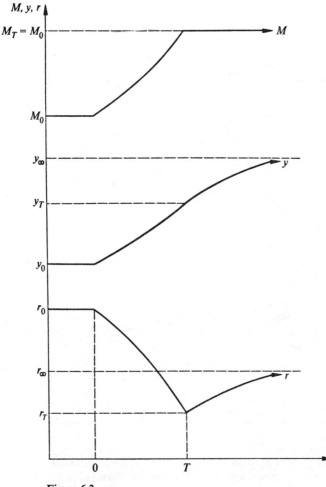

Figure 6.3
Time paths of M, y and r, with gradual adjustment of effective commodity demand: equations (6.3, 6.4, 6.5)

the only form of structural lag, the time path of y overshoots its final value. In figure 6.3, where gradual adjustment of effective commodity demand is the only form of structural lag, the time path of y lags behind the time path of M. These observations suggest, correctly, that in a more general model, these two forms of structural lags would tend to have

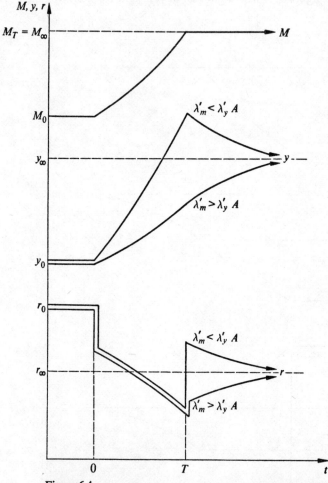

Figure 6.4
Time paths of M, y and r with gradual adjustment of effective commodity demand and money balances: equations (6.2, 6.3, 6.5)

offsetting effects on the time path of y. Figure 6.4 illustrates the time paths of M, y, and r which are implied by equations (6.2, 6.3, 6.5).[5] The

[5] The model represented by equations (6.2, 6.3, 6.5) represents a continuous analog of the discrete-time model formulated by Tucker (1966). Our results are also analogous to Tucker's.

net effect of the two forms of structural lag on the time path of y depends on the value of the adjustment speed for money balances relative to the adjustment speed for effective commodity demand weighted by a coefficient A. The coefficient A represents a positive combination of static structural parameters,

$$A \equiv 1 - y_y + \frac{M_y y_r}{M_r}.$$

Specifically, if λ'_m is larger than the product of λ'_y and A, y will lag behind M. Alternatively, if λ'_m is smaller than the product of λ'_y and A, y will overshoot its asymptotic value. Finally, if λ'_m exactly equals the product of λ'_y and A, the form of the time path of y will correspond exactly to the form of the time path of M.

The important implication of these results is that the existence of structural lags does not necessarily imply a lag in the response of y to changes in M. In the present context, the gradual adjustment of money balances causes a more exaggerated response of r to changes in M, which in turn tends to produce a more exaggerated movement in y. At the same time, the gradual adjustment of effective commodity demand tends to dampen the response of y to any given change in r. The net result can be either a greater or lesser response of y to M in the short run than in the long run.

The time path of r illustrated in figure 6.4 is rather complex. Because of the gradual adjustment of money balances, the given time path of M implies a discrete fall in r at date zero, a continual further decline in r until date T, and a discrete rise in r at date T. This much of the time path of r corresponds to figure 6.1. After date T, the further movement in r corresponds to the movement of y. If, as in figure 6.3, y lags and continues to increase after date T, r also increases after date T. Alternatively, if y overshoots and then decreases after date T, r also decreases after date T.

Mathematical note

The behavior of y and r described in figures 6.3 and 6.4 can be derived as follows: equations (6.5) and (6.2) can be written as

$$\begin{bmatrix} D + \lambda'_y(1 - y_y) & \lambda'_y y_r \\ \lambda'_m M_y & -\lambda'_m M_r \end{bmatrix} \begin{bmatrix} y \\ r \end{bmatrix} = \begin{bmatrix} 0 \\ (D + \lambda'_m)M \end{bmatrix},$$

where $D \equiv \dfrac{d}{dt}$.

Solving this pair of equations for y and r as functions of M yields

$$Dy + \lambda'_y Ay = \lambda'_y B \left(1 + \frac{D}{\lambda'_m}\right) M \text{ and}$$

$$Dr + \lambda'_y Ar = -\left(\frac{D}{y_r} + \lambda'_y \frac{1 - y_y}{y_r}\right) B \left(1 + \frac{D}{\lambda'_m}\right) M,$$

where $A \equiv 1 - y_y + M_y\, y_r/M_r$ and $B \equiv y_r/M_r$.

Given the time path of M specified by equation (6.3), these two differential equations become as follows:

$$Dy + \lambda'_y Ay = \begin{cases} \lambda'_y BM_0 & \text{for } t \leq 0, \\[2mm] \lambda'_y B \left(1 + \dfrac{\mu}{\lambda'_m}\right) M_0 e^{\mu t} & \text{for } 0 < t \leq T, \\[2mm] \lambda'_y BM_0 e^{\mu T} & \text{for } t > T. \end{cases}$$

$$Dr + \lambda'_y Ar = \begin{cases} -\lambda'_y \dfrac{1 - y_y}{y_r} BM_0 & \text{for } t \leq 0, \\[2mm] -\left(\dfrac{\mu}{y_r} + \lambda'_y \dfrac{1 - y_y}{y_r}\right) B \left(1 + \dfrac{\mu}{\lambda'_m}\right) M_0 e^{\mu t} & \\[1mm] & \text{for } 0 < t \leq T, \\[2mm] -\lambda'_y \dfrac{1 - y_y}{y_r} BM_0 e^{\mu T} & \text{for } t > T. \end{cases}$$

Assume an initial position of equilibrium and that the time path of y has no discontinuities. Notice that this model permits a continuous time path for y because it allows for discrete changes in r and dy/dt to absorb the discrete changes in dM/dt. Given these assumptions, the two differential equations have the following solutions:

$$y(t) = \begin{cases} \dfrac{B}{A} M_0 & \text{for } t \leq 0, \\[4mm] \dfrac{B}{A} \dfrac{M_0}{\lambda'_m(\mu + \lambda'_y A)} [\lambda'_y A(\lambda'_m + \mu) e^{\mu t} \\[1mm] \qquad + \mu(\lambda'_m - \lambda'_y A) \exp(-\lambda'_y At) & \text{for } 0 < t \leq T, \\[4mm] \dfrac{B}{A} M_0 \left\{ e^{\mu T} + \dfrac{\mu(\lambda'_m - \lambda'_y A)}{\lambda'_m(\mu + \lambda'_y A)} [1 - \exp\{(\mu + \lambda'_y A)T\}] \right. \\[2mm] \left. \qquad \exp(-\lambda'_y At) \right\} & \text{for } t > T. \end{cases}$$

$$r(t) = \begin{cases} -\dfrac{1-y_y}{y_r}\dfrac{B}{A}M_0 & \text{for } t \le 0, \\[2em] -\dfrac{1-y_y}{y_r}\dfrac{B}{A}\dfrac{M_0}{\lambda'_m(\mu + \lambda'_y A)}\left[\left(\dfrac{\mu A}{1-y_y} + \lambda'_y A\right)\right. \\[1.5em] \quad (\lambda'_m + \mu)e^{\mu t} - \dfrac{BM_y}{1-y_y}\mu(\lambda'_m - \lambda'_y A)\exp(-\lambda'_y At)\Big] \\[1em] \hspace{6em} \text{for } 0 < t \le T, \\[1.5em] -\dfrac{1-y_y}{y_r}\dfrac{B}{A}M_0\left\{e^{\mu T} - \dfrac{BM_y}{1-y_y}\dfrac{\mu(\lambda'_m - \lambda'_y A)}{\lambda'_m(\mu + \lambda'_y A)}\right. \\[1.5em] \quad [1 - \exp\{(\mu + \lambda'_y A)T\}]\exp(-\lambda'_y At)\Big\} \\[1em] \hspace{6em} \text{for } t > T. \end{cases}$$

Given $A > 0$, which follows from $y_y < 1$, these solutions have the following implications: regarding the time path of y,

$$y(\infty) \quad = \lim_{t \to \infty} y(t) = \frac{B}{A}M_0 e^{\mu T},$$

$$y(T) \quad > y(0), \text{ and}$$

$$y(T) \quad \gtreqless y(\infty) \text{ as } \lambda'_m \lesseqgtr \lambda'_y A.$$

Regarding the time path of r,

$$r(\infty) \quad = \lim_{t \to \infty} r(t) = -\frac{1-y_y}{y_r}\frac{B}{A}M_0 e^{\mu T},$$

$$r(0 + \varepsilon) \le r(0) \text{ as } \lambda'_m \lesseqgtr \infty,$$

$$r(0 + \varepsilon) \gtreqless r(\infty) \text{ as } \lambda'_m \gtreqless \mu A/(1 - y_y)(e^{\mu T} - 1),$$

$$r(T) \quad < r(0 + \varepsilon),$$

$$r(T) \quad < r(\infty),$$

$$r(T + \varepsilon) \ge r(T) \text{ as } \lambda'_m \le \infty, \text{ and}$$

$$r(T + \varepsilon) \gtreqless r(\infty) \text{ as } \lambda'_m \lesseqgtr \lambda'_y A.$$

6.3   Adaptive expectations

The analysis of chapter 3, which is serving as a point of departure for the present discussion, assumed expectations regarding output and income, real wages, and the rate of return to be static. Specifically, the representative household expected the level of profits and the constraint on the amount of employment obtainable to remain at its current level until date $\hat{N}$, and the representative firm expected the constraint on the level of sales to remain at its current level until date $\hat{N}$. In addition, the representative household and the representative firm expected no change in either the real wage rate or the rate of return over time. This section considers some implications of relaxing these assumptions about expectations. We first consider the distinction between current income and expected 'permanent' income. We then consider the distinction between the current rate of return and the expected 'normal' rate of return.

6.3.1   *Permanent income*

Recall briefly the derivation in chapter 3 of the effective commodity demand function. Effective commodity demand consists of effective investment demand plus effective consumption demand plus demand for financial services plus government demand. Effective investment demand, given by equation (3.29), depends on the difference between the actual capital stock and the effective target capital stock. The effective target capital stock depends in turn on the anticipated levels of the real wage rate, the rate of return, the level of public services, and the demand-determined constraint on sales. The derivation of equation (3.29) assumes that the representative firm expects this sales constraint to be effective at its current level until date $\hat{N}$ and that it expects no change over time in the other relevant variables.

Effective consumption demand, given by equation (3.36), depends on Ω_0', which measures the present value of lifetime nonwage resources and wage income until date $\hat{N}$, on the real wage rate, and on the rate of return. The derivation of equation (3.36) assumes that the representative household expects both the constraint on wage income and the level of profits to remain at the current level until date $\hat{N}$ and that it expects no change over time in the other relevant variables.

We now want to consider the possibility of nonstatic expectations regarding sales and income opportunities. Specifically, let us distinguish between current sales and income and expected average opportunities to make profitable sales and to earn income. For the representative firm, expected sales opportunities involve the expected time path of the sales constraint, where relevant, and the expected time path of the real wage rate. For the representative household, expected income opportunities involve the expected time path of the employment constraint, where relevant, and the expected time paths of profit income and the real wage rate. In common usage, the average in present value terms of these expected income opportunities for households is referred to as permanent income. For simplicity, denote permanent income by y^e, and let ye also represent the average value of expected sales opportunities for firms.

The possibility of y^e differing from y suggests immediately that effective commodity demand should be specified as depending on y^e, rather than on y. Thus, abstracting from gradual adjustment, the linear approximation for the determination of $y^{d'}$ and y becomes

$$y = y^{d'} = y_y y^e - y_r r. \qquad (6.6)$$

In addition, we must specify a procedure by which y^e is generated. Following the usual practice, we assume that this expectation is subject to linear adaptation – that is,

$$\frac{dy^e}{dt} = \theta_y (y - y^e), \qquad (6.7)$$

where the coefficient θ_y is positive and is treated, for simplicity, as a constant.[6]

As before, the existence of general excess supply implies that $y^{d'}$ determines y. The important new implication of equations (6.6) and (6.7) is that the feedback effect from changes in y to $y^{d'}$, which generates the demand multiplier, now involves a lag. Specifically, a change in y affects $y^{d'}$ only as y^e gradually adjusts towards y. Consequently, with regard to the time path of y and r, the effect of the introduction of permanent income into the effective commodity demand function is similar to the effect of gradual adjustment of effective commodity demand.

The precise implications of equations (6.6) and (6.7) for the time paths of y and r depend on the assumptions made regarding the effective demand for money balances. For example, if equations (6.6) and (6.7) are combined with equation (6.4),

$$M = M_y y - M_r r,$$

the only lag in the model would involve the effect of y^e on $y^{d'}$. This model would correspond closely to the model in which the only lag

---

[6] The essential analysis of the distinction between y and y^e, the relevant terminology of 'permanent' and 'transitory' income, and the linear adaptive expectations mechanism for generating y^e are all attributable to Friedman (1957). Friedman also utilizes an extension to the simple adaptive mechanism which allows for a long-term anticipated trend in income. We have previously utilized a linear adaptive expectations mechanism in section 6.4.1 to generate the expected rate of price change. The reader may refer to the discussion in that section as well as to the references noted there.

involved gradual adjustment of effective commodity demand, and the time paths of y and r would have the same form as those illustrated in figure 6.3 above.[7]

As another possibility, if the effective target money balance also depended on permanent income, equation (6.4) would be replaced by

$$M = M' = M_y y^e - M_r r.$$

The model would now correspond closely to the model in which gradual adjustment applied to both effective commodity demand and money balances. The lags involved in the effect of y^e on $y^{d'}$ and M' would tend to be offsetting, and the possible time paths of y and r would correspond to those illustrated in figure 6.4 above, with the substitution of θ_y for both λ'_m and λ'_y.[8]

[7] More precisely, the time path for y would correspond to that derived in the mathematical note to section 6.2, with the substitution of θ_y for both λ'_y and λ'_m, of

$$A' \equiv \frac{(1 - y_y)M_r + M_y y_r}{M_r + M_y y_r} \text{ for } A, \text{ and of } B' \equiv \frac{y_r}{M_r + M_y y_r} \text{ for B.}$$

In this case, given $0 < A' < 1$, which follows from $0 < y_y < 1$, y must lag behind M. In addition, the time path for r would also correspond to that derived in the mathematical note to section 6.2, with the substitution of θ_y for λ'_y, of A' for A, and of B' for B, and with $\lambda'_m = \infty$. If the variable r in equation (6.6) were replaced by the variable r^e, where $dr^e/dt = \theta_y (r - r^e)$, then the time paths of both y and r would correspond to those derived in the mathematical note to section 6.2, with only the substitution of θ_y for λ'_y and with $\lambda'_m = \infty$. We leave the verification of these results as an exercise for the reader.

[8] This model represents a continuous analog to the discrete-time model formulated by Laidler (1968). However, the dependence of M' on y^e would seem more plausible if the adjustment of money balances to the target level were gradual. In that case, the linear approximation for the equality between the effective flow demand and flow supply of money balances would be

$$\frac{dM}{dt} = \lambda'_m(M_y y^e - M_r r - M).$$

Combining this relation with equations (6.6) and (6.7) would yield possible time paths for y which correspond to figure 6.4, with the substitution of $(\lambda'_m + \mu + \theta_y)$ for λ'_y. The possible time paths for r would correspond to figure 6.4, with the substitution of θ_y for λ'_y. Again, we leave the verification of this result as an exercise for the reader. In addition, the introduction of gradual adjustment of effective commodity demand into the model incorporating permanent income would produce a second-order differential equation system and thereby create the possibility of oscillatory time paths for y and r. Laidler (1973) has analyzed such a model.

6.3.2   The disposition of transitory income

The preceding section considered the implications of substituting y^e, permanent income, for y, current income, within the effective demand functions which we had previously derived. However, the possibility that ye may not always be equal to y also suggests a basic reformulation of the effective demand for money balances. Equation (6.6), by assuming that the effective demand for commodities depends only on y^e and r, implies that all transitory income, which represents the difference between y and y^e, must be saved.[9] Like all other saving, the saving or dissaving which corresponds to transitory income can be used to accumulate either money balances or earning assets.

In the analysis developed in chapter 3, the rationalization and derivation of the representative household's demand for money balances involved the essential assumption that households incur transactions costs in buying and selling earning assets. These costs induced the representative household to economize on such transactions by initially accumulating its savings flow as money and only periodically exchanging this accumulated money for earning assets. These transactions costs also suggest an appropriate pattern for the disposition of transitory income. The transactions costs involved in exchanging money for earning assets induces the household to allow the savings corresponding to transitory income to accumulate initially as money balances. However, if the household is already buying or selling earning assets with the frequency v, at the end of the next interval l/v, the household may also find it worthwhile to exchange for earning assets the amount of its

---

[9] Transitory income may represent either an anticipated or an unanticipated deviation of current income from permanent income. Suppose that income is expected to fluctuate, in which case permanent income represents the expected average level of income. To the extent of these expected fluctuations, transitory income is anticipated and does not represent an addition to or subtraction from lifetime income receipts. If the representative household is currently receiving positive anticipated transitory income, it must have received in the past or expect to receive in the future negative anticipated transitory income of equivalent present value. For this reason, any accumulation of anticipated transitory income should be put to one side and should not affect the representative household's effective consumption demand. In contrast, transitory income in excess of these expected fluctuations of income about its expected average is unanticipated and represents a windfall. Any accumulation of such windfall transitory income should be reflected in Ω_0' and, once so accumulated, should affect the representative household's effective consumption demand.

money holdings which represent accumulated transitory income.[10] Thus, on average, the representative household adjusts its effective demand for money balances to accommodate some fraction of the flow of transitory income.

The formal respecification of the effective demand for money balances to allow for the optimal disposition of transitory income presents a challenging problem, which we leave for the reader's consideration. However, the general qualitative implications of assuming that the effective demand for money balances accommodates some fraction of the flow of transitory income seem clear enough. Specifically, this accommodation increases the immediate responsiveness of effective money demand to changes in income and, thus, serves to dampen the short-run response of y and r to monetary policy.[11]

6.3.3 *Speculative demand for money*

This section considers the possibility of non-static expectations regarding the rate of return on earning assets. Let r^e represent the normal rate of return which the representative household and the representative firm expect will obtain in the long run. Again following the usual practice, assume that r^e is generated by an adaptive expectations mechanism, similar to the mechanism which generates y^e. Such a mechanism would permit r^e to diverge from r. This divergence, in principle, would have a wide range of implications regarding the behavior of firms and households. The present section focuses on one of these implications – that reflecting the effect of a divergence between r and r^e on the alternative

---

[10] This motivation will be the stronger the longer the household expects this accumulation to remain as savings. The shorter the periodicity of fluctuations in transitory income relative to $1/v$, the more likely the household is to allow its money balance to absorb these savings. However, the accumulation of transitory income might also affect the optimal frequency of visits to the financial asset market. For example, if the amount of money holdings which represent accumulated transitory income became large enough, an extraordinary visit to the financial asset market would become worthwhile. Presumably, such visits would be more likely for accumulated windfall transitory income than for accumulated anticipated transitory income. In addition, the frequency of such visits would depend on rates of return and the level of transaction costs. Darby (1972) presents a more extensive study of the disposition of transitory income, with special attention to the role of durable consumer goods.

[11] If household purchases of consumer durables accomodate some part of the flow of transitory income, as is suggested by Darby (1972), there would be an offsetting force which would increase the short-run responsiveness of y to monetary policy.

costs of allowing savings to accumulate as money balances rather than as earning assets.

If r is not equal to r^e, the alternative cost of holding money balances would involve both the current rate of return on earning assets and an anticipated rate of change of the prices of earning assets. Suppose, for example, that r is less than r^e. In that case, the representative household would be anticipating that r will rise to its normal level. Recall that, given the flows of profits and interest payments, the prices of shares and bonds are inversely related to r.[12] Consequently, the representative household would also be anticipating that these prices, and hence the value of its earning asset holdings, will be falling. To the extent that the representative household holds its assets in the form of money it would avoid this anticipated capital depreciation.

In this way, speculative considerations enter into the determination of the effective demand for money balances. Specifically, effective money demand should be inversely related to the difference between r and r^e. Again, formal respecification of the effective demand for money balances to allow for this effect presents a challenging problem, which we leave for the reader's consideration. However, the general qualitative implications which are involved seem clear. Specifically, the speculative demand for money increases the immediate responsiveness of effective money demand to changes in r and, hence, serves to dampen the short-run response of y and r to monetary policy.[13] The similarity

[12] Neglecting anticipated changes in π and P, we have for equities, $P_e = P\pi/Er$, and for bonds, $P_b = i/Br$. These assets are perpetual. Alternatively, for assets with a finite maturity, the asset price becomes less sensitive to r as the time to maturity approaches zero. For very short-term assets, price is essentially constant and independent of r. However, even with the existence of short-term assets, such as call loans, which bear a positive rate of return, speculation on the price of long-term assets could still affect the demand for money if exchanges between money and these spot assets involve transaction costs.

[13] Previous authors, especially Keynes (1936) and Friedman (1961), have stressed these effects of a speculative demand for money. Keynes wrote, 'experience indicates that the aggregate demand for money to satisfy the speculative-motive usually shows a continuous response to gradual changes in the rate of interest... Indeed, if this were not so, "open-market operations" would be impracticable... in normal circumstances the banking system is in fact always able to purchase (or sell) bonds in exchange for cash by bidding the price of bonds up (or down) in the market by a modest amount...' (p. 197.)

In analyzing the initial part of the lag in the effect of monetary policy, Friedman wrote,

'Suppose the monetary authorities increase the stock of money by open-market purchases... An asset was sold for money because the

in this respect of the effect of speculation on asset prices and of the effect of the accommodation of transitory income is worth noting.

6.4   Gradual clearing of the financial asset market

The analysis of chapter 3, which continues to serve as a point of departure for the present discussion, assumed that the rate of return always took that value which was consistent with effective clearing of the financial asset market. This section considers some implications of relaxing this assumption. Specifically, we now assume that the rate of return adjusts gradually in response to any difference between the effective flow demand and the effective flow supply of financial assets – that is,

$$\frac{dr}{dt} = - \lambda_r (f^{d'} - f^{s'}), \tag{6.8}$$

where λ_r is positive, but finite, and is treated, for simplicity, as a constant. According to equation (6.8), r is decreasing when $f^{d'}$ exceeds $f^{s'}$ and r is increasing when $f^{s'}$ exceeds $f^{d'}$.[14]

Given that r adjusts only gradually to differences between $f^{d'}$ and $f^{s'}$, exchange may take place in the financial asset market under non-market-clearing conditions. In such a case, as was discussed in chapter 2, given voluntary exchange, the actual level of transactions will equal the smaller of the quantities supplied and demanded – that is,

$$f = \min (f^{d'}, f^{s'}).$$

From the standpoint of the individual, any divergence of actual quantities transacted from the quantities supplied or demanded appears as a constraint. For simplicity, we assume that government demand or

---

terms were favorable; however, the seller did not necessarily intend to retain the money indefinitely.' (p. 462).

Presumably, the willingness to absorb more money in the short run than in the long run, for a given reduction in the rate of return on earning assets, reflects a speculative demand.

[14] Because asset prices are inversely related to r, this specification implies that asset prices are rising when $f^{d'}$ exceeds $f^{s'}$ and that asset prices are falling when $f^{s'}$ exceeds $f^{d'}$. In reality, the size of λ_r would seem to vary widely among the various financial asset markets. In the organized exchanges, λ_r would seem to be very large, and our previous assumption that $f^{d'}$ always equals $f^{s'}$, which in effect implied that λ_r was infinitely large, would seem to be a good approximation. However, in other asset markets, such as the markets for mortgages and bank loans, λ_r would seem to be much smaller.

supply receives priority. Thus, if $f^{d'}$ exceeds $f^{s'}$, households will be unable to buy the quantity of earning assets which they demand, and, if $f^{s'}$ exceeds $f^{d'}$, firms will be unable to sell the quantity of earning assets which they supply.

As with the constraints implied by the failure of the labor or commodity market to clear, the constraints implied by the failure of the financial asset market to clear will also affect household or firm behavior in other markets. The focus of the present discussion is on the effect of a shift toward a more expansionary monetary policy. Given that the financial asset market is initially clearing, such a shift would cause $f^{d'}$ to exceed $f^{s'}$. Consequently, the representative household's actual purchases of earning assets will be $f = f^{s'} < f^{d'}$. Given this constraint, the representative household must choose some combination of two options regarding the disposition of the excess of $f^{d'}$ over $f^{s'}$. First, it can continue to add to its money balances at the rate $m^{d'}$ and add the amount $f^{d'} - f^{s'}$ to its effective consumption demand. Alternatively, it can continue to consume at the rate $c^{d'}$ and add the amount $f^{d'} - f^{s'}$ to its effective flow demand for money balances.[15] In the interest of brevity, let us simply assume that the representative household chooses a combination of both options. Specifically, assume that

$$y^{d''} = y^{d'} + \alpha(f^{d'} - f^{s'}) \text{ and} \tag{6.9}$$

$$m^{d''} = m^{d'} + (1 - \alpha)(f^{d'} - f^{s'}), \tag{6.10}$$

where $y^{d''}$ represents the revised effective commodity demand and $m^{d''}$ represents the revised effective flow demand for money balances. The spill-over coefficient α has a value in the interval, $0 < \alpha < 1$, and is treated, for simplicity, as a constant.[16]

Equations (6.9) and (6.10) are expressed in terms of the effective demand for commodities, the effective flow demand for money, and the

[15] Because we are dealing with a situation of excess supply of labor, so that employment is less than l^s, a reduction in effective labor supply would not serve to dispose of the excess of $f^{d'}$ over $f^{s'}$, unless the effective labor supply were reduced by more than the difference between l^s and l. For simplicity, we ignore this possibility.

[16] If, as in reality, firms hold money balances, the analysis of the effect of an excess supply of earning assets would be symmetrical to the effect of excess demand, at least in the sense that the analog to the coefficient α would have a value in the unit interval. However, if firms held no money balances, as we have been assuming for simplicity, the entire excess of $f^{s'}$ over $f^{d'}$ would have to be reflected in a reduction in effective investment demand. In that case, the analog to the coefficient α would be exactly equal to unity.

effective excess demand for earning assets. However, the economy-wide budget constraint, derived in chapter 3, and given by

$$(y^{d'} - y) + \frac{W}{P}(l^{d'} - l) + \frac{1}{P}(f^{d'} - f^{s'})$$

$$+ \frac{1}{P}\left(m^{d'} - \frac{dM}{dt}\right) = 0, \quad (3.45)$$

enables us to simplify these expressions by substituting for the effective excess demand for earning assets. Given $l^{d'} = l$ and $P = 1$, substituting from equation (3.45) into equation (6.9) yields

$$y^{d''} = y^{d'} - \alpha\left(y^{d'} - y + m^{d'} - \frac{dM}{dt}\right).$$

Thus, the condition of equality between actual output y and the revised effective demand $y^{d''}$ requires, assuming $\alpha < 1$,

$$y = y^{d'} - \frac{\alpha}{1 - \alpha}\left(m^{d'} - \frac{dM}{dt}\right). \quad (6.11)$$

Similarly, substituting for $f^{d'} - f^{s'}$ from equation (3.45) and for y from equation (6.11) into equation (6.8) yields, assuming $0 < \alpha < 1$,

$$\frac{dr}{dt} = \frac{\lambda_r}{1 - \alpha}\left(m^{d'} - \frac{dM}{dt}\right) = \frac{\lambda_r}{\alpha}(y^{d'} - y). \quad (6.12)$$

Given the linear approximations, $y^{d'} = y_y y - y_r r$ and $m^{d'} = \lambda'_m(M_y y - M_r r - M)$, and the behavior of M as specified by equation (6.3), equations (6.11) and (6.12) imply specific time paths for y and r.[17] The solid arrows in figure 6.5 illustrate these time paths. For purpose of comparison, the dashed lines in figure 6.5 reproduce from figure 6.1 the time paths of y and r with gradual adjustment of money balances, but with r continually adjusted to clear the financial-asset market. The mathematical note at the end of this section explains the derivation of figure 6.5.

The net relation between the time paths of r and M now depends on the offsetting effects of the gradual adjustment of money balances and the gradual clearing of the financial asset market. The net effect of

---

[17] Tucker (1968) analyzes a similar model, which also involves gradual adjustment of effective commodity demand. Grossman (1971) develops another similar but more general model in which P, rather than remaining fixed at a level which implies excess supply of commodities, also adjusts gradually to clear the commodity market.

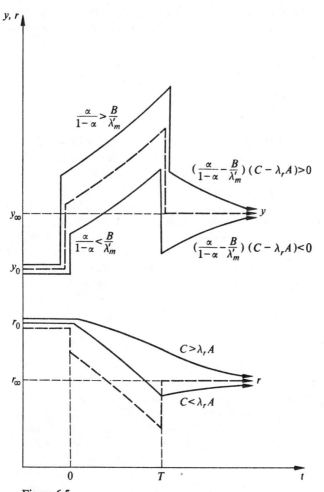

Figure 6.5
Time paths of y and r with gradual adjustment of money balances and gradual clearing of financial asset market: equations (6.3, 6.11, and 6.12)

these two forms of structural lag on the time path of r depends on the relative values of λ'_m incorporated into a coefficient C, and λ_r weighted by the coefficient A. The coefficient C represents a combination of λ'_m, the spill-over coefficient α, and various static structural parameters,

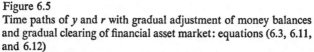

$$C \equiv (1 - \alpha)(1 - y_v)/M_r + \alpha \lambda'_m M_y/M_r.$$

By itself, the influence of gradual clearing of the financial asset market is to reduce the short-run response of r to the increase in M. Because r

is no longer constrained to keep $m^{a'}$ equal to dM/dt, the discrete changes in dM/dt at dates zero and T no longer imply discrete changes in r. If the product of λ_r and A is larger than C, r will still undershoot its asymptotic value. However, if the product of λ_r and A is smaller than C, r will lag behind M, and will continue to decline after date T. Finally, if the product of λ_r and A just equals C, the time path of r will correspond exactly to the form of the time path of M.

The net relation between the time paths of y and M also now depends on the combined effects of the gradual adjustment of money balances and the gradual clearing of the financial asset market. However, the influence on the time path of y of the gradual clearing of the financial asset market is rather complex, itself involving two offsetting effects. The first of these effects reflects the reduction in the short-run decline in r, which by itself would tend to reduce the short-run increase in y. The second of these effects reflects the influence, through the spill-over coefficient α, of the effective excess demand for earning assets on the effective demand for commodities. Because the discrete changes in dM/dt at dates zero and T imply discrete changes in the effective excess demand for earning assets, the spill-over effect will produce discrete changes in y at these dates. Moreover, the net short-run influence of the gradual clearing of the financial asset market on y depends on the size of α relative to the ratio B/λ'_m, where $B \equiv y_r/M_r$. Specifically, if the ratio $\alpha/1 - \alpha$ is smaller than B/λ'_m, the net effect will be to reduce the short-run rise in y. However, if $\alpha/1 - \alpha$ is larger than B/λ'_m, the spill-over effect will more than offset the effect of the reduced decline in r, and the net effect will be to increase the short-run rise in y. Finally, if $\alpha/1 - \alpha$ just equals B/λ'_m, the gradual clearing of the financial asset market will have no net effect, and the time path of y from date zero to date T will correspond to the time path depicted in figure 6.1.

After date T, the further movement in y corresponds to the further movement in r and the strength of the spill-over effect. Suppose, for example, that the product of λ_r and A is smaller than C, so that after date T the effective excess demand for earning assets is positive but diminishing, as r continues to decline. In that case, if the spill-over effect is strong, so that $\alpha/1 - \alpha$ is larger than B/λ'_m, y also decreases after date T. However, if $\alpha/1 - \alpha$ is smaller than B/λ'_m, y increases after date T.[18]

[18] If $\lambda_r A$ is larger than C, $f^{a'}$ will be smaller than $f^{s'}$ after date T. Figure 6.5 depicts this situation of positive excess supply for earning assets as symmetrical to the case of positive excess demand. However, as noted above, this symmetry requires symmetry between the behavior of firms and households.

Mathematical note

The behavior of y and r described in figure 6.5 can be derived as follows: equations (6.11) and (6.12) can be written as

$$
\begin{bmatrix}
(1 - y_y) + \dfrac{\alpha}{1 - \alpha}\,\lambda'_m M_y & y_r - \dfrac{\alpha}{1 - \alpha}\,\lambda'_m M_r \\[2ex]
\dfrac{\lambda_r}{\alpha}(1 - y_y) & D + \dfrac{\lambda_r}{\alpha} y_r
\end{bmatrix}
\begin{bmatrix} y \\[2ex] r \end{bmatrix}
$$

$$
= \begin{bmatrix}
\dfrac{\alpha}{1 - \alpha}\,(D + \lambda'_m) M \\[3ex]
0
\end{bmatrix},
$$

where $D \equiv \dfrac{d}{dt}$.

Solving this pair of equations for y and r as functions of M yields

$$
Dy + \lambda_r \lambda'_m \frac{A}{C} y = \lambda_r \lambda'_m \frac{B}{C}\left(1 + \frac{\alpha D}{\lambda_r y_r}\right)\left(1 + \frac{D}{\lambda'_m}\right) M \text{ and}
$$

$$
Dr + \lambda_r \lambda'_m \frac{A}{C} r = -\lambda_r \lambda'_m \frac{B}{C}\frac{1 - y_y}{y_r}\left(1 + \frac{D}{\lambda'_m}\right) M,
$$

where $A \equiv 1 - y_y + M_y y_r / M_r$, $B \equiv y_r / M_r$,

and $C \equiv (1 - \alpha)(1 - y_y)/M_r + \alpha\lambda'_m M_y / M_r$.

Given the time path of M specified by equation (6.3), these two differential equations become as follows:

$$
Dy + \lambda_r \lambda'_m \frac{A}{C} y =
\begin{cases}
\lambda_r \lambda'_m \dfrac{B}{C} M_0 & \text{for } t \leq 0, \\[3ex]
\lambda_r \lambda'_m \dfrac{B}{C}\left(1 + \dfrac{\alpha\mu}{\lambda_r y_r}\right)\left(1 + \dfrac{\mu}{\lambda'_m}\right) M_0 e^{\mu t} \\[1ex]
& \text{for } 0 < t \leq T, \\[3ex]
\lambda_r \lambda'_m \dfrac{B}{C} M_0 e^{\mu T} & \text{for } t > T.
\end{cases}
$$

$$
Dr + \lambda_r \lambda'_m \frac{A}{C} r =
\begin{cases}
-\dfrac{1 - y_y}{y_r} \lambda_r \lambda'_m \dfrac{B}{C} M_0 & \text{for } t \leq 0, \\[3ex]
-\dfrac{1 - y_y}{y_r} \lambda_r \lambda'_m \dfrac{B}{C} \left(1 + \dfrac{\mu}{\lambda'_m}\right) M_0 e^{\mu t} & \\[1ex]
& \text{for } 0 < t \leq T, \\[3ex]
-\dfrac{1 - y_y}{y_r} \lambda_r \lambda'_m \dfrac{B}{C} M_0 e^{\mu T} & \text{for } t > T.
\end{cases}
$$

Assume an initial position of equilibrium and that the time path of r has no discontinuities. Notice that this model permits a continuous time path for r because it allows for discrete changes in y and dr/dt to absorb the discrete changes in dM/dt. Given these assumptions, the two differential equations have the following solutions:

$$
y(t) =
\begin{cases}
\dfrac{B}{A} M_0 & \text{for } t \leq 0, \\[3ex]
\dfrac{B}{A} \dfrac{1 - y_y}{y_r} [(1 - \alpha)B - \alpha\lambda'_m] \dfrac{\mu(C - \lambda_r A)}{C(\mu C + \lambda_r \lambda'_m A)} & \\[2ex]
\quad \times M_0 \exp\left(- \lambda_r \lambda'_m \dfrac{A}{C} t\right) + \dfrac{(\lambda_r y_r + \alpha\mu)(\lambda'_m + \mu)}{M_r(\mu C + \lambda_r \lambda'_m A)} M_0 e^{\mu t} & \\[2ex]
& \text{for } 0 < t \leq T, \\[3ex]
\dfrac{B}{A} M_0 \left\{ e^{\mu T} + \dfrac{1 - y_y}{y_r} [(1 - \alpha)B - \alpha\lambda'_m] \dfrac{\mu(C - \lambda_r A)}{C(\mu C + \lambda_r \lambda'_m A)} \right. & \\[2ex]
\quad \left. \times \left[1 - \exp\left\{\left(\mu + \lambda_r \lambda'_m \dfrac{A}{C}\right) T\right\}\right] \times \exp\left(- \lambda_r \lambda'_m \dfrac{A}{C} t\right) \right\} & \\[2ex]
& \text{for } t > T.
\end{cases}
$$

$$
r(t) =
\begin{cases}
-\dfrac{1 - y_y}{y_r} \dfrac{B}{A} M_0 & \text{for } t \leq 0, \\[3ex]
-\dfrac{1 - y_y}{y_r} \dfrac{B}{A} \dfrac{M_0}{(\mu C + \lambda_r \lambda'_m A)} & \\[2ex]
\quad \times \left[\mu(C - \lambda_r A) \exp\left(- \lambda_r \lambda'_m \dfrac{A}{C} t\right) + \lambda_r A(\lambda'_m + \mu)e^{\mu t}\right] & \\[2ex]
& \text{for } 0 < t \leq T,
\end{cases}
$$

$$r(t) = \begin{cases} -\dfrac{1-y_y}{y_r}\dfrac{B}{A}\,M_0\left\{e^{\mu T} + \dfrac{\mu(C-\lambda_r A)}{(\mu C + \lambda_r \lambda'_m A)}\right. \\[2mm] \qquad \times \left[1 - \exp\left\{\left(\mu + \lambda_r \lambda'_m \dfrac{A}{C}\right)T\right\}\right]\exp\left(-\lambda_r \lambda'_m \dfrac{A}{C}\,t\right)\right\} \\[4mm] \hspace{9cm} \text{for } t > T. \end{cases}$$

Given $A > 0$ and $C > 0$, which follow from $y_y < 1$, these solutions have the following implications:

Regarding the time path of y,

$$y(\infty) \quad = \lim_{t\to\infty} y(t) = \frac{B}{A}\,M_0 e^{\mu T},$$

$$y(0 + \varepsilon) \;\geqq y(0) \text{ as } \frac{\alpha}{\lambda'_m} \geqq 0,$$

$$y(0 + \varepsilon) \;\gtreqless y(\infty) \text{ as } \frac{\alpha\mu}{(1-\alpha)(1-y_y) + \alpha\lambda'_m M_y} \gtreqless \frac{B}{A}(e^{\mu T} - 1),$$

$$y(T) \quad > y(0 + \varepsilon),$$

$$y(T + \varepsilon) \;< y(T), \text{ and}$$

$$y(T + \varepsilon) \;\gtreqless y(\infty) \text{ as } \left(\frac{\alpha}{1-\alpha} - \frac{B}{\lambda'_m}\right)(C - \lambda_r A) \gtreqless 0.$$

Regarding the time path of r,

$$r(\infty) \quad = \lim_{t\to\infty} r(t) = -\frac{1-y_y}{y_r}\frac{B}{A}\,M_0 e^{\mu T},$$

$$r(T) \quad < r(0), \text{ and}$$

$$r(T) \quad \gtreqless r(\infty) \text{ as } C \gtreqless \lambda_r A$$

7 *Output and employment with wage and price speculation*

This chapter considers the possibility that economic units have incomplete information regarding the spatial dispersion of wages and prices. Section 7.1 sketches an analytical framework, which produces such a spatial dispersion. Section 7.2 analyzes how incomplete information about this dispersion on the part of households generates speculative behavior in the determination of labor supply and consumption demand. Section 7.3 analyzes how such speculative household behavior affects the determination of output and employment. Section 7.4 considers speculative behavior on the part of firms.

7.1 The framework of wage and price speculation

In the basic model of chapter 1, changes in aggregate demand produced, say, by a change in the nominal money stock have no effect on either output, employment, the real wage rate, or the real values of other endogenous variables. This conclusion required two important assumptions. One of these assumptions was that exchange took place only under general-market-clearing conditions. The analysis in chapter 2 revealed how output and employment do depend on aggregate demand if exchange takes place when either wages or prices are not equal to their general-market-clearing values. The second important assumption of the basic model, which we have maintained until now, was that all economic units correctly perceive, pay, and receive the same wage rates and output prices. The purpose of the present chapter is to examine the implications of relaxing this second assumption. Specifically, we now assume that economic units have incomplete information regarding the relevant alternatives – that is, the wages and prices – which they face.

In order to rationalize this assumption, this chapter generalizes the analytical framework of the basic model by introducing decentralized markets for labor services and commodities. Consider a framework in which both the labor market and the commodity market involve a large number of spatially distinct market places, and in which demanders and suppliers distribute themselves randomly among these market places. In order to focus on the specific implications of this spatial dispersion, continue to assume, as in chapter 1, that labor services and commodities are homogeneous and that exchange takes place only under general-market-clearing conditions. The latter assumption means that the wage rate or commodity price at each market place is consistent with equality between the quantities supplied and demanded at that market place. However, at any time the wage rate or price level may differ from market place to market place depending on how demanders and suppliers have distributed themselves spatially at that time.[1]

The essential implication for households and firms of this spatial dispersion of labor and commodity markets is that individual economic units are now uncertain about the distributions of wages and prices over space. Both households and firms have only incomplete information, obtained from limited sampling, regarding these distributions. This uncertainty, combined with appropriate additional assumptions, generates speculative behavior in the determination of supplies and demands. This chapter analyzes the form of this speculative behavior and its implications. The discussion focuses first on the speculative behavior of households and then considers the speculative behavior of firms.

7.2 Wage and price speculation by households

In the basic model of chapter 1, notional labor supply and notional consumption demand depended only on nonwage wealth, Ω, and the real wage rate, W/P, in the forms

$$c^d = c^d(\Omega, W/P) \quad \text{and} \tag{1.9}$$
$$\underset{(+)\ \ (+)}{}$$

$$l^s = l^s(\Omega, W/P), \tag{1.10}$$
$$\underset{(-)\ \ (+)}{}$$

where $\quad \Omega \equiv \dfrac{M}{P} + N(\pi - \tau).$

In this formulation, a uniform wage rate was established at a centralized market for labor services, and a uniform commodity price was established at a centralized commodity market. Further, the representative household expected the levels of wages, prices, profits, and taxes to remain constant over time.

The present context departs from this basic framework in that wages and prices may now vary over space, and households have only

[1] Mortensen (1974) develops a formal analysis of such a market structure. The assumption that exchange takes place only under market-clearing conditions implies that our attention is limited to notional demands supplies. Note also that this chapter retains the assumption that both households and firms act as price takers and wage takers. Grossman (1973) develops a related model in which the firms set wages and prices.

incomplete information regarding these distributions. This uncertainty introduces speculative considerations into both the household decisions to accept employment – that is, to supply labor services – and to consume.

7.2.1   *The employment-acceptance decision*

Assume that the households' state of partial ignorance implies an employment-acceptance decision which satisfies two important properties. First, households, as suppliers of labor services, formulate subjective estimates of the distribution of nominal wage rates over space. These estimates are inelastic with respect to actual nominal wage rates sampled. The receipt of a wage offer which differs from the household's estimated mean wage causes a less than equiproportionate change in the household's subjective estimate of the mean wage. Second, given its subjective estimate of the distribution of nominal wage rates, the household's decision to supply labor services is sensitive to the actual wage offer which it receives. Specifically, the household will accept an actual wage offer which is high relative to its subjective estimate of the mean wage rate. However, it will reject an actual wage offer which is low relative to its subjective estimate of the mean.

Within the present analytical framework, we can rationalize this employment-acceptance behavior by focusing on the cost associated with the obtaining of information about alternative wage offers.[2] The crucial assumption here is that more and better information can be obtained more easily and quickly if the searcher is not currently employed. An obvious example of such a search-cost differential occurs

---

[2] Much of the existing literature on employment-acceptance behavior has utilized this assumption. See Phelps (1969), Alchian (1970), Mortensen (1970), and McCall (1970). An alternative rationalization for the employment-acceptance behavior assumed above would assume that households do not believe that wages are uniform over time, and would emphasize the intertemporal substitutability of leisure. Labor suppliers would choose to work intensively when they perceive the money wage obtainable to be relatively high and to leisure intensively when they perceive the money wage obtainable to be relatively low. In this context, given his subjectively estimated temporal distribution of wage offers, any change in the currently offered wage would prompt each labor supplier to alter his current allocation of time between labor and leisure. See Lucas and Rapping (1970) and Lucas (1972) for further development of this model. The existence of costs associated with accepting or quitting jobs or with varying the number of hours worked would discourage this intertemporal type of speculative behavior.

when a job searcher must travel during normal working hours in order to make inquiries of possible employers at alternative market places. Given such search-cost differentials, when confronted with a wage offer – either from his current employer or from a prospective employer if he is not currently employed – which is sufficiently low relative to his estimate of the distribution of money wages, the potential labor supplier will refuse employment while he engages in further job search.[3] Implicit in this formulation is the assumption that households do not believe that wage offers are uniform over space. Optimal policy is to continue searching until obtaining an actual wage offer above some critical value, where this critical or reservation wage depends on the subjectively estimated distribution of wage rates. Consequently, given the various households' subjectively estimated distributions, a leftward shift in the actual distribution of wage rates increases the mean duration of search, thereby decreasing the level of employment which is accepted.

The implications of this theory of employment acceptance can be formalized as follows. Let W now represent the mean of the actual spatial distribution of nominal wage rates. Similarly, let P now represent the mean of the actual spatial distribution of commodity prices. Let $\tilde{W}_i$ represent the mean of the ith household's estimated distribution of nominal wage rates and let $\tilde{W}$ represent the mean of the interhousehold distribution of the $\tilde{W}_i$. Similarly, let $\tilde{P}_i$ represent the mean of the ith household's estimated distribution of the prices of commodities and let $\tilde{P}$ represent the mean of the interhousehold distribution of the $\tilde{P}_i$. With regard to all these distributions, assume that the relation of all other parameters to the mean remains constant, so that the mean defines the entire distribution. As a convenient shorthand, denote $\tilde{W}$ as the normal money wage rate and $\tilde{P}$ as the normal price level.

Using these concepts, we can generalize the labor supply function of equation (1.10) to allow W and P to diverge, respectively, from $\tilde{W}$ and $\tilde{P}$. The labor supply function still involves a measure of nonwage wealth, Ω. In order to focus on the new elements which involve wage and price speculation, assume that the relevant measure of non-wage wealth now takes the form,

$$\Omega = \frac{M}{\tilde{P}} + N(\tilde{\pi} - \tau),$$

[3] In the absence of search-cost differentials, an employed labor supplier would not quit a low-wage job until he had located a higher wage job. However, even without search-cost differentials, a labor supplier who is currently employed might refuse a low-wage offer and remain unemployed while continuing to search for a higher wage offer if there are costs associated with accepting or quitting a job.

where $\tilde{\pi}$ denotes the normal level of profits. In this formulation, Ω involves only the normal levels of prices and profits. Implicitly, the representative household views divergences of P and π from $\tilde{P}$ and $\tilde{\pi}$ as transitory events, which have an insignificant impact on its lifetime asset-exhaustion condition. We continue to assume that the representative household expects τ to remain constant over time.

Given this specification of Ω and the above discussion of the employment-acceptance decision, we can now specify labor supply as depending on Ω and W/P, as in equation (1.10), and on $W/\tilde{W}$ and $P/\tilde{P}$, which represent the new speculative elements – that is,

$$l^s = l^s(\Omega, \underset{(-)}{W/P}, \underset{(+)}{W/\tilde{W}}, \underset{(+)}{P/\tilde{P}}). \tag{7.1}$$

We can explain the form of equation (7.1) as follows. With regard to nonwage wealth, given W/P, $W/\tilde{W}$, and $P/\tilde{P}$, an increase in Ω depresses l^s, as in equation (1.10). Consider next the real value of the mean of the actual spatial distribution of nominal wage rates. Given Ω, $W/\tilde{W}$, and $P/\tilde{P}$, an increase in W/P implies an increase in W relative to both P and $\tilde{P}$. In addition, given Ω, W/P, and $W/\tilde{W}$, an increase in $P/\tilde{P}$ also implies an increase in W relative to $\tilde{P}$, but no change in W relative to P. It is also useful to note that a decrease in P alone – with Ω, $\tilde{W}$, $\tilde{P}$, and W fixed – would imply an increase in W relative to P, but no change in W relative to $\tilde{P}$. All of these changes in the real value of actual wages involve offsetting substitution and income effects. As in equation (1.10), we assume that the substitution effects outweigh the income effects in the relevant range, so that the increase in W/P, the increase in $P/\tilde{P}$, and the decrease in P alone all tend to raise l^s. Finally, consider the relation between the actual mean money wage rate and the normal money wage rate. Given Ω, W/P, and $P/\tilde{P}$, an increase in $W/\tilde{W}$ motivates a speculative increase in the amount of employment accepted.

The crucial property of equation (7.1) for our purposes is that, given Ω, $\tilde{W}$, and $\tilde{P}$, an equiproportionate decrease in W and P implies a decrease in l^s. With $\tilde{W}$, $\tilde{P}$, and W/P fixed, a decrease in W makes current employment opportunities less attractive relative to both normal employment opportunities and the normal price of commodities. On both counts, speculative behavior produces a decrease in the current supply of labor services.[4]

---

[4] The above discussion of employment acceptance behavior emphasized the relation of W to $\tilde{W}$. However, some authors have emphasized the relation between W and $\tilde{P}$, which equation (7.1) also takes into account. See Friedman (1968), Almonacid (1971), Lucas (1973), and Sargent (1973).

7.2.2   Consumption demand

The above analysis of the employment-acceptance decision has parallel implications for the determination of consumption demand. An aggregate consumption demand function which, in allowing for wage and price speculation by households, would correspond to the labor supply function of equation (7.1) is

$$c^d = c^d(\Omega, W/P, W/\tilde{W}, P/\tilde{P}).$$ (7.2)
$$\quad\quad\quad (+) \; (+) \quad (-) \quad (-)$$

We can explain the form of equation (7.2) as follows. With regard to nonwage wealth, given W/P, $W/\tilde{W}$, and $P/\tilde{P}$, an increase in Ω raises c^d, as in equation (1.9). Consider next the price of consumption in terms of the leisure foregone. Given Ω, $W/\tilde{W}$, and $P/\tilde{P}$, an increase in W/P implies a decrease in P relative to both W and $\tilde{W}$. In addition, given Ω, W/P, and $P/\tilde{P}$, a decrease in $W/\tilde{W}$ also implies a decrease in P relative to $\tilde{W}$, but no change in P relative to W. It is also useful to note that an increase in W alone – with Ω, $\tilde{W}$, $\tilde{P}$, and P fixed – would imply a decrease in P relative to W, but no change in P relative to $\tilde{W}$. All of these changes in the real cost of consumption involve substitution and income effects which imply an increase in c^d. Finally, consider the relation between the actual mean price of commodities and the normal price of commodities. Given Ω, W/P, and $W/\tilde{W}$, an increase in $P/\tilde{P}$ motivates a speculative decrease in desired purchases of commodities.

In order to rationalize this speculative effect within the present framework, we can assume that the cost of obtaining information about prices at alternative commodity market places varies inversely with the intensity of current consumption.[5] In other words, consuming and searching, like working and searching, may represent alternative uses of time. Consequently, if a household confronts a price which is sufficiently high relative to its estimated distribution of prices, the household defers consumption while it searches for a lower price.

The crucial property of equation (7.2) for our purposes is that, given, Ω, $\tilde{W}$, and $\tilde{P}$, an equiproportionate decrease in W and P implies

---

[5] An alternative rationalization would assume that households do not believe that prices are uniform over time and would emphasize the intertemporal substitutability of consumption. Given significant substitution possibilities, households would consume lavishly when current prices are thought to be relatively low and live frugally when current prices are thought to be relatively high. A further possibility would arise if commodities were storable. In that event, even if intertemporal substitutability were limited, households would build up their inventories when prices were relatively low and run down their inventories when prices were relatively high.

an increase in c^d. With $\tilde{W}$, $\tilde{P}$, and W/P fixed, a decrease in P makes current commodity purchases more attractive relative both to normal opportunities to purchase commodities and to the normal nominal wage rate. On both counts, speculative behavior produces an increase in current consumption demand.

The notional labor supply and consumption demand functions of equations (7.1) and (7.2) also imply an aggregate saving function. Given the specification of saving as

$$\frac{m^d}{P} = \frac{W}{P} l^s + \pi - \tau - c^d,$$

the saving function has the following form:

$$\frac{m^d}{P} = \frac{m^d}{P} \underset{(-)\ (+)\ \ \ \ (+)\ \ \ \ (+)\ \ \ \ (+)}{(\Omega,\ W/P,\ W/\tilde{W},\ P/\tilde{P},\ \pi - \tau)}. \tag{7.3}$$

According to equation (7.3), given Ω, $\tilde{W}$, and $\tilde{P}$, an equiproportionate decrease in W and P, which decreases l^s and increases c^d, also produces a decrease in m^d/P. In other words, saving serves as a buffer which absorbs speculative changes in labor supply and consumption demand.

7.3 The determination of output and employment

This section is concerned with the short-run relations between the exogenous variables of the model and the values of the endogenous variables – wages, prices, output, and employment – which satisfy the market-clearing conditions. Short-run analysis in this context focuses on a time period sufficiently short that the households make minimal changes in the subjective beliefs represented by $\tilde{W}$, $\tilde{P}$, and $\tilde{\pi}$. For simplicity, the discussion which follows treats $\tilde{W}$, $\tilde{P}$, and $\tilde{\pi}$ as fixed. In the long run, in contrast, we would expect households to adjust $\tilde{W}$, $\tilde{P}$, and $\tilde{\pi}$ towards equality with W, P, and π. Thus, over time, speculative behavior would become less important and, in the long run, the basic model of chapter 1 would again become relevant.

A principal conclusion of this section is that wage and price speculation by households increases the responsiveness of output and employment to exogenous disturbances. For example, given speculative household behavior, the effect of a change in either the flow of money or the nominal stock of money on the real values of the endogenous variables is not neutral, even if transactions take place only under general-market-clearing conditions. Specifically, in the short run a decrease in either the flow of money or the nominal stock of money is likely to reduce the general-market-clearing levels of output and employment.

A second argument of this section is that speculative household behavior probably plays a relatively small role in the determination of the actual cyclical behavior of output and employment. This argument is based on the observation that certain qualitative implications of speculative household behavior are difficult to reconcile with actual experience. As we shall see in the following pages, these questionable implications concern behavior of the real wage rate and consumption.

7.3.1   *Market-clearing conditions*

The market-clearing conditions require a harmonization of the behavior of the firms, households, and government. The preceding section analyzed household behavior. Regarding firm behavior, it is convenient to postpone an analysis of wage and price speculation until section 7.4, below. Thus, assuming provisionally that speculative considerations are not relevant for firms, the demand for labor services and the supply of commodities depend only on the current real wage rate and level of public services, as in the basic model of chapter 1. Combining this assumption with the speculative behavior of households yields the following clearing conditions for the labor and commodity markets:

$$l^d \left(\frac{W}{P} \right) = l^s \left(\Omega, \frac{W}{P}, \frac{W}{\tilde{W}}, \frac{P}{\tilde{P}} \right) = l \quad \text{and} \tag{7.4}$$
$$\underset{(-)}{} \qquad \underset{(-)(+)(+)(+)}{}$$

$$y^s \left(\frac{W}{P}, g^d \right) = c^d \left(\Omega, \frac{W}{P}, \frac{W}{\tilde{W}}, \frac{P}{\tilde{P}} \right) + g^d = y, \tag{7.5}$$
$$\underset{(-)(+)}{} \qquad \underset{(+)(+)(-)(-)}{}$$

where $\Omega = \dfrac{M}{\tilde{P}} + N(\tilde{\pi} - \tau)$ and $\tilde{W}, \tilde{P},$ and $\sim$ are fixed.

Figure 7.1 provides a graphical representation of these market-clearing conditions in $(P, W/P)$ space. The solid lines depict combinations of P and W/P which satisfy the market-clearing conditions for given values of $\Omega, \tilde{W},$ and $\tilde{P}$. The labor-market-clearing locus is downward sloping. For a given value of W/P, a decrease in P, implying an equiproportionate decrease in W, would reduce l^s. Consequently, to maintain the labor-market-clearing condition, W/P would have to increase, causing l^s to increase and l^d to decrease. Thus, along the labor-market-clearing locus, a decrease in P is associated with an increase or less than equiproportionate decrease in W. The commodity-market-clearing locus, in contrast, is upward sloping. For a given value of W/P, a decrease in P would raise c^d. Correspondingly, to maintain the commodity-market-clearing condition, W/P would also have to decrease, causing c^d to decrease and y^s to increase.[6] Thus, along the commodity-market-clearing locus, a decrease in P is associated with a more than equiproportionate decrease in W. The intersection of these market-clearing loci shows the general-market-clearing price level to be P_1^* and the general-market-clearing real wage rate to be $(W/P)_1^*$.

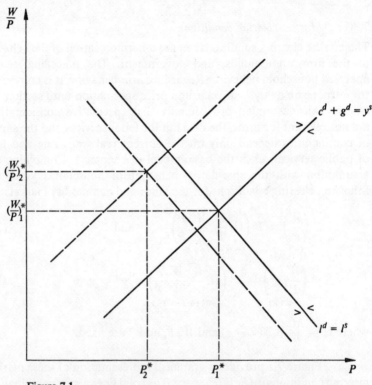

Figure 7.1
Effect of monetary contraction with speculative household behavior

7.3.2   *The effect of monetary contraction*

In order to emphasize the novel implications of wage and price speculation by households, consider the case of an exogenous change in

***

[6] It is clear that the decrease in W/P depresses c^d, because the effect of a decrease in W – given Ω, $\tilde{W}$, $\tilde{P}$, and P – would be to reduce c^d.

government behavior in the form of a decrease in m^s/P which is matched by an increase in τ. This disturbance highlights the essential differences between the model described by equations (7.4) and (7.5) and the basic model of chapter 1, as described by equations (1.13) and (1.14). Recall that in chapter 1 both a change in m^s/P and its cumulative effect on the stock of money caused W^* and P^* to change equiproportionately, but had no effect on $(W/P)^*$, l^*, or y^*.

In the present context, given $\tilde{W}$ and $\tilde{P}$, changes in W and P affect l^s and c^d through the speculative terms, $W/\tilde{W}$ and $P/\tilde{P}$. These effects imply that a change in m^s/P will generally alter $(W/P)^*$, l^*, and y^*. The dashed lines in figure 7.1 depict the effect of a decrease in m^s/P and increase in τ on the market-clearing loci. The increase in τ implies a decrease in Ω and, hence, an increase in l^s and a decrease in c^d. Consequently, the combination of values of P and W/P which originally satisfied the market-clearing conditions now implies excess supply of both labor services and commodities. Both market-clearing loci have shifted to the left. At the new intersection of the market-clearing loci, P_2^* is unambiguously lower than P_1^*. In addition, figure 7.1 depicts $(W/P)_2^*$ as higher than $(W/P)_1^*$, although this result is not unambiguous. In general, the change in $(W/P)^*$ depends on the relative magnitudes of the shifts and the relative slopes of the two market-clearing loci. In particular, an increase in $(W/P)^*$ results if the effect of Ω on l^s is relatively unimportant.

Consider next the implications of these adjustments of wages and prices for the levels of output and employment. If $(W/P)^*$ does increase, the firms' labor demand and commodity supply functions imply that l^d, l^*, y^s and y^* all decrease. Thus, given $\tilde{W}$ and $\tilde{P}$, in the context of speculative household behavior, a decrease in m^s/P can produce a decrease in the general-market-clearing levels of output and employment. The nature of the new general-market-clearing situation would be as follows. In the labor market, because W/P is higher, l^d is reduced. With respect to l^s, given $\tilde{W}$ and $\tilde{P}$, the decreases in W and P have a depressing speculative effect, which more than offsets the stimulus produced by the initial decrease in Ω and the increase in W/P.[7] In the commodity market, the increase in W/P implies a decrease in y^s. With respect to c^d, the initial decrease in Ω has a depressing effect, which more than offsets the stimulus produced by the increase in W/P and the decreases in W and P, given $\tilde{W}$ and $\tilde{P}$.

---

[7] It is clear that W decreases, because the effect of a decrease in P alone – given Ω, $\tilde{W}$, $\tilde{P}$, and W – would be to raise l^s.

7.3.3   *Quits and layoffs*

The above analysis demonstrates that wage and price speculation by households can generate a direct causal relation between changes in the money supply and changes in output and employment within a general-market-clearing context. In that respect the above results resemble the conclusions of section 2.2, which dealt with the case of excess supply in the labor and commodity markets. The purpose of the following sections is to bring out some important differences between the model of household speculation and the model of general excess supply.

In the present model of household speculation, exchange takes place only under general-market-clearing conditions. As a consequence of this specification, the quantity of employment accepted by labor suppliers effectively constrains the level of employment. The responsiveness of employment acceptances to changes in actual wage rates, reflecting the sluggish adjustment of the subjectively estimated distribution of wage rates, means that a contraction of demand would result in short-run reductions in both actual nominal wage rates and employment. The reduction in employment would presumably involve an increased quit rate and a prolongation of the average job search time of persons who are not employed, including new entrants to the labor market. Moreover, the analysis of employment-acceptance behavior implies a distinction between, on the one hand, normal quit rates and job search duration associated with subjective estimates of the distribution of wage rates which are correct on average and, on the other hand, abnormally high quit rates and job search duration associated with falling aggregate demand and subjective estimates of the distribution of wage rates which are correspondingly overly optimistic. Specifically, quit rates and the duration of job search should vary countercyclically. However, the evidence is that quit rates are relatively low, rather than relatively high, when employment is depressed.[8]

---

[8] See Sellier and Zarka (1966). Parsons (1973) has obtained direct estimates of a quit rate function based on the nominal wage rate and such real factors as relative wages and vacancy rates. He finds that the

'expectation hypothesis ... receives little empirical support. The effect of nominal wage changes had no systematic effect on quit rates when the "real factors" ... were controlled ... There is no evidence that any wage rate illusion, whether optimally motivated or otherwise, poses a serious market problem.' (p. 390).

These results suggest that the lag of $\tilde{W}$ behind W may not be an important source of variation in employment acceptances, at least as reflected in the quit rate.

An even more troublesome aspect of the depiction of employment as always governed by employment acceptance is its apparent inconsistency with the phenomenon of layoffs. In industrialized western countries, firms rarely cut wages and induce workers to leave employment voluntarily. Rather, significant declines in employment are typically effected through layoffs, unaccompanied by any change in the nominal wage rate.[9] The implied nonwage rationing of jobs is a pervasive aspect of declining employment for which analysis of employment-acceptance behavior makes no apparent allowance.

Some of the authors who have analyzed employment-acceptance friction have explicitly recognized this apparent discrepancy between fact and the implications of the theory, and, on this basis, have stressed that employment-acceptance friction does not offer a complete explanation for the relation between aggregate demand and employment.[10] However, other authors have argued that layoffs are an administrative veil which obscures the essential phenomenon, and, as such, are not inconsistent with the notion that employment acceptances govern employment.[11] These authors suggest that, regardless of superficial appearances, for analytical purposes we may always pretend that laid-off workers implicity have been offered and have declined an option to continue work at reduced wages.

These rationalizations, however, are not adequate to reconcile layoffs and nonwage rationing of jobs with the analysis of speculative household behavior. First, in this framework of analysis, the firm has no motivation to impose nonwage rationing. If a firm perceives an upward sloping supply curve of labor, laying off part of its labor force without cutting wages would imply paying higher wages than are apparently necessary to its remaining workers. Additional rationalizations for nonwage rationing of jobs are necessary. However, such

---

[9] In industrialized western countries. layoffs account for about two-thirds of total separations. See Sellier and Zarka (1966).

[10] For example, Mortensen (1970) says,
'The model presented in this paper purports to explain the flow of new hires, quits to search for new jobs, and intramarket turnover of employed participants as well as the dynamics of wage determination. Rehires and layoffs are neglected. Although the magnitudes involved are not small and the social importance of these flows is large, it seems to this author that an adequate explanation of these phenomena requires an additional hypothesis to that proposed in this paper.'

[11] See, for example, Alchian (1970) and Lucas and Rapping (1970). Alchian argues that firms know from experience that workers will not continue working at reduced wages, so they simply effect layoffs without bothering with wage negotiations.

rationalizations involve going beyond analysis of the employment-acceptance decision.[12]

Secondly, regardless of why firms effect layoffs without wage cuts, the effects of such a policy do not fit into the analytical framework developed to deal with employment-acceptance behavior. At the prevailing wages, laid-offs workers would prefer to be employed, but they are forced off their employment-acceptance schedule by a deficiency of demand. This nonwage rationing of jobs imposes a constraint on the household choice problem. This constraint does not arise if employment acceptances govern employment, but becomes a central consideration if labor markets fail to clear. On this score, the analysis of exchange under non-market-clearing conditions seems more satisfactory than does the model of speculative household behavior.[13]

7.3.4 The cyclical pattern of real wage rates

In the analysis of section 7.3.1, l^d is inversely related to W/P and, because exchange takes place only under general-market-clearing conditions, l is always equal to l^d. Consequently, the level of employment, l, and the real wage rate, W/P, are inversely related. In (l, W/P) space, changes in employment involve shifts in the l^s locus and movements along the l^d locus. Thus, the above analysis predicts a countercyclical movement of W/P.

Unfortunately, the absence of any consistent cyclical movement of W/P seems to be a well-established empirical observation.[14] Thus, it seems questionable that a model based on speculative household behavior and general market-clearing can provide a basic framework for analyzing the actual cyclical behavior of employment. In contrast,

---

[12] Recent papers by Azariadis (1974) and Baily (1974) represent attempts in this direction which stress the role of implicit long-term contracts for labor services.

[13] Some bits of quantititative evaluation of the implications of speculative household behavior may also be noted. Alchian (1970) points out, rather impressionistically, that employment-acceptance behavior cannot explain the slow rate of recovery from the trough of 1932. Lucas and Rapping (1972) present some econometric evidence regarding the experience of the 1930s. From this evidence they conclude,

> 'Our theory postulated lags in the adjustment of price-wage expectations as the *only* source of "rigidity" or of the persistence of unemployment. In fact, other important sources of rigidity were present in The Great Depression and, probably, in post-World War II recessions as well.'

[14] For a review of the evidence, see Kuh (1966) and Bodkin (1969).

the analysis developed in chapter 2, in which exchange took place under non-market-clearing conditions, was able to generate variations in employment even when W/P remained fixed. Specifically, in the general excess supply case of section 2.2, the effective labor demand function shifted with changes in effective commodity demand, and these shifts did not require inverse movements of the real wage rate.[15]

7.3.5 *The cyclical behavior of consumption and the demand multiplier*

In the example discussed in section 7.3.2, the increase in τ produced an initial decrease in c^d, but the subsequent decrease in P tended to offset the initial contraction of c^d. Consequently, the total change in c, which is equal to the total change in y, was smaller than the initial decrease in c^d. Unlike the case of the demand multiplier, which was generated in the general excess supply situation of section 2.2, the endogenous movements of the present model of household speculation imply counteracting effects to the original disturbance. Rather than an income multiplier, wage and price speculation by households produces a price-induced income dampener.[16]

The above example of an increase in τ involved an initial direct effect on Ω and c^d. As an alternative, consider a contractionary disturbance to aggregate commodity demand which does not involve Ω and c^d directly. An example of such a disturbance would be a decrease in g^d, matched by a decrease in m^s/P.[17] In the context of wage and price

[15] Attempts to avoid a stable relationship between l and W/P without allowing for excess supply of commodities have included Keynes' (1939) suggestion of cyclical variation in demand elasticities and Kuh's (1966) suggestion of a fixed-proportions production function in the short run.

[16] It should be noted that the unambiguous existence of a dampener requires the assumption that in the short run Ω is fixed. In fact, it is possible that changes in either π or P could affect Ω. First, in the above example, the increase in W/P implies a reduction in π. To the extent that Ω depends on current profits, either directly or through an induced revision of $\tilde{\pi}$, the reduction in π would depress Ω and c^d and produce a demand multiplier effect. However, this multiplier, which involves only profit income, would be smaller than the demand multiplier of section 2.2, which involved total income. Second, in the above example, the decrease in P implies an increase in M/P. To the extent that Ω depends on the current value of the real money stock, the increase in M/P would stimulate Ω and c^d and would tend to reinforce the dampener effect.

[17] Because g^d also enters into the production function, a decrease in g^d would depress current profits. Thus, the assertion that the decrease in g^d does not directly affect Ω requires either that Ω does not depend

speculation by households, the essential effect of a decrease in g^d would be the same as the effect of an increase in τ. Specifically, the endogenous response of P and W would imply decreases in l^d, l, and y.[18] However, the endogenous response of P and W would also imply an increase in c^d. Moreover, with no initial reduction in c^d, this endogenous response would represent the total effect on c^d of the decrease in g^d. Thus, a cyclical contraction which is initiated by a decrease in a non-consumption component of aggregate commodity demand leads to an increase in consumption demand. In this case, unlike the situation in the general excess supply case of section 2.2, wage and price speculation by households produces the possibility of a countercyclical pattern of consumption.

7.3.6 The effects of monetary expansion

The above discussion has concentrated on the effects of an exogenous reduction in aggregate demand, produced, say, by a monetary contraction, and has contrasted the implications of speculative household behavior with the implications of the general excess supply case of section 2.2. We saw that, although certain implications of general excess supply seem more consistent with actual experience, both models predict that a monetary contraction would depress output and employment. In actuality, the total effect of an exogenous reduction in aggregate demand on output and employment probably involves the combined effect of the factors analyzed in both models.

With this conclusion in mind, it is also interesting to consider the effects of an exogenous increase in aggregate demand, produced, say, by a monetary expansion. In this case, we want to contrast the implications of speculative household behavior with the implications of the general excess demand case of section 2.3. In this regard, the important aspect of the analysis in the present section is that wage and price speculation by households generates a continuous relation between changes in the money supply and changes in output and employment. Just as monetary contraction in the short run depresses W and P relative to $\tilde{W}$ and $\tilde{P}$ and reduces the market-clearing levels of l and y, so

---

on current profits or that τ is decreased sufficiently to offset the change in π. Another possible disturbance to aggregate commodity demand in an extended model would be a decrease in investment demand by firms.

[18] In this case, only the commodity market-clearing locus of figure 7.1 shifts. Consequently, W/P unambiguously increases.

monetary expansion in the short run raises W and P relative to $\tilde{W}$ and $\tilde{P}$ and boosts the market-clearing levels of l and y.

This latter implication contrasts sharply with the conclusions of section 2.3. In that context, given a wage-price vector initially consistent with general market clearing, a monetary expansion produces general excess demand. In this situation, the inability of the representative household to purchase the quantity of commodities which it notionally demands causes it to reduce its effective supply of labor services below its notional supply. Because in this situation the effective labor supply constrains employment, and employment in turn constrains output, this household behavior causes a contraction of employment and output. Thus, the model of wage and price speculation by households and the model of general excess demand imply opposite responses of output and employment to monetary expansion. To the extent that induced increases in prices and wages induce speculative household behavior, output and employment tend to rise. However, to the extent that these increases in prices and wages are insufficient to satisfy the general-market-clearing conditions, excess demand develops and output and employment tend to fall. This latter effect probably becomes more important the longer the excess demand persists. In any event, the net effect on output and employment of an exogenous increase in aggregate demand would involve a balancing of these two phenomena.

7.4 Wage and price speculation by firms

The analyses of the preceding sections assumed that the behavior of firms did not involve speculative considerations. Consequently, l^d and y^s depended only on W/P and g. This formulation accorded with the framework of the basic model, in which a uniform wage rate was established at a centralized market for labor services and a uniform commodity price was established at a centralized commodity market. The framework of the present chapter, however, departs from this basic framework in that wages and prices may now vary over space and firms have only incomplete information regarding these distributions. The purpose of the present section is to extend this analytical framework to allow for wage and price speculation by firms.

7.4.1 *Labor demand and output supply*

Assume that the firm's state of partial ignorance implies a hiring decision which satisfies two important properties. First, firms, like households, formulate subjective estimates of the distribution of nominal wage rates over space which are inelastic with respect to actual nominal wage rates encountered. Second, given its subjective estimate of the distribution of wage rates, the firm's decision to hire workers is sensitive to the actual wage which it must pay. Specifically, for a given real wage rate, the firm will hire more workers the lower is the nominal wage which it must pay relative to its subjective estimate of the mean nominal wage rate.

Within the present analytical framework, we can rationalize this hiring behavior by focusing on the costs associated with labor turnover.[19] One crucial element of these costs is that each firm must train new workers in order to integrate them into the firm's specific production routine. The costs of providing this training discourage the firm from filling vacancies temporarily at wages which it believes to be higher than normal.[20,21] Optimal policy is to continue searching until obtaining workers at a wage rate below some critical value, where this critical or reservation wage depends on the subjectively estimated distribution of wage rates, and to defer filling an existing vacancy until such a wage rate is located. Implicit in this formulation is the assumption that firms do not believe that wage offers are uniform over space. The effect of the firms' optimal hiring policy is that, given the various firms' subjectively estimated distributions, a leftward shift in the actual distribution of nominal wage rates decreases the mean duration of search by firms, thereby increasing the number of workers which the firms offer to hire.

The implications of this theory of firm behavior can be formalized by specifying labor demand as depending on W/P as in equation

[19] Differential search costs, which we used to rationalize speculative household behavior, do not seem relevant as a rationalization for speculative firm behavior, because firms, unlike workers, are not indivisible. In particular, we would not expect that the typical firm would benefit by specialization in search activities at certain points in time. However, another possible way to rationalize wage and price speculation by firms would be to treat entrepreneurial services as a separate input into the productive process. The behavior of suppliers of entrepreneurial services would be analogous to the household behavior analyzed in section 7.2 above. Almonacid (1971) provides an analysis of such speculative entrepreneurial behavior.

[20] A vacancy can be defined as a situation in which the marginal product of an additional worker exceeds the real wage rate which the firm would have to pay him.

[21] Another important element of labor turnover costs is that workers must incur search costs in order to look for a higher paying job. These costs mean that the firms have some assurance that the workers whom they hire will not tend to leave immediately.

(1.3), and on the speculative elements $W/\tilde{W}$ and $P/\tilde{P}$ – that is,

$$l^d = l^d(\underset{(-)}{W/P},\ \underset{(-)}{W/\tilde{W}},\ \underset{(-)}{P/\tilde{P}}). \tag{7.6}$$

We can explain the form of equation (7.6) as follows. Consider first the profitability of hiring additional workers. Given $W/\tilde{W}$ and $P/\tilde{P}$, an increase in W/P implies an increase in W relative to both P and $\tilde{P}$. In addition, given W/P and $W/\tilde{W}$, an increase in $P/\tilde{P}$ implies an increase in W relative to $\tilde{P}$, but no change in W relative to P. It is also useful to note that a decrease in P alone – with W, $\tilde{W}$, and $\tilde{P}$ fixed – would imply an increase in W relative to P, but no change in W relative to $\tilde{P}$. All of these effects involve an increase in the wage rate relative to either actual prices or normal prices, and imply a reduction in the current demand for labor services. Consider next the relation between the actual mean money wage rate and the normal money wage rate. Given W/P and $P/\tilde{P}$, an increase in $W/\tilde{W}$ motivates a speculative decrease in the current demand for labor services.

The crucial property of equation (7.6) for our purposes is that, given $\tilde{W}$ and $\tilde{P}$, an equiproportionate decrease in W and P implies an increase in l^d. With $\tilde{W}, \tilde{P}$, and W/P fixed, a decrease in W makes current employment more profitable relative to both the normal price of commodities and the normal wage rate. On both counts, speculative behavior produces an increase in the current demand for labor services. Finally, given the production function, $y = \Phi(l, g)$, the labor demand function of equation (7.6) implies an output supply function of the form

$$y^s = y^s\,(\underset{(-)}{W/P},\ \underset{(-)}{W/\tilde{W}},\ \underset{(-)}{P/\tilde{P}},\ \underset{(+)}{g}).^{22} \tag{7.7}$$

7.4.2   *Output and employment*

Consider the implications of firm speculative behavior for the short-run relations between the exogenous variables of the model and the values of the endogenous variables which satisfy the market-clearing conditions. To highlight the short-run nature of the analysis, we again treat $\tilde{W}, \tilde{P}$,

---

[22] Further possibilities for speculative firm behavior would arise if output were storable. The storability of output would allow current production to differ from current sales. The optimal choice of inventory level over time, which determines the relation between production and sales, would depend primarily on the relation between P and $\tilde{P}$. In particular, given W/P and $W/\tilde{W}$, an increase in P/P would motivate a decumulation of inventories, so that sales could rise despite a reduction in labor demand and production. For simplicity, the present discussion assumes as in the basic model that output is not storable.

and $\tilde{\pi}$ as fixed. The labor supply and commodity demand functions of equations (7.1) and (7.2) together with the labor demand and commodity supply functions of equations (7.6) and (7.7) imply the following market-clearing conditions:

$$l^d \left(\underset{(-)(-)(-)}{\frac{W}{P}, \frac{W}{\tilde{W}}, \frac{P}{\tilde{P}}} \right) = l^s \left(\underset{(-)(+)(+)(+)}{\Omega, \frac{W}{P}, \frac{W}{\tilde{W}}, \frac{P}{\tilde{P}}} \right) = l \quad \text{and} \qquad (7.8)$$

$$y^s \left(\underset{(-)(-)(-)(+)}{\frac{W}{P}, \frac{W}{\tilde{W}}, \frac{P}{\tilde{P}}, g^d} \right) = c^d \left(\underset{(+)(+)(-)(-)}{\Omega, \frac{W}{P}, \frac{W}{\tilde{W}}, \frac{P}{\tilde{P}}} \right) + g^d = y, \qquad (7.9)$$

where $\quad \Omega = \dfrac{M}{\tilde{P}} + N(\tilde{\pi} - \tau)$, and $\tilde{W}$, $\tilde{P}$, and $\tilde{\pi}$ are fixed.

Figure 7.2, which may be contrasted with figure 7.1 above, provides a graphical representation of these market-clearing conditions in $(P, W/P)$ space. The solid lines again depict combinations of P and

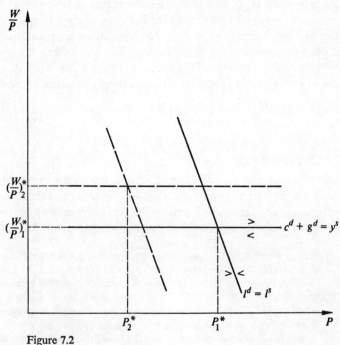

Figure 7.2
Effect of monetary contraction with speculative household and firm behavior

W/P which satisfy the market-clearing conditions for given values of Ω, $\tilde{W}$, and $\tilde{P}$. The labor-market-clearing locus is again downward sloping. The presence of speculative terms in the l^d function makes this locus more steep than before. However, the sign of the slope of the commodity-market-clearing locus is now ambiguous, because the speculative terms in the y^s function counteract the speculative terms in the c^d function. If the effects of firm and household speculative behavior are approximately offsetting, this locus would be horizontal, as shown in figure 7.2.[23]

Consider again the monetary-contraction example of section 7.3.2, which involved a decrease in m^s/P and an increase in τ. The dashed lines in figure 7.2 again depict the effects of this disturbance on the market-clearing loci. This disturbance again produces a decrease in P^* and an increase in $(W/P)^*$.[24] Thus, the introduction of wage and price speculation by firms does not alter the qualitative relation between shifts in aggregate demand, caused in the present example by monetary contraction, and the resulting adjustments of wages and prices.

The differences which do derive from the introduction of wage and price speculation by firms involve the implications of the adjustments of wages and prices for employment and output. In order to focus on these new implications, assume for the moment that speculative considerations are not relevant for households, so that the supply of labor services and the demand for commodities depend only on nonwage wealth and the actual real wage rate. In this case, monetary contraction has apparently paradoxical implications. Specifically, the decrease in m^s/P and increase in τ unambiguously produce an increase in the market-clearing level of employment and output. The nature of the new labor-market-clearing situation would be as follows. The combined effect of the increase in W/P and the decrease in Ω, produced by the increase in τ, would insure an increase in l^s.[25] With respect to l^d, given $\tilde{W}$ and $\tilde{P}$, the

---

[23] In this context, inventory speculation by firms would reinforce the speculative elements in the c^d function. Hence, if inventory speculation were an important force, it is likely that the commodity-market-clearing locus in figure 7.2 would be upward sloping. However, this modification to the model would not alter the conclusions which we reach below regarding the effects of monetary contraction on the real wage rate, output, and employment. The main new element would be the possibility that sales can move in a direction opposite to output.

[24] Because of the change in the relative slopes of the market-clearing loci in figure 7.2, $(W/P)^*$ can increase even if the effect of Ω on l^s is relatively large.

[25] Alternatively, if $(W/P)^*$ were to decrease, the combined effect of the decreases in W/P and W would insure an increase in l^d. Thus, in either event, employment increases.

decreases in W and P produce a speculative stimulus, which more than offsets the depressing effect of the increase in W/P.[26] Through the production function, the increase in l, given the level of g, implies an increase in output.

These results enable us to contrast the effects of household and firm speculative behavior. In both cases, monetary contraction causes W and P to decline, and probably causes W/P to increase. If both households and firms engage in wage and price speculation, these effects would be reinforced. However, the important result is that, in terms of the effects on employment and output, the implications of firm speculative behavior are opposite to the implications of household speculative behavior. In the case of household speculative behavior only, the decline in W produced a leftward shift in the l^s curve along an l^d curve which was fixed versus W/P. In that case employment fell while W/P increased. In the case of firm speculative behavior only, the decline in W produced a rightward shift in the l^d curve along an l^s curve which was fixed versus W/P. In that case, l and W/P both increased.

Because of these opposite effects on employment, if both households and firms engage in wage and price speculation, a monetary contraction produces a decline in employment and output only if speculation by households, who are the suppliers of labor services, is the more important force. However, even in this case, the analysis would still have the implications, discussed in section 7.3 above, which are difficult to reconcile with experience. These difficulties involved the phenomenon of layoffs and the cyclical patterns of quits, real wage rates, and consumption. Alternatively, if speculation by firms, who are the demanders of labor services, is the more important force, exogenous shifts in aggregate demand and induced changes in the level of employment, contrary to experience, would be inversely related.[27] On the basis of these results, it seems likely that speculative firm behavior, like speculative household behavior, plays a relatively small role in the determination of the actual cyclical behavior of output and employment.

---

[26] It is clear that W decreases in this case, because the effect of a decrease in P alone–given $\tilde{W}$, $\tilde{P}$, and W – would be to reduce l^d.

[27] Note that, in this case, the level of employment and the real wage rate would not be inversely related.

References

Alchian, A. A., 'Information Costs, Pricing, and Resource Unemployment', in E. S. Phelps, *et. al.*, *Microeconomic Foundations of Employment and Inflation Theory* (New York: Norton, 1970).

Allais, M., 'A Restatement of the Quantity Theory of Money', *American Economic Review*, **56**, December, 1966, 1123–57.

Almonacid, R. D., 'Nominal Income, Output, and Prices in the Short Run', Ph.D. Dissertation, University of Chicago, 1971.

Azariadis, C., 'Implicit Contracts and Underemployment', unpublished manuscript, June, 1974.

Bailey, M. J., *National Income and the Price Level*, 2nd edition (New York: McGraw-Hill, 1971).

Baily, M. N., 'Wages and Employment under Uncertain Demand', *Review of Economic Studies*, **41**, January, 1974, 37–50.

Barro, R. J., 'A Theory of Monopolistic Price Adjustment', *Review of Economic Studies*, **39**, January, 1972, 17–26.

Barro, R. J., 'The Control of Politicians: An Economic Model', *Public Choice*, **14**, Spring, 1973, 19–42.

Barro, R. J., 'Are Government Bonds Net Wealth?', *Journal of Political Economy*, **82**, November/December, 1974.

Barro, R. J. and H. I. Grossman, 'A General Disequilibrium Model of Income and Employment', *American Economic Review*, **61**, March, 1971, 82–93.

Barro, R. J. and H. I. Grossman, 'Suppressed Inflation and the Supply Multiplier', *Review of Economic Studies*, **41**, January, 1974a, 87–104.

Barro, R. J. and H. I. Grossman, 'Consumption, Income and Liquidity', read at Conference on 'Equilibrium and Disequilibrium in Economic Theory', Institute for Advanced Studies, Vienna, July, 1974b.

Barro, R. J. and A. Santomero, 'Transaction Costs, Payments Periods, and Employment', in H. G. Johnson and A. R. Nobay, eds., *Issues in Monetary Economics* (New York: Oxford, 1974).

Bodkin, R. G. 'Real Wages and Cyclical Variations in Employment', *Canadian Journal of Economics*, **2**, August, 1969, 353–74.

Buchanan, J. M. and G. Tullock, *The Calculus of Consent* (Ann Arbor: University of Michigan Press, 1962).

Burmeister, E. and A. R. Dobell, *Mathematical Theories of Economic Growth* (New York: Macmillan, 1970).

Cagan, P., 'The Monetary Dynamics of Hyperinflation', in M. Friedman, *Studies in the Quantity Theory of Money* (Chicago: University of Chicago Press, 1956).

Carr, J. and L. B. Smith, 'Money Supply, Interest Rates, and the Yield Curve', *Journal of Money, Credit, and Banking*, **4**, August, 1972, 582–94.

Clower, R. W., 'The Keynesian Counterrevolution: A Theoretical Appraisal', in F. Hahn and F. Brechling, eds., *The Theory of Interest Rates* (London: Macmillan, 1965).

Darby, M. R., 'The Allocation of Transitory Income Among Consumers' Assets', *American Economic Review*, **62**, December, 1972, 928–41.

Edgeworth, F. Y., *Mathematical Psychics* (London: Kegan Paul, 1881).

Fand, D., 'High Interest Rates and Inflation in the U.S.: Cause or Effect?', *Banca Nazionale del Lavoro-Quarterly Review*, **25**, March, 1972, 3–44.

Feige, E. L. and M. Parkin, 'The Optimal Quantity of Money, Bonds, Commodity Inventories, and Capital,' *American Economic Review*, **61**, June, 1971, 335–49.

Ferguson, J. M., ed., *Public Debt and Future Generations* (Chapel Hill: University of North Carolina Press, 1964).

Fischer, S., 'Money, Income, Wealth, and Welfare', *Journal of Economic Theory*, **4**, April, 1972, 289–311.

Flemming, J. S., 'The Consumption Function when Capital Markets Are Imperfect: The Permanent Income Hypothesis Reconsidered', *Oxford Economic Papers*, **25**, July, 1973, 160–72.

Friedman, M., *A Theory of the Consumption Function* (Princeton: Princeton University Press, 1957).

Friedman, M., 'The Lag in the Effect of Monetary Policy', *Journal of Political Economy*, **69**, October, 1961, 447–66.

Friedman, M., 'The Role of Monetary Policy', *American Economic Review*, **58**, March, 1968, 1–17.

Friedman, M., 'Factors Affecting the Level of Interest Rates', in *Savings and Residential Financing*, 1968 *Conference Proceedings* (Chicago: US Savings and Loan League, 1968).

Gogerty, D. C., and G. C. Winston, 'Patinkin, Perfect Competition, and Unemployment Disequilibria', *Review of Economic Studies*, **31**, April, 1964, 121–6.

Grossman, H. I., 'Reserve Base, Reserve Requirements, and the Equilibrium Rate of Interest', *Quarterly Journal of Economics*, **81**, May, 1967, 312–20.

Grossman, H. I., 'Theories of Markets Without Recontracting', *Journal of Economic Theory*, **4**, December, 1969, 476–9.

Grossman, H. I., 'Money, Interest, and Prices in Market Disequilibrium', *Journal of Political Economy*, **79**, September/October, 1971, 943–61.

Grossman, H. I., 'Was Keynes a "Keynesian"?', *Journal of Economic Literature*, **10**, March, 1972a, 26–30.

Grossman, H. I., 'A Choice-Theoretic Model of an Income-Investment Accelerator', *American Economic Review*, **62**, September, 1972b, 630–41.

Grossman, H. I., 'Aggregate Demand, Job Search, and Employment', *Journal of Political Economy*, **81**, November/December, 1973, 1353–69.

Grossman, H. I., 'The Nature of Quantities in Market Disequilibrium', *American Economic Review*, **64**, June, 1974a, 509–14.

Grossman, H. I., 'The Cyclical Pattern of Unemployment and Wage Inflation', *Economica*, **41**, November, 1974b, 403–13.

Grossman, H. I. and R. F. Lucas, 'The Macroeconomic Effects of Productive Public Expenditures', *The Manchester School*, **42**, June, 1974, 162–70.

Hansen, B., *A Study in the Theory of Inflation* (New York: Rinehart, 1951).

Hansen, B., 'Excess Demand, Unemployment, Vacancies, and Wages', *Quarterly Journal of Economics*, **84**, February, 1970, 1–23.

Intriligator, M. D., *Mathematical Optimization and Economic Theory* (Englewood Cliffs, NJ: Prentice-Hall, 1971).

Karni, E., 'Inflation and Real Interest Rate: A Long-Term Analysis', *Journal of Political Economy*, **80**, March/April, 1972, 365–74.

Keynes, J. M., *The General Theory of Employment, Interest, and Money* (New York: Macmillan, 1936).

Keynes, J. M., 'Relative Movements of Real Wages and Output', *Economic Journal*, **49**, March, 1939, 34–51.

Kuh, E., 'Unemployment, Production Functions, and Effective Demand,' *Journal of Political Economy*, **74**, June, 1966, 238–49.

Laidler, D., 'The Permanent Income Concept in a Macro-Economic Model', *Oxford Economic Papers*, **20**, January, 1968, 11–23.

Laidler, D., *The Demand for Money: Theories and Evidence* (Scranton: International, 1969).

Laidler, D., 'Expectations, Adjustment, and the Dynamic Response of Income to Policy Changes', *Journal of Money, Credit, and Banking*, **5**, February, 1973, 157–72.

Leijonhufvud, A., *On Keynesian Economics and the Economics of Keynes* (New York: Oxford, 1968).

Lipsey, R. G., 'The Relationship between Unemployment and the Rate of Change of Money Wage Rates in the U.K., 1862–1957: A Further Analysis', *Economica*, **27**, February, 1960, 1–41.

Lucas, R. E., 'Optimal Investment Policy and the Flexible Accelerator', *International Economic Review*, **8**, February, 1967, 78–85.

Lucas, R. E., 'Expectations and the Neutrality of Money', *Journal of Economic Theory*, **4**, April, 1972, 103–24.

Lucas, R. E., 'Some International Evidence on Output-Inflation Tradeoffs', *American Economic Review*, **63**, June, 1973, 326–34.

Lucas, R. E., and L. A. Rapping, 'Real Wages, Employment, and Inflation' in E. S. Phelps, *et al.*, *Microeconomic Foundations of Employment and Inflation Theory* (New York: Norton, 1970).

Lucas, R. E., and L. A. Rapping, 'Unemployment in the Great Depression: Is There a Full Explanation?', *Journal of Political Economy*, **80**, January/ February, 1972, 186–91.

Marshall, A., *Principles of Economics*, 1890; 8th edition (London: Macmillan, 1930).

McCall, J. J., 'Economics of Information and Job Search', *Quarterly Journal of Economics*, **84**, February, 1970, 113–26.

Metzler, L. A., 'Wealth, Saving, and the Rate of Interest', *Journal of Political Economy*, **59**, 1951, 93–116.

Mortensen, D. T., 'A Theory of Wage and Employment Dynamics', in E. S. Phelps, *et al.*, *Microeconomic Foundations of Employment and Inflation Theory* (New York: Norton, 1970).

Mortensen, D. T., 'Job Matching Under Imperfect Information', read at conference on 'Evaluating the Labor Market Effects of Social Programs', Princeton, May, 1974.

Mundell, R. A., 'A Fallacy in the Interpretation of Macroeconomic Equilibrium', *Journal of Political Economy*, **73**, February, 1965, 61–6.

Muth, J. F., 'Rational Expectations and the Theory of Price Movements', *Econometrica*, **29**, July, 1961, 315–35.

Niskanen, W. A., *Bureaucracy and Representative Government* (Chicago: University of Chicago Press, 1971).

Oi, W. Y., 'Labor as a Quasi-Fixed Factor', *Journal of Political Economy*, **70**, December, 1962, 538–55.

Parsons, D. O., 'Specific Human Capital: An Application to Quit Rates and Layoff Rates', *Journal of Political Economy*, **80**, November/December, 1972, 1120–43.

Parsons, D. O., 'Quit Rates Over Time: A Search and Information Approach', *American Economic Review*, **63**, June, 1973, 390–401.

Patinkin, D., *Money, Interest, and Prices*, 1956; 2nd edition (New York: Harper and Row, 1965).

Perry, G. L., 'Changing Labor Markets and Inflation', *Brookings Papers on Economic Activity*, 1970, no. 3, 411–41.

Phelps, E. S., 'Phillips Curves, Expectations of Inflation, and Optimal Unemployment Over Time.' *Economica*, **34**, August, 1967, 254–81.

Phelps, E. S., 'The New Microeconomics in Inflation and Employment Theory', *American Economic Review*, **59**, May, 1969, 147–60.

Phillips, A. W., 'The Relationship between Unemployment and the Rate of Change of Money Wage Rates in the U.K., 1862–1957', *Economica*, **25**, November, 1958, 283–99.

Robertson, D. H., *Banking Policy and the Price Level* (London: King, 1926).

Samuelson, P. A., *Foundations of Economic Analysis* (Cambridge: Harvard University Press, 1947).

Santomero, A. M., 'A Model of the Demand for Money by Households', *Journal of Finance*, **29**, March, 1974, 89–102.

Sargent, T., 'Rational Expectations, the Real Rate of Interest, and the Natural Rate of Unemployment', *Brookings Papers on Economic Activity*, 1973, no. 2, 429–72.

Sargent, T. and N. Wallace, 'Rational Expectations and the Dynamics of Hyperinflation', *International Economic Review*, **14**, June, 1973, 328–50.

Schultze, C. L., *Recent Inflation in the United States* (Government Printing Office: Washington, 1959).

Sellier, F. and C. Zarka, *International Differences in Factors Affecting Labor Mobility* (Geneva: International Labor Organization, 1966).

Stein, J., *Money and Capacity Growth* (New York: Columbia University Press, 1971).

Sweezy, P. M., 'Demand Under Conditions of Oligopoly', *Journal of Political Economy*, **47**, August, 1939, 568–73.

Tobin, J., 'The Burden of the Public Debt: A Review Article', *Journal of Finance*, **20**, December, 1965, 679–82.

Tobin, J., 'Inflation and Unemployment', *American Economic Review*, **62**, March, 1972, 1–18.

Tucker, D. P., 'Dynamic Income Adjustments to Money Supply Changes', *American Economic Review*, **56**, June, 1966, 433–49.

Tucker, D. P., 'Credit Rationing, Interest Rate Lags, and Monetary Policy Speed', *Quarterly Journal of Economics*, **82**, February, 1968, 54–84.

Walras, L., *Elements of Pure Economics*, 1874; translation by W. Jaffe (London: Allen & Unwin, 1954).

Yeager, L., 'The Keynesian Diversion', *Western Economic Journal*, **11**, June, 1973, 150–63.

Index of names